Narcissism and the Literary Libido

Literature and Psychoanalysis
General Editor: Jeffrey Berman

Narcissism and the Literary Libido

Rhetoric, Text, and Subjectivity

Marshall W. Alcorn, Jr.

NEW YORK UNIVERSITY PRESS
New York and London

NEW YORK UNIVERSITY PRESS
New York and London

Library of Congress Cataloging-in-Publication Data
Alcorn, Marshall W., 1949–
Narcissism and the literary libido : rhetoric, text, and
subjectivity / Marshall W. Alcorn, Jr.
p.   cm. — (Literature and psychoanalysis)
Includes bibliographical references and index.
ISBN 0-8147-0614-2 (alk. paper)
  1. Psychoanalysis and literature.   2. Narcissism in literature.
3. Subjectivity in literature.   4. Narration (Rhetoric)   I. Title.
II. Series.
PN56.P92A46   1994   93-25793
801'.92—dc20   CIP

New York University Press books are printed on acid-free paper,
and their binding materials are chosen for strength and durability.

Manufactured in the United States of America

10 9 8 7 6 5 4 3 2 1

For Janis, Skye, and Sean

Contents

Foreword

As New York University Press inaugurates a new series of books on literature and psychoanalysis, it seems appropriate to pause and reflect briefly upon the history of psychoanalytic literary criticism. For a century now it has struggled to define its relationship to its two contentious progenitors and come of age. After glancing at its origins, we may be in a better position to speculate on its future.

Psychoanalytic literary criticism was conceived at the precise moment in which Freud, reflecting upon his self-analysis, made a connection to two plays and thus gave us a radically new approach to reading literature. Writing to his friend Wilhelm Fliess in 1897, Freud breathlessly advanced the idea that "love of the mother and jealousy of the father" are universal phenomena of early childhood (*Origins*, 223–24). He referred immediately to the gripping power of *Oedipus Rex* and *Hamlet* for confirmation of, and perhaps inspiration for, his compelling perception of family drama, naming his theory the "Oedipus complex" after Sophocles' legendary fictional hero.

Freud acknowledged repeatedly his indebtedness to literature, mythology, and philosophy. There is no doubt that he was a great humanist, steeped in world literature, able to read several languages and range across disciplinary boundaries. He regarded creative writers as allies, investigating the same psychic terrain and intuiting similar human truths. "[P]sycho-analytic observation must concede priority of imaginative writers," he declared in 1901 in *The Psychopathology of Everyday Life* (*SE* 6213), a concession he was generally happy to make. The only exceptions were writers like Schopenhauer, Nietzsche, and Schnitzler, whom he avoided reading because of the anxiety of influence. He quoted effortlessly from Sophocles, Shakespeare, Goethe, and Dostoevsky, and was himself a master prose stylist, the recipient of the coveted Goethe

Prize in 1930. When he was considered for the Nobel Prize, it was not for medicine but for literature. Upon being greeted as the discoverer of the unconscious, he disclaimed the title and instead paid generous tribute to the poets and philosophers who preceded him.

And yet Freud's forays into literary criticism have not been welcomed uniformly by creative writers, largely because of his allegiance to science rather than art. Despite his admiration for art, he viewed the artist as an introvert, not far removed from neurosis. The artist, he wrote in a well-known passage in the *Introductory Lectures on Psycho-Analysis* (1916–17), "is oppressed by excessively powerful instinctual needs. He desires to win honour, power, wealth, fame and the love of women; but he lacks the means for achieving these satisfactions" (*SE* 16376). Consequently, Freud argued, artists retreat from reality into the world of fantasy, where they attempt to make their dreams come true. While conceding that true artists manage to shape their daydreams in such a way as to find a path back to reality, thus fulfilling their wishes, Freud nevertheless theorized art as a substitute gratification. Little wonder, then, that few artists have been pleased with Freud's pronouncements.

Nor have many artists been sympathetic to Freud's preoccupation with sexuality and aggression; his deterministic vision of human life; his combative, polemical temperament; his self-fulfilling belief that psycho-analysis brings out the worst in people; and his imperialistic claim that psychoanalysis, which he regarded as his personal creation, would explore and conquer vast new territories. He chose as the epigraph for *The Interpretation of Dreams* (1900) a quotation from *The Aeneid* "Flectere si nequeo superos, Acheronta movebo" ("If I cannot bend the Higher Powers, I will move the Infernal Regions"). Although he denied that there was anything Promethean about his work, he regarded himself as one of the disturbers of the world's sleep. The man who asserted that "psycho-analysis is in a position to speak the decisive word in all questions that touch upon the imaginative life of man" (*SE* 19208) could hardly expect to win many converts among creative writers, who were no less familiar with the imaginative life of humankind and who resented his intrusion into their domain.

Freud viewed psychoanalysts as scientists, committed to the reality principle and to heroic self-renunciation. He perceived artists, by contrast—and women—as neurotic and highly narcissistic, devoted to the pleasure principle, intuiting mysterious truths which they could not rationally understand. "Kindly nature has given the artist the ability to express his most secret mental impulses, which are hidden even from himself," he stated in *Leonardo da Vinci and a Memory of His Childhood* in 1910 (*SE* 11 107). The artist, in Freud's judgment, creates beauty, but the psychoanalyst analyzes its meaning and "penetrates" it, with all the phallic implications thereof. As much as he admired artists, Freud did not want to give them credit for knowing what they are doing. Moreover, although he always referred to artists as male, he assumed that art itself was essentially female; and he was drawn to the "seductive" nature of art even as he resisted its embrace, lest he lose his masculine analytical power. He wanted to be called a scientist, not an artist.

From the beginning of his career, then, the marriage Freud envisioned between the artist and the analyst was distinctly unequal and patriarchal. For their part, most creative writers have remained wary of psychoanalysis. Franz Kafka, James Joyce, and D. H. Lawrence were fascinated by psychoanalytic theory and appropriated it, in varying degrees, in their stories, but they all remained skeptical of Freud's therapeutic claims and declined to be analyzed.

Most artists do not want to be "cured," fearing that their creativity will be imperiled, and they certainly do not want psychoanalysts to probe their work; they agree with Wordsworth that to dissect is to murder. Vladimir Nabokov's sardonic reference to Freud as the "Viennese witch doctor" and his contemptuous dismissal of psychoanalysis as black magic are extreme examples of creative writers' mistrust of psychoanalytic interpretations of literature. "[A]ll my books should be stamped Freudians Keep Out," Nabokov writes in *Bend Sinister* (xii). Humbert Humbert speaks for his creator when he observes in *Lolita* that the difference between the rapist and therapist is but a matter of spacing (147).

Freud never lost faith that psychoanalysis could cast light upon a wide variety of academic subjects. In the short essay "On the Teaching of Psycho-Analysis in Universities" (1919), he maintained that his new science has a role not only in medical schools but also in the "solutions of problems" in art, philosophy, religion, literature, mythology, and history. "The fertilizing effects of psycho-analytic thought on these other disciplines," Freud wrote enthusiastically, "would certainly contribute greatly towards forging a closer link, in the sense of a *universitas literarum*, between medical science and the branches of learning which lie within the sphere of philosophy and the arts" (*SE* 17173). Regrettably, he did not envision in the same essay a cross-fertilization, a desire, that is, for other disciplines to pollinate psychoanalysis.

Elsewhere, though, Freud was willing to acknowledge a more reciprocal relationship between the analyst and the creative writer. He opened his first published essay on literary criticism, "Delusions and Dreams in Jensen's *Gradiva*" (1907), with the egalitarian statement that "creative writers are valued allies and their evidence is to be highly prized, for they are apt to know a whole host of things between heaven and earth of which our philosophy has not yet let us dream" (*SE* 98), an allusion to his beloved Hamlet's affirmation of the mystery of all things. Conceding that literary artists have been, from time immemorial, precursors to scientists, Freud concluded that the "creative writer cannot evade the psychiatrist nor the psychiatrist the creative writer, and the poetic treatment of a psychiatric theme can turn out to be correct without any sacrifice of its beauty" (*SE* 9:44).

It is in the spirit of this equal partnership between literature and psychoanalysis that New York University Press launches the present series. We intend to publish books that are genuinely interdisciplinary, theoretically sophisticated, and clinically informed. The literary critic's insights into psychoanalysis are no less valuable than the psychoanalyst's insights into literature. Gone are the days when psychoanalytic critics assumed that Freud had a master key to unlock the secrets of literature. Instead of reading literature to confirm psychoanalytic theory, many critics are now reading Freud to discover how his understanding of literature shaped the evolution of his theory. In short, the master-slave relationship traditionally implicit in the marriage between the literary critic and the psychoanalyst has given way to a healthier dialogic relationship, in which each learns from and contributes to the other's discipline.

Indeed, the prevailing ideas of the late twentieth century are strikingly different from those of the late nineteenth century, when literature and psychoanalysis were first allied. In contrast to Freud, who assumed he was discovering absolute truth, we now believe that knowledge, particularly in the humanities and social sciences, is relative and dependent upon cultural contexts. Freud's classical drive theory, with its mechanistic implications of cathectic energy, has given way to newer relational models such as object relations, self psychology, and interpersonal psychoanalysis, affirming the importance of human interaction. Many early psychoanalytic ideas, such as the death instinct and the phylogenetic transmission of memories, have fallen by the wayside, and Freud's theorizing on female psychology has been recognized as a reflection of his cultural bias.

Significant developments have also taken place in psychoanalytic literary theory. An extraordinary variety and synthesis of competing approaches have emerged, including post-Freudian, Jungian, Lacanian, Horneyan, feminist, deconstructive, psycholinguistic, and reader response. Interest in psychoanalytic literary criticism is at an all-time high, not just in the handful of journals devoted to psychological criticism, but in dozens of mainstream journals that have traditionally avoided psychological approaches to literature. Scholars are working on identity theory, narcissism, gender theory, mourning and loss, and creativity. Additionally, they are investigating new areas, such as composition theory and pedagogy, and exploring the roles of resistance, transference, and countertransference in the classroom.

"In the end we depend / On the creatures we made," Freud observed at the close of his life (*Letters*, 425), quoting from Goethe's *Faust;* and in the end psychoanalytic literary criticism depends on the scholars who continue to shape it. All serious scholarship is an act of love and devotion, and for many of the authors in this series, including myself, psychoanalytic literary criticism has become a consuming passion, in some cases a lifelong one. Like other passions, there is an element of idealization here. For despite our criticisms of Freud, we stand in awe of his achievements; and even as we recognize the limitations of any single approach to literature, we find that psychoanalysis has profoundly illuminated the human condition and inspired countless artists. In the words of the fictional "Freud" in D. M. Thomas's extraordinary novel *The White Hotel* (1981), "Long may poetry and psychoanalysis continue to highlight, from their different perspectives, the human face in all its nobility and sorrow" (143n.).

Jeffrey Berman
Professor of English
State University of New York at Albany

Works Cited

Freud, Sigmund. *The Letters of Sigmund Freud.* Ed. Ernst Freud. Trans. Tania and James Stern. New York:Basic Books, 1975.

———. *The Origins of Psychoanalysis.* Ed. Marie Bonaparte, Anna Freud, and Ernst Kris. Trans. Eric Mosbacher and James Strachey. New York:Basic Books, 1954; rpt. 1977.

———. *The Standard Edition of the Complete Psychological Works of Sigmund Freud.* Ed. James Strachey. 24 vols. London:Hogarth Press, 1953–74.

Nabokov, Vladimir. Introduction to *Bend Sinister.* New York:McGraw Hill, 1974.

———. *Lolita.* London:Weidenfeld and Nicolson, 1959.

Thomas, D. M. *The White Hotel.* New York:Viking, 1981.

Acknowledgments

No argument is ever fully finished, and this book is no exception. There is still more to be said, more support to give to claims, more examples needed for clarity. Yet this book has evolved with the help of many friends: It has gained strength and maturity over more than a few years as it has benefited from revisions, reconsiderations, and turns of argument. Paragraphs that now seem to follow a rather simple (and I hope) logical development are really the final products of a taxing dialectical process; I responded to a reader's intelligent comment, which was itself a response to a response I made to an earlier reader's intelligent comment, which responded to an earlier primitive and undeveloped idea I thought was my own after I forgot who prompted me to think it. I am incapable of the monologic discourse essential for the production of a book. I am now somehow listed as the "author" for this present work only because I struggled to be obsessive enough to knit together the ideas of different people sharing a common interest.

Four friends have given careful attention to more recent drafts of this manuscript. Jeffrey Berman at SUNY, Albany, has long been a wise and supportive guide; his advice, his psychoanalytic expertise, and his three books on literature and psychoanalysis, as well as his forthcoming book on psychoanalytic effects in the classroom, both educated and inspired me. Jim Mellard at Northern Illinois University read this manuscript with care and intelligence; chapter titles and sentence wording often reflect the clarity of his thinking and not my own. Claudia Tate at George Washington University has a talent for asking intelligent questions; her marginal comments helped me see clear relationships where I foundered in imprecision. Jean Wyatt at Pomona College helped me focus and develop my central argument; her generous, intelligent advice and her own recent book helped me to appreciate the breadth and depth of reader-response theory. I would also like to thank an anonymous reader who gave careful attention to the manuscript and directed my attention to facets of the argument that needed more clarity and more support.

Each chapter has its own personal history. A few were published elsewhere and, before publication, went through their own slow process of revision and alleged transfiguration.

Chapter 1 benefited from suggestions from Mark Bracher at Kent State University, Geoffrey Harpham at Tulane University, and Mark Kipperman and Jasper Neel, both at that time at Northern Illinois University. Jim and Tita Baumlin at Southwest Missouri University asked me for an essay on *ethos* several years ago. At the time I had never given a moment's thought to the concept of *ethos*, but with their help I discovered an engaging theoretical concept. They gave enormous attention and much help to developing an earlier version of chapter 2. I wish I could be so intelligent and industrious an editor. Jon Quitslund and Patrick Cook, colleagues at George Washington University, also read the manuscript carefully, offering much advice. Mark Bracher, Norman Holland at the University of Florida, and Teresa Toulouse at Tulane gave careful and plentiful response to chapter 3 as it developed into the essay that was later published in *College English* (February 1987, Copyright 1987 by the National Council of Teachers of English and reprinted with permission). Mark Bracher and Geoffrey Harpham also gave helpful advice with early drafts of chapter 4. Mark taught me to be a more careful writer and vigilant thinker. Geoff gave me an appreciation for the rhetorical energy and creativity of good writing. Walter Reed, John Farrel, Jim Kaufmann, Louis Mackey, and Charles Rossman—all at that time at the University of Texas at Austin—gave helpful advice for the earliest version of chapter 5. This was later published in a shorter form in *Conradiana* (16, 1984, copyright 1984 by *Conradiana* and reprinted with permission). I sometimes think I have been driven to write an entire book of theory in order to support an initially promising but muddled and unfinished reading of *Heart of Darkness*. Mark Bracher helped with the development of chapter 6. His expertise with Lacan was constantly useful for both this chapter and the progress of this book.

All of this thinking really began more than 14 years ago at the University of Texas at Austin when a group of graduate students and instructors —Mark Bracher, Jackie Byars, Harney Corwin, Terry MacDonald, and

Rosa Turner—met weekly under the instruction of Jim Kaufmann to better understand relationships between literature and psychoanalysis. These meetings overcame my own resistance to Freud and shifted my research interests from philosophical to psychoanalytic inquiry.

George Washington University provided the professional stability I needed to finish this book. I appreciate their trust in granting me tenure before this book was accepted for publication. I would like to thank our department chairpeople, Chris Sten and Judy Plotz, for their support. The administrative staff, Connie Kibler and Lucinda Kilby, were generous with their time and attention.

Finally, I would like to thank my family. My wife Janis Alcorn offered encouragement and support despite being busy with her own books and articles. My father, Marshall W. Alcorn, Sr., provided many years of encouragement. If I have come to write a book about storytelling, it is in part because I heard so many stories from him. My own sons, Sean and Skye Alcorn constantly remind me that language is not mere signification, but a medium for telling stories, a medium for forming bonds, making promises, and establishing trust. It is a means by which we construct identity, community, and personal values. If I have not discussed Donald Duck (Skye and Sean's favorite literary character) in this book, it is only because I have found no rhetorically effective way to explode or marginalize the academic pomposity that insists on situating such a discussion. I have been told that Wittgenstein suggested that, in regard to that which we cannot talk, we must remain silent. Donald Duck, I suspect, would energetically insist, "quack, quack, quack." I am always happy to see fools rush in where philosophers of language fear to tread. Donald, like many of us, cannot contain what he cannot say.

Narcissism and the Literary Libido

Political Ties and Libidinal Ruptures: Narcissism as the Origin and End of Textual Production

Ideology necessarily implies the libidinal investment of the individual subject.

Jameson, *The Political Unconscious*

This book is about change—changes in people, changes in value, changes in thinking, changes in perception, changes in attention, and changes in the intensity of attention. This subtle continuum between changes in people and changes in the intensity of attention is part of the complexity of change. Because readers and teachers direct (and to some extent control) acts of attention, a better understanding of this continuum is important. We need a theoretical framework that will help us understand how changes in the intensity of attention affect social action and value.

There are many simple ways to explain changes in human behavior. People will change what they do if they are threatened by weapons or their paychecks are withheld. People will also change as a result of changes in the material conditions of their life. New technologies can change jobs and in so doing often change attitudes as well. In the liberal arts, however, there has been a long-standing assumption that language, in and of itself, can cause change. This power, located ambiguously in language, has been traditionally termed *rhetoric*. Rhetoric designates a force in language manipulating how people experience value. Too often, this assumption about the power of rhetoric to affect change is either totally dismissed as wishful thinking or so crudely believed that different political groups are willing to harm others in their attempt to control or regulate language use.

I

Because of the importance of human change, both social and psychological, we must investigate more thoroughly the subtle resources of rhetoric. For many scholars, rhetoric refers to a formal study of language and communication. Rhetoric is concerned with the rules, strategies, and structures of discourse. For others, rhetoric describes the experience of a discourse stimulating change. This often ignored relationship between the structure and the experience of language is another concern of my study. The theoretical ideas that we entertain need to be supported by our experiences and our empirical observations. Theoretical discussions of language should help us make better sense of day-to-day experiences.

Kenneth Burke, whose study of rhetoric was broadened by his study of psychoanalytic theory, made an important contribution to understanding puzzling relations between language and experience when he equated the mechanism of rhetoric with identification. We are prompted to agree with speakers, he says, when we come to identify with them. In many respects, this book pursues Burke's interest in the relationship between rhetoric and identification.[1] Identification, however, is a complex and unwieldy concept. The term applies equally well to situations where we imagine ourselves as different from what we are, as we try to imagine ourselves as like another, and situations where we imagine others as different from what they are, because we want them to be like ourselves. In the former case, we try to change ourselves in order to be more like others. In the latter case, we try to change—or perceive others differently—in order treat them like ourselves. Identification is crucial for all rhetorical functions, but the term *identification* oversimplifies the complexity of the psychological processes involved in responding to the discourse of others. For reasons I soon make clear, I have decided to elaborate on Burke's term, *identification,* by giving special emphasis to another related term, *narcissism.* Recent study of narcissistic processes has yielded a more complete understanding of the various forms and intensities of identification.

The term *narcissism* is associated with the Greek myth of Narcissus and its theme of self-love, and is used by both psychoanalysts and literary critics to describe a wide range of conscious and unconscious, interpersonal and intrapersonal phenomena. If we turn to Freud to discover precisely what narcissism means, however, we are likely to turn away more confused. In his 1910 footnote to "Three Essays on the Theory of Sexuality," Freud associated narcissism with autoerotic self-stimulation and speculated that such tendencies could explain homosexuality.[2] By 1914 Freud saw wider applications for the concept of libidinal "self-love." In "On Narcissism: An Introduction," Freud used the concept of narcissistic cathexis (the self's investing energy in itself) to explain narcissistic rewards to be gained from sleep, schizophrenia, and hypochondria.[3] These conditions, Freud postulated, offer satisfaction because they offer a regressive experience of returning to early childhood's blissful oneness with the mother. Freud still imagined narcissism as a particularly self-reflexive dimension of experiencing and pursuing desire, but he began to take an interest in the concept's potential to make sense of various transformations of libido. In his account of mourning in 1917, Freud explained the mourner's loss of "libidinal" interest in the external world in terms of narcissism. Mourners, he suggested, lose interest in the outside world because they have "narcissistically" withdrawn libido into the self.

Freud's concern for the puzzling symptoms of mourning, profound dejection, cessation of interest in the external world, inability to love, general inhibition of all activity, and a lowering of self-esteem, indicates an important truth about the nature of human libidinal attachments. People seldom respond to major loss by simply choosing and pursing a new object of desire. Instead, people suffer a feeling of emptiness that must be "worked through" before "transformed libido" can be directed to new objects. A physically painful experience of emptiness must be suffered by the self; a complex process of suffering must be accepted and endured before "libido" can be redirected again to the outside world. If an old refrigerator quits working, people typically junk it and eagerly go out to buy a new model. If "Lassie" dies, however, no one quickly dumps the body and walks happily to a well-stocked pet store. Changes in deeply invested objects of human desire are not simple affairs. Changes in desire often require complicated changes in people. To explain these changes adequately, one must understand Freud's observations about "transformations in libido" and its relation to narcissism.

Literary theory and rhetorical theory most often talk about transformations in value, rather than transformations in libido. We often think of changes in value as a rational (or an irrational) process that proceeds forward as if the subject were an inert appendage being dragged along by other very different forces. In some cases this is true; but it is not true in those cases that affect us most. As Jameson's quote (see chap. epigraph) suggests, major transformations in value must occur first at the level of transformations in the "libidinal investment of the individual subject." The changes that most require rhetorical skill, those made difficult because of deep investments in ideas and values, require complex libidinal transformations.

My intention in this book is to demonstrate that the central focus for rhetorical study should not be language exclusively, but should include the relations between language and libidinal structures. Libidinal structures are the components of self-structure. These structures are composed by our interaction with language and experience and they modify our sense of both ourselves and the world. If we look carefully at literary language, we can see interactions between self-structure and libidinal structure driving rhetorical operations. In order to understand this claim, however, we must develop a greater understanding of libido. I have claimed that the concept of identification can be more thoroughly understood by examining psychoanalytic research on narcissism. I also want to suggest that narcissism can be more thoroughly understood if we examine its relationship to libidinal transformations.

The concept of *libido* has always been charged with ambiguity, but psychoanalytic theory has found the term very handy for discussing the flow of human desire and for describing changes in the object or intensity of desire. Heinz Kohut talks of libido as a force that makes people and objects seem interesting. Libido is an energy investing objects (both human beings in the psychoanalytic sense of the term and material everyday objects like cars and clothes) with appeal and desirability.[4] In the crudest sense, libido is the force of sexual attraction. This sexual dimension should not be underestimated. Stephen Mitchell points out that "sex is a powerful organizer of experience," subtly affecting the tone of our perceptions.[5] In common experience, however, the sexual energy of libido often seems quite diffuse. People are libidinally invested in many objects—clothes, cars, computers, guns, coffee makers. This does not mean that there is an explicit sexual experience generated by these objects. But it does mean that the investments made in these objects are not trivial. How can we understand this attachment? How can we understand, for example, the reluctance of the adult to junk an old coffee maker?

Mitchell's discussion of the child's early "sexual" experiences is helpful here: "Bodily sensations, processes, and events dominate the child's early experience. . . . The child draws on and generalizes from the major patterns of bodily experience in constructing and representing a view of the world and other people."[6] These early constructions and representations are linked to strong feelings of pleasure and pain, and are "libidinal" systems of fantasy and memory that become building blocks for experience and self-identity. Because infantile sexuality is so poorly understood, libidinal perception and libidinal experience are also poorly understood. But it is clear that some modes of thinking and perceiving are especially energetic and linked to bodily experience. This form of experience seems related to the idea of "gut level" experience. It is similar to the child's experience of the world, because this form of thinking is experienced in the body, not just in the mind. It is more "attached" to things—attached, for example, to old clothes or old coffee makers. Consequently, it is a mode of thinking more vivid, more intense, and more interesting than usual.

In addition, it operates according to its own principles, often indifferent to the demands of rational thought. Both Freud and Lacan argued that humans develop logical abstract thought in order to free themselves from childlike attachments to objects and images. But logic and abstract thought do not end more primitive thought attached to objects; it simply pushes it into the unconscious. According to Freud, "The system Ucs contains the thing-cathexes [the libidinal investments] of the objects, the first and true object-cathexes."[7] We might thus consider the unconscious not simply as a reservoir of repressed or forgotten memories, but as a system of unconscious libidinal attachments that affects our attention to and response to conscious objects.

Understood in the broadest sense, libido is a "psychic energy" that can invest almost anything with an attractiveness that does not at all seem sexual. Both advertising and art attempt to orchestrate the flow of libido in order to reposition or revalue particular cultural items, ideas, or situations. The glamorous blonde draped languorously over the hood of the red sports car may be "sexy" in the literal sense of the word, but her presence bestows the car with a "sexiness" of another order. The car becomes the center of an acquisitive gaze that makes all its details seem glamorous and noteworthy. Clearly, an understanding of libidinal "flow" can contribute to our understanding of rhetoric. The car ad example makes it clear that the cold metallic and mechanical structures of a vehicle can become rhetorically enhanced by means of libidinal manipulations.

Advertisers know they can manipulate us into feeling an attachment for the car if they can first elicit an attachment we already have for the blonde.

Although narcissism is usually associated with self-love, it is rather easy to see how the admiration of cars and many other fashionably produced objects can be as narcissistic as gazing in a mirror. When we are libidinally invested in cars, it is often not the cars that we actually care about; we care about ourselves. In looking at the car, we are concerned about our own self-image.[8] The car takes on value because we project something narcissistic about ourselves into it. The blonde does not give the car her sex appeal simply by appearing with it. We create the glamour of both the woman and the car because we project glamour onto the object. We are creatures of history and culture, and this makes us active and not passive in the creation of our own feelings. We project libidinal qualities onto objects—cars and blondes—according to complicated rules of status, gender, memory, and mood.

In the *Analysis of the Self*, a ground-breaking book on the concept of narcissism, Kohut observes that whereas narcissism is usually associated with self-love (or the libidinal investment of the *self*), narcissism actually supports a wide array of libidinal investments. People, material objects, human activities, and even thoughts can be invested with "narcissistic libido." Narcissistic libido, not only for Kohut (unlike Freud), contributes to "mature object relationships" (to healthy human relationships). It also forms "the main source of libidinal fuel for some of the socioculturally important activities which are subsumed under the term creativity."[9] Artists, Kohut argues, direct and invest "narcissistic libido" when they spend enormous time and effort in shaping a work—an apparently inconsequential flow of words or a squat block of wood—that becomes singularly important because it seems to "contain" or "express" a deeply human feeling.

Narcissistic libido helps to produce a work of art, and, in a different way, makes a work of art interesting. Narcissistic libido accounts for the laborious attention that critics give to such seemingly inconsequential products. The uninitiated often find art criticism tiresome, but the art critic usually takes great pleasure in the inspection, analysis, and discussion of art. Minute details that would seem accidental or irrelevant to many people appear full of meaning and consequence. Artworks repay such attention because they, in some manner, initiate complex imaginative experience and "gratify" the narcissistic libido of those who invest time in them.

People who appreciate art claim that it prompts them to see things differently, that is, to experience events differently. We sometimes imagine that these events are caused by the external object, but in reality these experiences are caused by the interaction between the observer and the object observed. These experiences occur when observers "invest" something of themselves in the object.

This notion of "investment" is an important idea; we might understand it best by considering our relationship to people. When narcissistic libido is invested in people, narcissistic needs can give people a special aura of "grandeur" or desirability. Kohut argues that this grandeur is the result of narcissistic libidinal investments. This grandeur is produced by an investment of "narcissistic libido" because an unconscious aspect of the observer's self-structure makes the person observed seem attractive. Part of the psychic structure missing in the observer is perceived as existing in the object observed. Kohut points out:

The intensity of the search for and of the dependency on these objects [people] is due to the fact that they are striven for as a substitute for the missing segments of the psychic structure. They are not objects (in the psychological sense of the term) since they are not loved or admired for their attributes, and the actual features of their personalities, and their actions, are only dimly recognized.[10]

In Arthur Miller's *Death of a Salesman*, Linda Loman's attachment to Willy illustrates the commonplace truth of Kohut's ideas. Linda "more than loves" Willy, Miller writes, "she admires him as though his mercurial nature, his temper, his massive dreams and little cruelties served her only as sharp reminders of the turbulent longings within him, longings which she shares but lacks the temperament to utter and follow to their end."[11] Because Willy serves Linda as a substitute for a missing part of her own nature, Linda does not see him fully. She is repeatedly hurt by his failings and his "little cruelties." But, as Miller observes, she has developed an "iron repression of her exceptions to Willy's behavior."

In this example, as in many others, the investment of narcissistic libido in objects operates to make objects seem grand or valuable. At the same time, however, this investment can disguise the real nature of the thing admired. Certain people or objects are needed because of narcissistic need, but this same need dictates that these people or objects cannot be seen realistically.

This overinflation of the object or person should be an interesting theme for rhetoricians. I suggested earlier that narcissistic libido makes objects seem valuable primarily by disguising their true qualities; but I should draw more careful attention to this behavior. Narcissistic libido seems to disguise an object because it encourages us to pay only selective attention to it. Narcissistic libido can be considered a sort of light that, when shone on an object, can partly hide it by revealing it according to a particular and limited effect of shade and shadow; some facets are accentuated, other facets are hidden. Rhetoric constantly makes use of this lighting effect as it presents objects in particularly crafted ways in order to make them appear useful or valuable.

Rhetoric, I argue at some length, is facilitated through the libidinal manipulations of an object. Other psychoanalytic accounts of rhetoric emphasize the importance of fantasy, transference, and identification.[12] These phenomena are indeed important, but consideration of libidinal manipulation offers an added tool to investigate rhetorical transactions. It allows us to examine texts more closely, to see interactions between signifiers and experience, to see links between particular words and wider patterns of signification found in plots, characters, and even readers. For example, when Conrad's Marlow first describes his impressions of Kurtz he says:

I had heard Mr. Kurtz was in there. I had heard enough about it, too—God knows! Yet somehow it didn't bring any image with it—no more than if I had been told an angel or a fiend was in there. I believed it the same way one of you might believe there are inhabitants in the planet Mars.[13]

A few pages later, however, when Marlow hears the manager and his nephew talk about Kurtz, Marlow suddenly gets a vivid image:

I seemed to see Kurtz for the first time. It was a distinct glimpse: the dugout, the four paddling savages, and the lone white man turning his back suddenly on the headquarters, on relief, on thoughts of home—perhaps; setting his face towards the depths of the wilderness.[14]

The image appears when Marlow makes a narcissistic and a libidinal investment in Kurtz. The image makes Kurtz "real." It is produced when Marlow, who wants to be a great explorer, identifies with Kurtz's apparently brave decision to set "his face towards the depths of the wilderness." Marlow has had some firsthand experience of the "depths of the wilderness," and he begins to understand and take a real interest in Kurtz when he sees him turning to this exotic, threatening, and fascinating darkness. Kurtz therefore becomes real for Marlow when there is a narcissistic libidinal investment in his representation.

Many things in daily experience are made more real, alive, and important because of narcissistic investments. As teachers, we know the importance of this moment of special "recognition," a moment when students feel that they can "relate" to the text. This is a crucial event for classroom discussions—in its own terms and in terms of the critical resources we can bring to bear on it. Yet this event is infrequently discussed, and too often negotiated in intuitive terms only.

Most often our libidinal investments are relatively fixed by the structures of our character. We might consider character as something very much like an organization of libidinal investments. These investments are relatively stable, so we see the world according to customary patterns of perception and value. In reading, as I argue in some detail in the following chapters, rhetorical strategies make libidinal investments fluid so that libido can shift to new objects, allowing us to consider as "interesting" objects we might in other situations dismiss or recognize only according to established patterns of habit. Through rhetorical manipulation, things not otherwise invested with narcissistic libido become invested with narcissistic libido.

Just as the blonde can make the car seem interesting, a Romantic lyric about the wind can suddenly seem important when it engages rhetorical structures that promote identification and shifts in libidinal investment. Students who may initially care little about Shelley's meditations on the west wind in Italy can often identify with the mood changes described in the poem and soon come to feel that the experiences described are very much like their own. In "light" of this perception, metaphors such as the "breath of Autumn's being" and images such as "dead leaves," "winged seeds," and "sweet buds" become the focus of a caring attention that frequently deepens and intensifies the reader's own appreciation of both nature (the objects of nature are visualized more acutely) and inner experience. Students sometimes comment that after reading the poem they experience a kind of rejuvenation, a feeling that can accompany a mood change when it is no longer something passively endured, but something actively anticipated and cultivated.

My discussion of Conrad and Shelley indicates that shifts in libidinal investment help students (and people in general) to take a more particular interest in the subjects of discourse. In the following chapters I describe rhetorical structures as devices that allow libido to be more "fluid," more able to move from one location to another. We often think of a text's rhetoric as equivalent to the value it endorses: A text's rhetoric is its message or its meaning. But we might more usefully think of a text's rhetoric as broader and more encompassing, something quite different from message or meaning. Rhetoric, considered from this perspective, is not the message of a text, but the specific ways—often present in the form of textual scenes, structures, or vocabulary—by means of which texts prompt readers to *entertain*, in the literal sense of the word, a new argument about value.

If we think of rhetoric as a force that pulls a reader or listener from one value to another, then the rhetorical power of a text would reflect its ability first to divide readers from their own customary self with its rigidly invested values, and second, make them feel that such a customary self is not desirable. Rhetoric works by convincing us that, although we have not considered it seriously before, we are really happier with a new perspective. This new perspective is something we have hitherto disregarded or seen as undesirable, but by means of the text's modification of our perceptions, we now see it as more compatible with our larger system of value. In the case of Shelley's "Ode to the West Wind," a student participating in the strategies and libidinal shiftings of the poem may come to see that poetry is not dead and unimaginative, but relevant and engaging.

Textual rhetoric is aided by the mechanisms with which literary texts promote a "fluidity" of libidinal investments.[15] When the rhetoric of a text is successful, the libidinal structures of the reader are modified by the libidinally charged linguistic structures of the text. Texts that promote a fluidity of libidinal investments have more rhetorical power than texts that simply and rigidly assert a value position. Many literary works, such as Melville's *Billy Budd*, for example, labor to promote fluidity by encouraging multilayered conflictual and complex judgments on values, each position inviting identification. When texts simultaneously both invite a play of identification and structure a perception of conflict, they put pressure on fixed patterns of libidinal attachments. Barbara Johnson comments on *Billy Budd:* "The effect of . . . explicit oscillations of judgment within the text is to underline the importance of the act of judging while rendering its outcome undecidable."[16] Often texts seem to need critics to encourage readers to appreciate such "fluid" modes of judgment that Johnson describes. But often enough, writers consciously discuss the importance of encouraging contradictory perceptions. For example, in *The Crack Up,* Fitzgerald argues that "the test of a first-rate intelligence is the ability to hold two opposed ideas in the mind at the same time, and still retain the ability to function."[17]

Literature is a verbal genre that is conspicuous in its ability both to induce identification and promote a conflictual vision of value. Literature is also a verbal genre that encourages us to appreciate and take aesthetic pleasure in an ambiguity or conflict that, in other contexts, we might find too stressful and disorienting. Thus, at the same time that it structures a perception of conflict, literature typically reduces our anxiety about it. As Aristotle observed long ago, we can take pleasure in literary representations of the tragic. Simon Lesser argues that

when we read fiction we are ordinarily relaxed and secure, so that we can see things that might elude us at other times. In imagination we can experiment, try out various approaches to our problems, alter this or that circumstance to see what results ensue.[18]

When the rhetoric of a text is successful, it weakens the rigidity of value commitment as it encourages satisfying narcissistic alliances and provides a secure space for entertaining new concerns, interests, and values.

The reading of literature offers a protected space for what Stephen Mitchell calls "self-regulation": "Human beings are simultaneously self-regulating and field regulating."[19] Humans attempt, at the same time, to maintain a coherent sense of self and a coherent sense of their relations with others. "We are concerned," Mitchell says:

with both the creation and maintenance of a relatively stable, coherent sense of self out of the continual ebb and flow of perception and affect, and the creation and maintenance of dependable, sustaining connections with others, both in actuality and as internal presences. The dialectic between self-definition and connection with others is complex and intricate, with one or the other sometimes being more prominent. Self-regulatory and field regulatory processes sometimes enhance each other and sometimes are at odds with other, forming the basis for powerful conflicts.[20]

This dialectic between internal and external world is central and inescapable for human thought. Too often in daily life, however, the human ego is too rigid and inflexible to be fully responsive to needed adjustments.

better position to understand the configurations of perception, emotion, and cognition that fund rhetorical transformations. The work of Kohut and Kernberg distinguishes between narcissistic personality disorders and narcissistic strategies for defense or development common to all people.[24] Kohut diverges more radically from classical psychoanalytic theory than Kernberg, but both men propose a theory of ego development emphasizing the role of narcissistic investments in the formation of the internal structure of the self. The particular nature of our libidinal investments in processes such as empathy, identification, idealization, loss, and mourning, for example, can alter who we are and what we think. It seems only too true, thus, that the "rhetoric" of early character formation is the work of libidinal investment.

This theory of development (found in different ways in both object-relations theory and self-psychology) emphasizes that the structure of the self develops initially in terms of the child's earliest identifications. Identification means, as Thomas Ogden states, not only "a modeling of oneself after the external object, but, as in the case of superego formation, a process by which the functions of the external object are instated within the psyche."[25] The self thus takes its internal structure, its being, its emotions, fears, and motivations, from its interaction with others in its world. Identification is not simply a gesture that identity performs; it is a gesture that can form and transform identity.

Freud's work indicates that identifications follow the paths of our libidinal investments.[26] Our most profound identifications, however, seem to be in response to the experience of loss. First of all, we suffer when a person close to us is lost because, as Freud says, we are "unwilling to abandon" our libidinal attachment to the object (the person). Though the object is gone, we cannot abandon it, and we are unwilling to accept substitutions. The object is present in our imaginations, and we persist in our attachment to it.

We are able to "work through" the experience of loss gradually as we come to internalize the lost properties of the object. Internalization occurs when libido attached to the object is not abandoned, but instead withdrawn to the self-structure of the mourner. The person in mourning, instead of giving up that which is lost, appropriates for subjectivity particular qualities belonging to one lost. A mourner *internalizes* for self-structure certain qualities of the person lost. In many cases, these are "admired" qualities" and they become self functions; for example, we may internalize a parent's discipline or nurturing concern when we lose that parent. Human character is thus changed because of this narcissistic "transformation of libido."

Acts of identification are not always as consequential as those acts of identification that heal the psychic wound of loss. But all acts of identification, attachment, and admiration can be considered narcissistic. Narcissism, in the broadest sense, does not refer to a specific model of deviant behavior. It refers to a theoretical understanding of the dynamic relationships between our "internalizations" of "external" objects and our libidinal models of aspiration and identity. Although many theorists continue to emphasize the primary importance of early childhood experience in the development of self-structure, contemporary theorists are more open to considering the impact of adult experience on character.

Theories of narcissism seek to understand the ways various needs and self-images are activated or adopted in times of stress. Narcissism refers most fundamentally to a process: "the cathexis of the self," the self's libidinal involvement with itself, its mode of investing energy in evaluative, protective, and developmental functions. In order to develop, the ego must cathect itself and must have itself as the object of its own aspirations. If the ego did not cathect itself there would be no superego, no ego ideals, and no truly *human* behavior. Thus the growth of human identity is necessarily "narcissistic" in the broad sense of the term. Such a usage does not imply a negative character disorder; it merely characterizes the necessarily self-referential psychodynamics of individuation.

I use the concept of narcissism, as the new post-Freudian psychoanalytic studies have come to understand it, to examine a web of phenomena affiliated with the rhetorical dynamics of identification and libidinal investment.

If an understanding of narcissism helps us to understand the particular shifts in attention and interest that direct a reader's response to a text, an understanding of narcissism also can help to explain the larger force that makes rhetoric operate as a force of change. In certain respects, self-identity is enormously conservative and resistant to change. Freud emphasizes the ego's desire to preserve itself. But at the same time, the ego wants to be greater and more powerful. Narcissism thus emerges as a form of desire in which the ego is willing to entertain change as a movement toward that ever mythical "greater being." Narcissism presides over a state of affairs in which—because we always want to be more than we are—some aspect of the self, at some level, desires change. Of course, the permutations and duplicities of change are enormously complex, but the central motive for change would seem to be narcissistic in nature. We accept or embrace change only because we think it will somehow effect for us a "better" state of affairs.

This observation indicates that, as a term, narcissism should imply dialogical—not solipsistic—relationships. The attention we give the word *narcissism* usually triggers a dismissal of the ineluctably social nature of narcissistic relations. Such a dismissal vastly oversimplifies narcissistic phenomena. Narcissism needs an other. It needs an other to impress, to model the self on, or to respond to. Narcissistic behavior is thus especially involved with social fashion and social status. However, the social dimensions of narcissistic behavior, with their emphasis on vanity, are larger in scope than these terms suggest.

Freud's concept of primary narcissism, with its emphasis on a blissful oneness with an imagined other, suggests the self in isolation. But secondary narcissism, which derives from primary narcissism, is emphatically social in its concerns. Ellie Ragland-Sullivan explains that according to Lacan "secondary narcissism, with its attributes of permanence as manifest in ego ideals . . . [is] the basic process of humanization as well as the cornerstone of human relations."[27] This insistence on a profound relationship between narcissism and "human relations" may seem surprising. But if narcissism seeks to improve an image of the self by looking elsewhere for identification, then narcissism is an essentially social mechanism. Narcissism, apparently the most private and individual of psychological forces, is also the most social, because it marks the self's most fundamental response to an image of otherness. It is the primary force working at the cutting edge of the self's differing from itself. The implications of these observations are important.

In serving to enhance the self, narcissism has the goal of enlargement of being. But narcissism has no innately specific direction. Nothing and no one, in and of itself, delivers increased being to the self. Plenty of people and things *promise* increased being. But this promissory status is infinitely paradoxical.

The "things" that "deliver" increased being to the self are largely imaginary. Given this state of affairs, narcissism becomes closely tied to the imagination. Imaginative experience helps to "supplement" objects and events with narcissistic promise. This dynamic relationship between narcissism and imaginative needs cannot be overemphasized. Narcissistic energy is usually bound, although precariously, by rather specific signifiers or representations supported in their roles by culture, the family, or the singular nature of individual experience. In such cases of binding, however, the terms for signification are seldom fully adequate. Narcissistic desire generally wants more than the formulations it accepts. Freud speaks of narcissism in terms of "his majesty" the child. Kohut emphasizes the "grandiose" and "idealizing" gestures of narcissism. Because of what one theorist called "the narcissistic pursuit of perfection," narcissistic energy actively and constantly exercises the imagination in order to see, grasp, and respond to people and situations in new and more desirable ways.[28] Narcissistic energy funds both discourse and perception actively seeking to create a social and material world that can more fully satisfy narcissistic need.

In this context, writing becomes a rather powerful medium for transferring narcissistic needs into a social space. Narcissistic needs motivate the creation of rhetorically effective discourse structures, and the narcissistic energy activated by such rhetoric makes language a socially shared imaginative space where narcissistic needs are shaped and explored.

Rhetorical language, in both its production and its reception, is especially haunted by both narcissistic investments and the turnings—that is, the libidinal fluidity—of narcissistic investments. In any example of discourse, textuality is "sculptured" by a subject's (reader or author) narcissistic investments: Some words or phrases are weighted, other words or phrases are elided or relegated to marginal positions by selective acts of attention. In any act of writing, writers perform this sculpting, and in any act of reading, readers configure the meanings of texts by enacting their own investments.

This sculpturing of value in language is universal. Language comes to an author from a social world that structures emotion as it libidinally invests language with "living" form, shape, and weight. As it is reworked by an author, however, language develops its own unique form, shape, and weight. Furthermore, as readers respond to discourse produced by another, they libidinally edit and configure, according to their own interests, the sculptured "messages" they perceive in the discourse.

To the extent that literary products are linguistic mediums for narcissistic investments, they are also mechanisms for the social interaction of narcissistic investments. Literary texts bring diverse readers together in shared concerns. They designate a space where cultural values, ideological claims, and even cultural discourse itself, under the pressure of conflicting social and personal concerns, undergoes conception, debate, and evolution. Whereas private narcissistic investments often help us to appreciate texts, it is also true that rhetorical interactions with others give texts added depth and importance. Such interactions encourage us to objectify our narcissistic investments—to state what we think and how we care about texts. In these interactions we often discover that we idealize what others repress, just as others may idealize what we repress. In this manner, literary texts can, and usually do, become a space where individual narcissistic investments are vigorously and socially negotiated.

The particular form of a text's rhetorical resources for shifting libidinal investments derives—at least in part—from the narcissistic nature of textual production itself. An author produces a language invested with narcissistic concerns and this sculpting affects a variety of verbal structures—character, plot, imagery, theme, and signification itself. Jeffrey Berman points out that the Narcissus myth dramatizes all the "fundamental oppositions of human existence: reality/illusion, presence/absence, subject/object, unity/disunity, involvement/detachment."[29] As these "fundamental oppositions" play out their themes in regard to character, plot, imagery, and language in all literary texts, they provide a structure for an author's narcissistic concerns and—as I argue—both a structure and a stimulus for a fruitful dialogical relationship between the codings of an author's narcissistic text and a reader's narcissistic interest.

Various empirical and theoretical resources could be used to support the claim that writing begins as a narcissistic gesture. But it may be most efficient to develop my argument by exploiting the work of Jacques Derrida. Although Derrida's work is no longer as influential as it once was, it provides me with philosophical language which serves as a sort of shorthand representation for ideas that would be more cumbersome to develop in a psychological vocabulary. For Derrida, the center of writing speaks the futile attempt of the being of a subject to come into being through the presence of language. Writing is, in effect, a narcissistic crutch: "When Nature as self-proximity comes to be forbidden or interrupted, when speech fails to protect presence, writing becomes necessary. It must be added to the word urgently."[30]

Considered from this perspective, writing offers a narcissistic compensation for a sensed failure in presence and being.[31] Writing becomes a compromise formation that both expresses the ontological insecurity of being and ameliorates that insecurity through the production of signification. Writing allows a self to augment its anxiously depleted self-presence, by the supplement of the word. Writing is a libidinal investment whose form seeks to extend and increase libidinal investments. From a Lacanian perspective, the word is a particularly apt ontological gamble. Writing is a "want to be," but it is a "want to be" that wants to be read. Writing always courts an other; writing seeks to be "the desire of the other."

Writing produces, magnifies, and extends the presence of self-consciousness by seeming to represent it in language for others. In seeming to represent self-consciousness in language, writing converts it into a commodity and places this commodity (self-consciousness) outside the self for consumption. Writing thus offers an imaginary representation of self-consciousness as a commodity for recognition and appropriation. The text, as a "representation" of self-consciousness, provides a space, a habitation (in the form of signifiers), inviting an other to take up presence. It offers, in a subtle form, a verbal body to shore up the insecurity of a self's presence. Writing, then, begins as a narcissistic crutch; it is a verbal, artificial prop for self. Successful writing, however, becomes much more than a prop or a crutch. It produces for the artist a kind of social recognition that mitigates narcissistic fears. As Freud points out, the reality of the artist's social recognition is a very powerful force. We must understand why the artist is given such recognition and admiration.

Fundamentally, the text mediates between the narcissism of a writer and the narcissism of a reader. The text links the insecure presence of a reader to the insecure presence of the author. Both come to the signifier for substance and, according to their appetites, both find something of value. But this process is curiously paradoxical: The writer (among other goals) seeks to appropriate being and status by attracting the reader's recognition; readers, on the other hand, seek to appropriate being and status by recognizing themselves in the signification produced by the writer. Both come to signification, the word, because of what they lack. Yet, when the libidinal shifting of the texts is fruitful, the interaction between the reader and author (at the locus of the text) seems able to manufacture a commodity, an experience of "satisfaction" not available to either. If both author and reader feel themselves "recognized" in a satisfactory way, the pain of inner lack is ameliorated and a certain mysterious absent commodity, "being," is satisfactorily produced and consumed (even though it may or may not be, in a strict sense, shared).

If desire, as Lacan says, needs an other, then there is a fundamental reciprocity linking the producer and consumer of literary productions. An author's desire is essentially an expression seeking to elicit and draw power from the desiring response of a reader. Just as the child seeks recognition and narcissistic support from the mother and gains such support through both self-expression and the expression of frustration, artists seek both to gain recognition and to express their conflictual consciousness.

Just as the writer's desire gestures toward a reader, the reader's desire gropes toward an otherness desired and apparently configured in the text. Both author and reader are divided from themselves by their turning toward an otherness beyond them, in the text. This divergence of the author and reader from themselves, however, becomes the basis for a convergence of both author and reader on a textual medium that dramatizes, problematizes, reformulates—and in some paradoxical way satisfies—questions of being and value. This convergence of both author and reader in the text provides the basis for a metaphysically complex community established by the fantastic nature of the text.

Writing, we want to say, produces a message. But some messages, the kind we like to call literature, seem to multiply their meanings and, further, survive temporal interpretive transformations. Readers keep coming back to the ancestral bodies of many texts, thus keeping them relevant as they comment on and reinvest something of themselves in them. We could outline a history of the natural selection of texts, including the historical, political, and psychological forces that determine their character, their survival, and mode of reproduction. But such an outline is not my purpose here. I do wish to suggest that as authors and readers experience the various effects of recognition through textual production and response, literary texts become forms for reformulating libidinal investments. Literature becomes a vehicle whereby feelings, thoughts, and social arrangements that may not be initially a part of the discourse of a culture can become expressed, debated, and made "real" via the libidinal power of literary expression.

As teachers, we often get to see the generative effects of literary discourse in action in the classroom. It is interesting to see how highly personal literary recognitions quickly become a medium for social bonds between students. In response to texts, students often come to recognize what they care about and with whom they share this feeling. Psychologists argue that recognition is a very powerful and important experience. Recognition gives legitimacy to aspects of the self that may be unacknowledged or disowned. But we do not often acknowledge the wider social implications of recognition. Personal images and social visions are not disparate and isolated phenomena; they are intertwined and interactive. As a result of textual identifications, people come to fantasize about themselves differently, to define themselves differently, to act differently, and to have different ideas about an ideal community. They adjust their self-images and form bonds with like-minded people and begin to argue with others. They engage in politics. They formulate new definitions of authority and morality to justify the new visions of self and society that they have come to embrace.

Both readers and authors, I suggest, come to texts for substance; the substantial text is one that fills a certain emptiness within the self. The ability of texts to fill a certain emptiness within selves is a purely imaginary event, an event of "vision." Yet this event can have real and practical consequences.

As the imaginary "form" produced by texts takes up habitation in human bodies, imaginary "form" gives definition to very practical things: law courts, governments, armies. Texts are imaginary verbal artifacts, but they give a culture and a community a language to discuss its concerns. James Boyd White argues that "the community that a text establishes . . . has a real existence in the world."[32] We might say, then, that writing does not merely attempt to appropriate an imaginary entity— "being"—from an other by means of a circular and reciprocal act of empathy and communication; it often succeeds. Through the effects of recognition, social reciprocity, and shared fantasy, literary texts and other art forms produce linguistic codes necessary for the social reshaping—the libidinal rebinding—of communal being.

Ontological insecurity may be the center for the production of writing. But this unstable center produces an imaginary product that produces the metaphors of value necessary for every cultural change and identity. Rhetoric originates from an ontological emptiness, but it moves toward an imaginary and verbal structure that fabricates the true "material" of social and personal being. Readers respond to certain texts strongly because they feel they themselves are somehow "at issue" (as indeed they are) in the imaginative form and social consequence of that text; they respond to complete or define themselves; and they respond to banish the vertiginous and uneasy experience that the rhetoric of the text produces within them.

To understand textual rhetoric, we must appreciate its powerful emotional force. But we must also free ourselves from the immediacy of our initial response to it. As scholars we should do more than provide yet another reading or another ideological analysis of some particular text. We must seek to describe the nature of this entity, rhetoric, that produces the various contradictory sundering and repairing effects described here. The study of rhetoric should take a broad perspective on the subject. It should venture into a interdisciplinary investigation of its various mechanisms and operations.

Writing creates rhetoric and puts pressure on libidinal attachments as it dramatizes sites of psychological conflict, demands recognition from an other, and compensates the neediness of the self. A theory of rhetoric, thus, must concern itself with psychological events. It must examine the psychological mechanisms that produce the "experience" of such textual supplementation.

A good theory of rhetoric must avoid positivistic assumptions that would cut off certain lines of inquiry at the outset. I suggest that literary texts offer a supplementation for depleted being. From a positivist perspective this claim must sound ridiculous. The self cannot in any real sense get more "being" than it already has. In a certain sense the biological body is all the "being" that the self will ever achieve. But these complaints miss the point by failing to understand the point of narcissistic concerns. The question that needs to be answered here is not whether or not the experience of compensation or self-supplementation has some final ontological ground, but how the imagined experience (false though it may be) becomes produced. Even if the need for being more fully "alive" is purely an imaginary need or experience, we must take it seriously and investigate its dialogical implications for signification.

We must examine the various complexities of the experience of being more fully alive. There are numerous paradoxes to consider. Not every imaginary image of the fulfillment of being more fully alive, for example, can satisfy the imaginary need for being alive. Some images for the fullness of being can be shared between people, some images cannot. Some imaginary presences *seem* full, others *seem* empty. This is one of many paradoxes that surround this curious linguistic production. Many signified presences change their appearances as readers change. And many readers change in response to the ideological structures produced and marketed by cultures. Interpretation theory should explore these paradoxes. Interpretation theory should patiently and methodically explore the variety of psychological mechanisms that are the ground of textual rhetoric. Interpretation theory should seek to explain the psychological mechanisms that produce the effect of an experienced self-supplementation. A theory of textual rhetoric would thus appropriate another discourse explaining how rhetoric is an effect compensating for a depletion of being.

From a strictly economical point of view, writers write because they gain more reward than loss from the process. The same is true for readers: They read because they gain more than they lose.

How do we examine the complex psychological issues behind this simple gain? This question brings us back to the concept of narcissism. Narcissism is a name for a dialectical function presiding over an event we might call the *transference of being*. A species of narcissism occurs whenever being is transferred from one entity that has it (or seems to have it) to another entity that does not. This "thing" that is transferred from one self to another self is apparently imaginary. It does not exist in any "real" sense. Yet this "thing" that does not exist is central to human life and action, and is essential to the rhetorical functions of language.

How does one transfer something imaginary from one person to another? How does the receiver of the imaginary something acknowledge the receipt of a nonexistent entity? How does the receiver of an imaginary something sense, initially, the nonpresence of the nonexistent entity? These may or may not be valid metaphysical questions, but they are valid psychological questions. They characterize transactions we experience everyday. They describe experiences we take for granted, things that, as Fish says, "go without saying." They also, I think, characterize many of the implicit, unspoken assumptions about existence and signification shared by writers and readers. If writers can rhetorically manipulate the hidden agenda of readers' ontological or narcissistic concerns, they can find mechanisms for binding readers to texts, and readers to particular visions of life and community. If writers can induce us to narcissistically invest in imaginary things, these imaginary things can become real things.

The protected "narcissistic" space of literary enjoyment can insulate literary experience from real-world experience. But it need not. Many nineteenth-century readers saw Conrad's skeletal image of Kurtz intensely, and saw this image as a clear political message, a fit representation of the Belgian rape of the Congo.[33] When experiences such as these are noted and discussed in newspapers, as they often are, they are a clear force for propaganda. They influence a culture's image of itself and influence political action. We should not underestimate the degree to which literary response can be "absorbing" and transformative. We should not underestimate how literary experience, unlike the usual experience of reading a newspaper, can manipulate libidinal shifts and cultivate new value perceptions in a manner not commonly managed by nonliterary modes of representation.

An enduring theme of religious art shows Mary, the mother of Jesus, looking down with care into her son's eyes. The gaze from child to mother is transparent. The babe does not look *at* his mother. More properly, he participates in her being. He is surrounded and supported by her presence. He bathes in the resonance of her joy. Psychologists have argued that this unspoken and largely unspeakable experience is the ground of the emergence of the self. Children take on being as they take in the being of the mother. The mother offers her being to her children's need for being. Children are at one with the mother's inner life, and in this inwardness they develop their own inwardness. The mother–infant bond is, as they say, a narcissistic bond. Narcissism, in this case, characterizes the exchange of being from mother to child and from child to mother. Both participants are unusually "safe" but also vulnerable and receptive, unusually empathic. They give what they do not "really" have and receive that which could not exist except in the relationship between the two.

All bonds are narcissistic. All development and transformation are grounded initially in the receipt of nonexistent supplies. At the turning points of our self-development, we often have little more than a sense of inner emptiness and the faint glimpse of an idea. Our response to emptiness and our "regulation" of these ideas and images is both delicate and subtle. But this response and our regulation of it is enormously important. If we fail to organize and regulate our ideas and images, others will do this for us. Advertising and politics thrive on the marketing and manipulation of libidinal attachments and imaginary "images."

The narcissistic transference of being does not usually designate the portage of some homogenous substance "being" from one subject to another. Rather, being always has texture, style, and particularity. In this sense, there are countless varieties of narcissistic themes, countless forms of rhetorical structures. The mother has love, or anger, and usually both together, and these things come into her children as the substance of their being. The mother also has ideas, work, and values, which also "position" her children's identity. It is crucial to note that the child, or adult, may be surrounded by various and numerous experiences, that is, surrounded by many people who can become objects of identification. But the self cannot by a simple process identify with all or take in all (or even the best) that is without.

Neither parents, nor politicians, nor advertisers fully control the self-system of the subject. Only certain things can be ferried across the gulf that separates one person from another. Only certain things will come to count as being. The study of narcissism requires a study of what things can count, how they come to count, and what the consequences are.

Notes

1. Kenneth Burke, *A Rhetoric of Motives* (Berkeley and Los Angeles: University of California Press, 1969), 55.
2. Sigmund Freud, *Three Essays on the Theory of Sexuality* (1905), in *The Standard Edition of Complete Psychological Works of Sigmund Freud*, ed. and trans. James Strachey (London: Hogarth Press, 1963), 7: 145. Henceforth all references to Freud come from the twenty-four-volume *Standard Edition* (London: Hogarth Press, 1953–74).
3. Sigmund Freud, "On Narcissism: An Introduction" (1914), *The Standard Edition* 14: 83–84.
4. In this book I have chosen to generally ignore the distinction between "narcissistic libido and sexual libido." Freud sharply distinguished between attachments based on sexual instincts (erotic cathexis) and attachments based on ego need (narcissistic cathexis). See Sigmund Freud, "Mourning and Melancholia" (1917), *The Standard Edition* 14: 249. According to Freud, the subject has an original libidinal investment in itself that is later transformed and invested in objects. Freud's distinction is clearly an oversimplification of the mechanisms involved, but it does seem to have merit. Both Kohut and Kernberg are very persuasive in their analysis of such distinctions operating in analysis. Texts, however, do not offer the same concrete access to experience as analysis. For this reason I have not attempted to consistently

work with this distinction. There are moments when I feel secure about describing an investment in terms of narcissistic as opposed to sexual libido, but for the most part I use only the term *libido* and emphasize the similarities rather than the differences between these two modes of cathexes.

5. Stephen Mitchell, *Relational Concepts in Psychoanalysis: An Integration* (Cambridge: Harvard University Press, 1988), 103.

6. Ibid., 102.

7. Sigmund Freud, "The Unconscious" (1915), *The Standard Edition* 14: 201.

8. A long complicated article could be written at this juncture about the distinction between "object libido" and "narcissistic libido." As our understanding of narcissism has deepened, these ideas have undergone considerable readjustment and debate. I do not attempt to summarize an immense wealth of detailed discussion, but I can give a good sense of the range of these ideas by quoting from Mitchell, *Relational Concepts in Psychoanalysis:* "In classical drive theory," he says, innate instincts make us who we are by driving our response to the sexual power of appropriate objects:

> psychosexual urges and wishes propel experience and behavior, and one's sense of self is derivative of the expression of these underlying motives. Various authors from different traditions have turned this causal sequence around, arguing that the maintenance of a sense of identity and continuity is the most pressing human concern and that sexual experiences often derive their meaning and intensity by lending themselves to this project. (99)

Some theorists want to make all examples of libidinal investment examples of object seeking behavior. Other theorists, however, see all examples of attachment as expressions of self-identity. I must admit that I can neither synthesize these two views nor choose between them. In the example of the blonde by the car I would not want to insist that, for heterosexual men, biology plays no role in "determining" the woman's appeal as an example of "object libido." I would, however, insist that glamour, which shapes sexual experience, is heavily determined by our culturally conditioned response to details—clothes, poise, body image, hair color—fashioned by dominant social value. These details—examples I presume of "narcissistic libido"—undoubtedly provide cues for sexual arousal.

9. Heinz Kohut, *The Analysis of the Self: A Systematic Approach to the Psychoanalytic Treatment of Narcissistic Personality Disorders* (New York: International Universities Press, 1971), 40.

10. Ibid., 45.

11. Arthur Miller, *Death of a Salesman* (New York: Penguin, 1985), 12.

12. For a discussion of fantasy and rhetoric, see Jean Wyatt, *Reconstructing Desire: The Role of the Unconscious in Women's Reading and Writing* (Chapel Hill: University of North Carolina Press, 1990), and Ernest B. Borman, *Discussion and Group Methods: Theory and Practice* (New York: Harper & Row, 1975). For a discussion of transference and rhetoric, see Peter Brooks, "The Idea of a Psychoanalytic Literary Criticism," *Critical Inquiry* 13 (1987):

334–48; and Meredith Ann Skura, *The Literary Use of the Psychoanalytic Process* (New Haven, Conn.: Yale University Press, 1981). For a discussion of identification and rhetoric, see Burke, *A Rhetoric of Motives.*

13. Joseph Conrad, *Heart of Darkness,* in *Youth and Two Other Stories* (Garden City, N.Y.: Doubleday, Page & Co., 1921), 81.

14. Ibid., 90.

15. I see this fluidity of cathexes promoted by literary texts as the product of something present in the artist's self-structure. Heinz Kohut, for example, describes the artist as having a fluidity of narcissistic cathexes; see Heinz Kohut, "Creativeness, Charisma, Group Psychology." In *Self Psychology and the Humanities: Reflections on a New Psychoanalytic Approach,* ed. Charles B. Strozier (New York: Norton, 1985), 189.

16. Barbara Johnson, *The Critical Difference* (Baltimore: Johns Hopkins University Press, 1980), 101.

17. F. Scott Fitzgerald, *The Crack Up,* ed. Edmund Wilson (New York: New Direction, 1956), 69. I am indebted to Jeffrey Berman for drawing my attention to these issues of splitting and contradiction in relation to Fitzgerald's comment.

18. Simon O. Lesser, *Fiction and the Unconscious* (Chicago: University of Chicago Press, 1957), 55.

19. Mitchell, *Relational Concepts in Psychoanalysis,* 35.

20. Ibid., 35.

21. Otto Kernberg, *Borderline Conditions and Pathological Narcissism* (New York: Jason Aronson, 1975), 342.

22. Ibid., 339–40.

23. Heinz Kohut, *The Restoration of the Self* (New York: International Universities Press, 1980), 82.

24. Kernberg, *Borderline Conditions;* also Otto Kernberg, *Object Relations Theory and Clinical Psychoanalysis* (New York: Jason Aronson, 1976); Otto Kernberg, *Internal World, External Reality* (New York: Jason Aronson, 1980); Kohut, *The Analysis of the Self;* and Kohut, *Restoration of the Self.* Further useful studies from France include Bela Grunberger's *Narcissism: Psychoanalytic Essays* (New York: International Universities Press, 1979); and Janine Chasseguet-Smirgel, *The Ego Ideal: A Psychoanalytic Essay on the Malady of the Ideal* (New York: Norton, 1985).

25. Thomas H. Ogden, *The Matrix of the Mind* (Northvale, N.J.: Jason Aronson, 1986), 134.

26. See Mitchell, *Relational Concepts in Psychoanalysis,* 48–51, for a thorough discussion of Freud's attempt to make sense of narcissism and identification.

27. Ellie Ragland-Sullivan, *Jacques Lacan and the Philosophy of Psychoanalysis* (Urbana: University of Illinois Press, 1986), 35.

28. Arnold Rothstein, *The Narcissistic Pursuit of Perfection* (New York: International Universities Press, 1984).

29. Jeffrey Berman, *Narcissism and the Novel* (New York: New York University Press, 1990), 1.

30. Jacques Derrida, *Of Grammatology*, trans. Gayatri Spivak (Baltimore: Johns Hopkins University Press, 1976), 144.

31. For a broad discussion of theoretical and clinical support for the origin of artistic production in narcissistic compensations, see Lynne Layton and Barbara Ann Schapiro, eds., "Introduction," in *Narcissism and the Text: Studies in Literature and the Psychology of Self* (New York: New York University Press, 1986), 1–35.

32. James Boyd White, *When Words Lose Their Meaning: Constitutions and Reconstitutions of Language, Character, and Community* (Chicago: University of Chicago Press, 1984), 15.

33. Ian Watt, *Conrad in the Nineteenth Century* (Berkeley and Los Angeles: University of California Press, 1979), points out: *"Heart of Darkness* was, among other things, an early expression of what was to become a worldwide revulsion from the horrors of Leopold's exploitation of the Congo" (139). Captain Otto Lutken, a Danish sea captain who had commanded ships on the upper Congo for eight years, wrote a response to Conrad's work: "It is in the picture Conrad draws of Kurtz, the *tropenkollered* [maddened by heat] white man, that his authorship rises supreme. The man is lifelike and convincing—heavens, how I know him! I have met one or two 'Kurtzs' in my time in Africa, and I can see him now," (from *London Mercury* 22 (1930): 350). Patrick Brantlinger, *Rule of Darkness* (Ithaca, N.Y.: Cornell University Press, 1991), 259, points out that "much of the horror either depicted or suggested in *Heart of Darkness* represents not what Conrad saw but rather his reading of the literature that exposed Leopold's bloody system between Conrad's return to England and his composition of the novella." Conrad wrote in the context of this British expose literature, and he wrote for the reading public that was responding to such literature. Chinua Achebe's, "Image of Africa: Racism in Conrad's *Heart of Darkness*," *Massachusetts Review* 18 (1977): 782–94, is a useful corrective to many overidealizations of Conrad's clearly compromised moral posture. But Achebe's argument should not prompt us to overlook the propaganda effect present in the work's historical context. The novel written with Ford Madox Hueffer, *The Inheritors: An Extravagant Story* (New York: Doubleday, Page & Co., 1925), is aggressively explicit in expressing emphatic repulsion with Leopold's imperialism.

Self-Structure as a Rhetorical Device: Modern *Ethos* and the Divisiveness of the Self

Emancipate yourself from mental slavery; none but ourselves can free our minds.

Bob Marley, "Redemption Songs"

Contemporary scholarship in English has begun to show an increasingly sophisticated attentiveness to the forces of politics and persuasion. It is not simply that Marxists like Terry Eagleton pronounce literary theory dead and rhetoric alive; many traditional scholars, people deeply committed to politically disinterested New Critical views of art, have begun to recognize political forces and rhetorical patterns in texts long considered distant from such concerns. In keeping with this new interest in the operations of rhetoric, it is useful to examine the traditional concept of *ethos*. *Ethos* seems especially fitted to advance an understanding of textual rhetoric because it focuses attention on a simple question often neglected by traditional literary theory: How do people persuade other people to change their values?

Although our understanding of *ethos* has changed over the years, one feature remains constant: Often it is not a person's *ideas* but a person's *character* that changes people. Thinkers as diverse as Aristotle and Kenneth Burke agree on this point. Aristotle formulated three modes of argumentative support (logos, *ethos,* and pathos) and discussed *ethos* (persuasion stemming from the personal qualities of the rhetor) as a highly effective rhetorical tool. A speaker's character, Aristotle points out, "may almost be called the most effective means for persuasion he [she] possesses."[1] Like Aristotle, Kenneth Burke insists on the importance of the speaker's character: "You persuade a man only insofar as you can talk his language by speech, gesture, tonality, order, image, attitude, idea, identifying your ways with his."[2] For Burke, persuasion works via mechanisms of identification or "consubstantiality." When people identify with speakers, they can be manipulated into accepting their ideas and values. For both Aristotle and Burke a key impetus for persuasion lies, not in a conscious response to logical and factual reasoning, but in the prior (more primitive, and often unconscious) gesture of identification.

In many ways identification is a fundamental narcissistic gesture. We identify with people we want to be like; we want to imagine ourselves as better or more powerful by assuming the properties of people we admire. Our identifications, because they demonstrate our need for a desirable self-image, are narcissistic modes of desire. Aristotle's insistence on the importance of *ethos* and Burke's insistence on the gesture of identification thus give powerful support to an argument linking narcissism to rhetoric.

Theoretical Considerations

If identification is the key to persuasion, then any response to human character is a formidable rhetorical power. This response, as many argumentation theorists see it, is not something *behind* the force of an argument; it *is* the force of an argument. This chapter attempts to clarify this claim and support it in detail.

If *ethos* refers to the manner in which the character of the speaker or writer is featured in persuasive activity, then we must examine how character can be fashioned by language to serve a rhetorical function in a text. Second, we must examine, at the most fundamental level possible, the relationships between language and human character. This examination of relationships between human character and language is crucial to the larger argument of this book. Rhetoric, as I argue, is fundamentally concerned with the way self-structures participate in, and become reformed by, verbal structures.

What is self-structure? How is it related to a "self"? Unfortunately, contemporary discussion of relationships between language and the self is often confined within the assumptions and parameters of two models: the traditional Aristotelian theory of *ethos* and the current poststructuralist account of intertextuality. Neither of these models of character understand self-structure. Both lack the theoretical flexibility needed for an adequate explanation of rhetoric.

Classical consideration of *ethos* frequently links three separate ideas closely together: the development of self, the development of *ethos*, and the development of ethical habits. The classical message seems to be that people are the roles they habitually play. Rhetoricians, for both moral and practical reasons, are instructed to learn "good," or "ethical," roles. Quintilian argues that the good orator should be "a good man [woman]; and consequently we demand of him [her] not merely the possession of exceptional gifts of speech, but of all the excellence of character as well."[3] This quotation works in two ways. First, Quintilian is exhorting his reader: "Be a good man [woman]." Second, Quintilian is making what he takes to be a factual statement: "A good rhetorician is a good man [woman]." Taken together, these two messages implicitly define the self. A "person" is what he or she strives and learns to be. As a "person" learns and repeatedly plays a role (a "good" role, it is assumed), he or she becomes the person embodied by that role. The self is thus an effect of learning, a coherent behavioral role acquired through repeated performances.

This idea of the self may be popular because it has flattering implications for teachers of rhetoric. In a recent article on *ethos,* for example, S. Michael Halloran supports the claim that "habituation" is the means by which both character and *ethos* develop. Because Aristotle's theory of learning seems intuitively correct, Halloran urges teachers to give students training in "rhetorical action" and to encourage the interaction between rhetorical training and self-development. Students will develop character, Halloran argues, by becoming educated through rhetorical models:

If *ethos* is manifested in rhetorical action, and if *ethos* is formed by choosing ethical modes of action, it follows that educating a person in rhetorical action, schooling him [her] in proper rhetorical habits, is a means of forming his [her] character.[4]

This image of the self, common among rhetoricians, may be partly true, but it is an overly simple perspective distorting the complex relations existing between rhetoric and self-structures.

Poststructuralists see the self very differently from Halloran: The self is not a freely chosen social role, but a linguistic accident. Selves do not emerge as they choose to do things with rhetoric; rather, rhetoric continually does things to selves. Selves are not creative agents working within the inner core of the rhetorical process; instead, selves are the effects of rhetoric, a sort of epiphenomena constituted by an interplay of social, political, and linguistic forces. There is no inner entity, the self, that chooses its character. Instead, the self reflects the particular character of larger social forces that determine its nature and movement.

In addition, the self is not something that needs constancy or consistency over time. Different social situations trigger different self-structures; it is a mistake to assume that there is an inner core to the self that somehow grounds the various roles assumed by the self. Paul Smith, a theorist describing the implications of certain Lacanian and Althusserian ideas, suggests that a person can be "conceived as a colligation of multifarious and multiform subject-positions situated along, but not united by, temporal experience."[5] Such a self is little more than a simple collector of random and diverse exposure to social interaction. Memory and "character" play no role in giving a characteristic "shape" to self experience.

Not all Aristotelian and poststructuralist perspectives on the self are as tenaciously reductive as I have described. But as these models are disseminated in a formulaic manner, they pose serious limitations to any coherent theory of *ethos*. Both models fail to recognize the rhetorical complexity of the human structures they seek to explain. The Aristotelian view envisions an overly strong self able to choose freely its own nature, able to become whatever model it can imagine. Such a notion is a pleasurable and at times useful fantasy, but it is unable to account for the limitations of human nature—those moments when humans encounter their lack of freedom, their inability to be and do what they imagine. The poststructuralist view emphasizes the self's lack of freedom, but in doing so it imagines an overly weak self. A self composed entirely of collected social discourse is infinitely plastic. It conforms effortlessly to textual influence, changes easily and constantly, and offers no determined or "characteristic" resistance to the discourses that assault it. This view of the self helps us appreciate the social determination of selfhood, but it implies that the self, once formed, has no organized and enduring inner structure. The traditional and poststructuralist accounts of the self are useful for some purposes, but they are not particularly useful for a theory of *ethos*.

I describe *ethos* as a relationship existing between the discourse structures of selves and the discourse structure of "texts." Before I develop my argument, however, I want to clarify my claims in relation to the theoretical problems I have just raised. Aspects of my argument rely on assumptions antithetical to both traditional and poststructuralist accounts of the self. Rather than simply revealing these assumptions in the course of the argument, I want to argue in advance for their validity. I want to challenge traditional assumptions by arguing that the self is not something universal, but something deeply crafted by history and changing social formations. Second, however, I want to make it clear that my own position is not that of a poststructuralist. I want to challenge poststructuralist assumptions by suggesting that whereas various forms of the self change over time, the particular selves formed within particular historical conditions have relatively stable self structures.

Historical perspectives on the self are important because too often we consider the self a stable entity that does not change over time. This conditions us to assume that all different perspectives on the self reflect different ideas about one and the same thing. It may well be, however, that there are many distinctly different socially conditioned versions of the self. We often think of *ethos* as a concept defining a single stable relation between language and the self. But if the nature of both language and the self undergo historical change, then it must follow that *ethos* also undergoes historical change. The concept of *ethos*, thus, should not be imagined as some fixed reality approached by different perspectives, but as something assuming different shapes and structures over time.

Our interest in Aristotle's concept of *ethos* should reflect not only an interest in his understanding of the concept, but an interest as well in the social and psychological context that made the concept meaningful for him. Numerous scholars have increased our awareness of the historical and social context of Aristotle's ideas. Less has been done to describe the particular historical character of the ancient Greek self. Of course, it is impossible to recover a complete description of the historically situated Greek self. Nonetheless, we need to consider the information available, seeking to understand the differences between ancient Greek and modern selves. In an essay in *The Identities of Persons*, Amelie Rorty offers help by providing a broad overview of the kinds of concerns an historical consideration of *ethos* should engage.

Rorty traces the historical changes in four different literary concepts of the self. These literary concepts, Rorty argues, reflect not simply changes in the way we imagine selves, but changes in the phenomenon itself. She names these different entities the "character," the "person," the "self," and the "individual." In unreflective moments we describe all these differently structured entities as the self.

The early Greek world, Rorty suggests, imagined people as "characters."[6] Characters have a certain coherency at the level of behavior, but they have little psychological inwardness that takes responsibility for behavior. Characters

are the predictable and reliable manifestations of their dispositions; and it is by these dispositions that they are identified. Their natures form their responses to experiences, rather than being formed by them. Nor do characters have identity crises; they are not presumed to be strictly unified. Dispositional traits form an interlocking pattern, at best mutually supportive but sometimes tensed and conflicted. There is no presumption of a core that owns these dispositions.[7]

The concept "character" suggests a primitive structure of self-definition. Characters do not grow from experience; they are simply "manifestations" of "dispositions." Rorty's point is not simply that characters are primitive notions of selves, but that there is a reciprocal relation between what people really are and what other people imagine them to be. Cultures that imagine people as characters, because they have less demanding social expectations than other cultures, create different kinds of people. Characters have less "inner discipline." Culture and society neither expect nor create the psychological structures that provide such discipline.

More complex cultures begin to define social roles in terms of the "person."[8] The person evolves primarily in a society with a more elaborate legal system. Because laws require stricter social roles, the person is given impetus to be more responsible than the character, to conform more painstakingly to publicly approved roles. Rorty explains:

The person . . . comes to stand behind his [her] roles, to select them and to be judged by his [her] choices and his [her] capacities to act out his [her] personae in a total structure that is the unfolding of his drama. The person is the idea of a unified center of choice and action, the unit of legal and theological responsibility. Only when a legal system has abandoned clan or family responsibility, and individuals are seen as primary agents, does the class of persons coincide with the class of biological individual human beings.[9]

Persons are more complex entities than characters. They facilitate smoother social interaction because they are predictable; they are not chaotic or undisciplined eddies of emotion held together by virtue of one's name.

In many respects Rorty's person resembles Aristotle's self. This self has coherence but not self-division (that is, it is defined neither by an experience of inner conflict nor by an awareness of plural inner voices— both defining features of the "modern self"). Also, when Aristotle says that "we believe good men more fully and more readily than others," he seems to imagine *ethos* as some positive quality fully identified with the speaker's character.[10] *Ethos* achieves authority by virtue of acting out a particular role (a trusted "person"); *ethos* is not a complex and fully particularized experience produced by the distinctive self-structure of a fully individualized speaker. It is as if, for Aristotle, character does not *itself* trigger a distinctive emotional response in an audience. For Aristotle, in fact, the rhetor's ability to manipulate an audience's emotion is not considered as *ethos* (an expression of character) but as *pathos,* an argument consciously contrived in order to appeal to emotion. Consequently, in Aristotle there is a curiously sharp and unprofitable theoretical separation between a speaker's real person and the emotions that speaker can use to move an audience. In Aristotle's discussion of *pathos* human character does not *reveal* in a rhetorically effective manner the real emotion it "contains"; instead speakers, quite independently of their own feelings, consciously and purposefully direct words toward another's emotion.

To appreciate further how Aristotle's limited concept of the self restricts his understanding of *ethos,* we should consider Rorty's other categories of selfhood. The person is the characteristic mode of self that thrives before the advent of capitalism and social mobility. Capitalism provides new conditions that change the rules in the game of social status. And in changing the rules of this game, it contributes to the change of the self. As the self gains status through the acquisition of money and property, the "person" gives way to the "self" per se.[11] "Selves" develop, Rorty says, as individuals identify with their ownership of property, not with their roles. The evolution of a self identified with property allows the "self" a certain freedom. Selves transcend the limitation of proper public roles and become able to assume various roles:

When a society has changed so that individuals acquire their rights by virtue of their powers, rather than having their powers defined by their rights, the concept of person has been transformed to a concept of self. At first, the primary possession is that of land, and a person of substance is one of the landed gentry.

But when a man's industry determines whether he is landed, the story of men's lives are told by their achievements rather than by their descent. The story of fulfilled ambition is shaped by an individual's capacity to amass goods, by the extent of his properties.[12]

Capitalism, by changing social and economic relationships, therefore changes the shape of selfhood. As a new culture evolves, people both expand their ability to play roles and grant socially legitimate entitlement to other people who can play a multitude of roles in culturally approved ways.

In time, new social and cultural forces encourage a different version of selfhood. The self of early capitalism gives way to the modern "individual":

From the tensions in the definition of the alienable properties of selves, and from the corruptions in societies of selves—the divergence of practice from ideological commitments—comes the invention of individuality. It begins with conscience and ends with consciousness.

Individuals actively resist typing: they represent the universal mind of rational beings, or the unique private voice. Invented as a preserve of integrity, an autonomous *ens,* an individual transcends and resists what is binding and oppressive in society and does so from an original natural position. . . .

Because they are defined by their freedom, they no longer choose from their natures but choose their identities. But since such choice is itself ungrounded, they are simply the act of choosing.[13]

The last category of self, the individual, gives Rorty's argument a strikingly evolutionary cast. The essay thus describes a self evolving by gaining greater ontological freedom from, and control of, various forms of experience.

Characters simply react to experience. They have a measure of freedom, because their lack of "self-discipline" enables them to respond "freely" to any event. But in merely reacting to experience they do not learn from it; they are forced to repeat themselves in all they do. Persons, in contrast, have self-structures that mediate between experience and personality. The social roles given to persons allow them to take "positions" in relation to experience; they are not determined by the immediate emotional power of the experience. Selves have more freedom than persons, and they can play various roles. Individuals, finally, seem to have the most freedom. They have no core being, and are free from all constraints to choose their own "inner" being.

We can imagine, from Rorty's discussion, a kind of economy in the change or evolution of the self whereby desire, rhetoric, ideology, and social structure interact to produce the various real forms the self can take. These various agencies change as they adapt and respond to each other in their competition for power. And as they change in order to compete more successfully for power, they formulate social conditions that require evermore inventive changes and responses to change. Such a situation, perhaps, is most characteristic of contemporary life.

Rorty's analysis of the self should not be taken as a definitive description of the evolution of the concept of the self. Many of her terms appear to be overly idealized abstractions. Clearly, more precise work needs to be done on the relationship between social reality and literary representation. The historical difference among these categories of selfhood may also be less important than Rorty suggests. One mode of self may be prominent in a certain historical period, but all modes might exist in any one period. We might imagine, also, that a culture's discourse promotes complex relationships between rhetorical illusions that sustain conceptualizations of the self and real self-structures that are in part produced by rhetorical illusions.

Rorty's work may be inaccurate, but it encourages us to acknowledge that different cultures not only imagine and define selves differently but also formulate social and cultural conditions that allow for the creation of disparate selves. These varied self-structures reflect distinct models of libidinal organization and utilize diversely structured self-components to organize and regulate desire. By providing for different organizations of self components, cultures generate different strategies for structuring selves.

Social history plays a role in determining self-organization, but the individual history of a particular subjectivity also plays a powerful role in determining self-organization. While culture provides models for self-structure, selves also develop these models according to the particular workings of self-functions. Different self-structures, for example, are the consequence of particular selves responding to the cues of culture. Particular selves therefore internalize unique social ideals, unique self-images, and uniquely encountered particular role models. The individual self thus plays its own role in the development of self-structure at the same time that this role responds to the larger system of a particular culture. In all cases, the social rewards provided by a culture regulate those libidinal investments that contribute to a suitable self-structure and within each social context, there develops a reciprocal relation between the fictional self a culture imagines and the real shape of a particular lived self-structure.

"We are different entities," Rorty argues, as we conceive ourselves in light of different concepts of the self "our powers of actions are different, our relations to one another, our properties and proprieties, our characteristic successes and defeats, our conceptions of society's proper strictures and freedoms will vary with our conception of ourselves as characters, persons, selves, individuals."[14] Rhetoricians will readily see that Rorty's remarks are not simply remarks about selves. They are remarks about the nature of *ethos*. They implicitly suggest that *ethos*, as a concept, should describe relationships between differing ideas of the self and differing abilities of selves to act rhetorically in a society.

When considering the self, we must examine the various historical determinations brought to the concept. Historical consideration of the self demonstrates how models of selfhood have enormous flexibility and fluidity as the self responds to changing social conditions. Too often, however, this useful perspective on the self suggests that a particular self formed by social conditions has the same fluidity and flexibility that self-structure itself shows over centuries of change. The self, as an abstract psychological structure, indeed has enormous fluidity, but a particular self does not have the same fluidity. As a result of its relatively constant and particular organization of components, a particular individual self is much more stable in structure than that same abstract entity "the self," considered in terms of its historical permutations.

Scholars who take an historical or sociological perspective on the self see fluidity in self-structure as a result of self-structure changing from one generation to the next. This fluidity changing across generational lines is quite different from the fluidity within the self-structure of a particular self. History and social interaction give shape to selves, but these forces do not fully explain how *particular* and *discrete* self-structures interact with particular structures of language. To understand the rhetorical nature of a particular self, we must shift from an historical to a psychoanalytic perspective.

A particular self is not, as in poststructuralist terms, a simple, random, and constantly changing collection of texts shaped by historical forces. A particular self is not an infinitely changing collection of voices housed within a biological organism. It is a relatively stable organization of voices. Although we need not adopt the various models of the self-structure advocated by psychoanalysis, if we are sensitive to the nature of rhetoric we should acknowledge that the self has a relatively stable inner organization. Indeed, the idea of rhetoric requires a theory of a relatively stable self-structure.

The different modes of the self vary enormously according to time and place, but each self seems to have a distinctive character—a characteristic self-structure—that gives it a distinctive quality. Many poststructuralist theorists will find this claim about self-structure unsettling. New theories of language make it difficult to see the self in terms of stability, agency, or consistency—qualities we associate with self-structure. The self, thus considered, is a passive effect of language, something "subjected" to language use or a site where discourse collects. This emphasis on the self's passivity has prompted some thinkers to argue that it is time to abandon the concept "self" altogether. Other theorists retain the concept but describe the self as "dissolved." Jonathan Culler, paraphrasing claims made by Levi-Strauss, points out that whereas structuralist thought investigates the self, it also erases it: "As the self is broken down into component systems, deprived of its status as source and master of meaning, it comes to seem more and more like a construct: a result of systems of convention."[15] The new structuralist and poststructuralist ways of accounting for the self are useful, but they oversimplify the issues most important to rhetoric theory. They fail to grasp the self as an essentially rhetorical entity, a site of conflict in discourse organization.

Although it makes good sense to see the self as an entity composed of "component systems," as Culler suggests, it is also important to see the self as a conflictual *organization* of such components. The idea of conflictually organized self-components explains how and why selves act rhetorically. It explains why selves sometimes "take in" or internalize discourse, but also sometimes resist and deflect the linguistic structures and social formations that surround them. Clearly, selves are not mere radio receptors for social discourse. They are not passive vehicles constantly animated in different patterns by the passing-through of ceaselessly changing social discourse. Selves do not become each and every socially constructed discourse formation they encounter; something within its own inner organization prompts the self to identify with certain social forms and to reject others.

In some ways the account of the self offered by Culler and others is compatible with the account of self-structure given by contemporary psychoanalytic thinkers. Theorists who maintain a lively interest in the self understand it, not in terms of some authoritatively unified and dominating ego, but (much like Culler) as poorly organized self-components that interact with variable consequences. These same theorists frequently maintain that the "voice" of the ego has no existence prior to the voice of others. The self is not some homunculus that stands outside and beyond all social interaction. Instead, the self gains "form" as it is "informed" by the speech of others. The self indeed is a function of self-components that participate in and reflect psychologically significant nodules of social discourse. But these components, although they change over time as a result of social interaction, nonetheless maintain relatively stable configurations within the self. The relative stability of these configurations allows the self to dialectically engage and resist—rather than passively submit to—social interaction.

Poststructuralist descriptions of the self and the accounts given by Kohut and Lacan, for example, differ in their emphasis on language. For most poststructuralists, the self is nothing but speech. For Kohut and Lacan, speech is central to self formation, but the human person is more than speech; it is a biological organism whose desires, goals, and ambitions are organized by linguistic structures that overlay and complicate more primordial biological and preverbal structures. The self is not just a "text"; it is an active and complex organization of libidinal investments. It is, as well, a process of disorganized organization, a moving, interacting effect of discordant self-components.

Rhetoric might be defined as a well-focused and carefully crafted strategy for changing self-organization. It seeks to participate in the modification of self-components in order to produce changes in human action or belief. As an activity, rhetoric requires discipline—strategy, organization, planning, complexity—because selves are not passive receptors of discourse. Selves do not simply adopt the discourse systems they encounter; they admire, resist, or reject discourse according to their own unique character. Selves are clearly organized by forces that are not fully disclosed in any purely linguistic analysis of the organization of language.

A properly complex understanding of the self is important for a theory of rhetoric. If the discipline of rhetoric is to have the coherency it aspires to, the self must be imagined as having a self-structure held in place by organizing principles that are responsive to the forces operating in rhetorical transactions.

Major concepts in rhetoric reflect the discipline's longtime interest in relationships between self-structure and rhetorical structure. Style, for example, is an important rhetorical concept reflecting assumptions that rhetoricians hold in regard to the relative stability of self-structure. Style indicates a certain distinctiveness in the manner (as opposed to the content) of expression. At times this distinctiveness can refer to socially learned qualities, for example, when a writer is described as having a Romantic style. In this sense, style helps us to understand how human character is informed by social custom. Equally often, style posits a certain uniqueness of character itself. In this sense, style shows how each subject, although informed by social custom, also reformulates the patterns of social custom in distinctive ways. Ben Jonson, for example, insists that "this my style no living man shall touch."[16] In a similar fashion (but using a more theoretical vocabulary) Paul Valery argues, "Style signifies the manner in which a man [woman] expresses [her-] himself, regardless of what he [she] expresses, and it is held to reveal his [her] nature, quite apart from his [her] actual thought—for thought has no style."[17] Jane Gallop, after discussing Lacan's interest in style, suggests that "the object of psychoanalytic study reveals itself as style."[18] Style, in this case, reflects the manner in which content of any sort is appropriated by the symptoms of subjectivity.

The self has a relatively stable self-structure, and therefore a recognizable style. Rhetoricians frequently describe and analyze this property in linguistic structures produced by writers. Style is important not simply because it is a distinctive property of selves; it is important because it describes a linguistic site where self-structure, engaging social discourse, produces rhetoric. Rhetoricians examine how the style of the self is "characteristically" carried forward (consciously and unconsciously) into language to achieve rhetorical effects. Terry Eagleton emphasizes that much of Frederic Jameson's rhetorical force derives from his personal rhetorical style. "Jameson," he observes, "composes rather than writes his texts, and his prose . . . carries an intense libidinal charge, a burnished elegance and unruffled poise, which allows him to sustain a rhetorical lucidity through the most tortuous, intractable materials."[19] Although it expresses the "subjectivity" of the writer, style composes also the "subject" of sentences, and at least momentarily (and, when effective, more than momentarily), a unique subjectivity within the reader.

Other facets of rhetorical study imply a similar co-responsive relationship between self-structure and rhetorical language. Because selves respond to rhetorical discourse in complicated patterns of pleasure, censorship, attention, and belief, rhetorical activity attempts to control and direct these complex interwoven patterns of response. When speakers prepare speeches, for example, they typically seek to learn the attitudes, feelings, and values of their audience in order to promote certain intended rhetorical effects. Audiences, rhetoricians argue, can be most easily moved when they are flattered by a speaker who seems to promote their own values. Flattery is not a mere ornamental device. As Burke argues, "Persuasion by flattery is but a special case of persuasion in general."[20] This assumption indicates something important about rhetorical transactions: Rhetorical structures work best when they "fit into" or "work on" psychological structures already in place.

The beliefs of an audience are important to know because we assume that the self, as a result of deeply held beliefs, can resist rhetorical manipulation. Real people, unlike the passive creatures often conceived by structuralist theory, are not easily "subjected" to rhetorical effects of language. Real people resist that which they sense to be "rhetoric." The self seems to have a relatively stable structure that identifies with particular feelings and ideas in a predictable way, so it actively resists other opposing feelings and ideas. Rhetoricians acknowledge this fact and seek to develop rhetorical strategies that can overcome resistance.

Human value and belief—character itself—are not easily changed because of self-structure. Self-structure reflects those organizations of libidinal investment and libidinal control that define subjectivity. These organizations are durable and not easily changed. Rhetoricians, however, believe effectively planned discourse can overcome the resistance these systems have to rhetoric. When resistance is overcome, the stability of human character is an ally rather than an enemy to rhetoric.

Consider for a moment how the temporal stability of the self contributes to rhetorical effects. It seems clear that rhetoric can work—that it can have practical effects on the ways people act and behave. But what makes these effects possible? How does mere language have lasting effects on a biological organism? It must be the case that effective rhetoric is something like self-structure itself. It is not a mere collection of words

and voices, not a passive structure of language; rhetoric—like self-structure—manipulates the properties of linguistic form that organize (articulate the emotional and linguistic components of) the self. Both structures, rhetoric and the self, actively employ language to organize human
feeling and behavior.

Rhetorical form "works" when it operates psychological mechanisms
that inform self-structure. More importantly, rhetorical form can work
only when its effect survives the temporal moment of language exposure,
is preserved in certain components of self-structure, and is carried forward temporally into some larger horizon of thought and planning.

For most people, human experience is not like an afternoon at the
circus, a dizzy disorganized collection of momentary rides, that once
ridden, are immediately left behind. Some principle organizes and focuses human experience. Self-structure is precisely such a principle. It
gives meaning, focus, and organization to diverse segments of human
experience. Effective rhetoric, in a similar manner, makes use of this
same principle of focus and organization. Effective rhetorical transactions, like strongly remembered experiences, stand out as an ordering
center for an otherwise less impressive collection of dispersed impressions. They draw disorganized elements of memory and emotion into
their patterned structure. Admittedly, people are often only momentarily moved by rhetoric. But people can be affected in ways that move
them to vote or act in conformity with rhetorical aims at moments much
later than the time of the rhetorical experience. Effective rhetoric is not a
momentary and quickly emptied thing, and this fact requires more theoretical attention. Through language, such rhetoric taps the energy that
organizes self-structure. It can radically and lastingly change people's
attitudes because, much like strong experience itself, it makes use of
language to build self-structure.

All these observations lead me to a simple generalization important to
describing relationships between rhetoric and self-structure. There is a
sense in which people change and a there is a sense in which people do
not change. This assumption is essential for rhetorical theory. The self is
stable enough to resist change and changeable enough to admit to rhetorical manipulation, but not so changeable as to be in constant chameleon-
like response to each and every social force. Rhetoric therefore needs a
theory of the self that is sufficiently complex to conceptualize these

features. A theory of rhetoric needs an understanding of the self that appreciates the relative stability and instability of self-structure.

Implications

I have argued that the self has a relatively stable self-structure. I have also argued that self-structure is given particular shape by historical processes. These claims have implications for an understanding of the nature of *ethos*. Let me now make these implications more explicit.

A "modern" self differs from the Aristotelian self, and, because of this, an Aristotelian *ethos* differs from a modern *ethos*. Let me be more emphatic: It is not simply that Greeks and moderns have different selves, but that the larger structure of *ethos*—the particular mechanisms governing how personality can itself be persuasive—is quite different in the two models.

Aristotle's ideas are not outdated, but they are restrictive. These ideas were formulated within a particular social and psychological moment. The Greek self, Greek culture, and Greek rhetoric are interactive units that function differently than the modern self, modern culture, and modern rhetoric. Clifford Geertz argues that the human animal is an incomplete thing that finds its completion only in culture.[21] We should assume that different cultures "complete" selves in different ways, and provide different structures for rhetorical interaction.

To understand the form of modern *ethos* (though it is difficult to give "modern" a specific date) we must first, following the implications of Rorty's argument, consider the particular nature of modern culture in its relation to the modern self and modern rhetoric. How does modern culture give form and direction to both self-structure and self-activity?

An important aspect of modern culture is its prodigious diversity, plurality, and multiplicity. This cultural diversity is not simply something "outside" us. It is part of us, part of our consciousness. Geertz argues that "the hallmark of modern consciousness . . . is its enormous multiplicity."[22] Geertz points out that in premodern societies human actions are governed by "primordial attachments" defined by blood, race, language, region, religion, and custom. Traditionally, these attachments establish social groups, and probably also determine the values held by these groups. These traditional attachments have been very strong rhetorical tools. For most of the developed world these ties and their corresponding rhetoric are much diminished. Racial, religious, and linguistic conflict continue, and in some areas increase in intensity, but nation states of the West have minimized or simply reformulated the terms for racial, religious, and linguistic identification.

Extreme social mobility now allows and encourages people to situate themselves within and identify with a much wider diversity of relationships. It is no longer uncommon for children to leave their parents, marry outside of their religion or race, abandon old customs, and move to new regions. As the authority of primordial ties diminish, new forces work to situate and regulate the self. One of these forces is modern culture itself, which, characterized by diversity and plurality, reduces the emphasis given to the unquestioned authority of primordial identifications.

Aristotle was aware of conflicts among authorities, but demonstrated an attachment to a "primordial" authority; he idealized "truth" both as a voice of authority and as a single voice. By comparison, modern American culture does not idealize any single voice as the fountainhead of authority. Instead, many different and distinct voices are empowered, and all clamor to speak with authority. Modern culture, as a consumer culture, has in fact become a consumer of the "truth" voices of other cultures. Just as we buy the physical products of other cultures, we commodify, in a hybridized form, the thought of other cultures. The world becomes a vast supermarket of artifacts, discourses, and values, all available for consumption.

Ihab Hassan sees "postmodern pluralism" as powerfully disruptive, insisting that "pluralism . . . has become the irritable condition of postmodern discourse."[23] He describes "postmodern" culture as a scene where authoritative guides for human action and value no longer preside. In place of authority, Hassan finds indeterminacy, fragmentation, decanonization of authority, irony, and hybridization. As modern or postmodern selves become caught in the conflictual linguistic codings of modern culture, they confront the psychological effects of a radical disorder.

Modern culture "informs" self-structure. The cultural and social life of the modern developed world is especially informed by plurality and diversity, and this experience characterizes the modern self. Such a self is torn and disordered by many different styles of authority and personality. It hears, remembers, and internalizes many different styles of voice.

As the modern self develops, it seeks to establish identity in relation to the many voices competing for its attention. Rorty argues that the modern self "is" (at the level of self-representation, anyway) nothing more than a set of actions or choices; moderns, in other words, identify their selves not with some concrete entity, but with the *act* of choosing an identity. Postmoderns dispute the self's "freedom" to choose its identity. Nonetheless there is agreement that the modern (and postmodern) self is fractured by conflictual self-images. Perhaps, for this reason, the modern self seems especially characterized by anxiety, internal diversity, and conflict.

Heinz Kohut, a psychoanalyst, finds evidence for the fragmented nature of the modern self in literature. Like Rorty, he believes literature reflects self-structure. He also believes that the literary products of modern culture differ markedly from older forms. He argues that whereas artists of the past wrote drama in which a "relatively strong self" is exposed to "loves and hates, . . . triumphs and defeats," many modern artists "have begun to deal with a new set of issues": "This set of issues, to speak of it in the most gross terms, is the falling apart of the self and of the world and the task of reconstituting the self and the world."[24] Kohut's psychoanalytically informed observation echoes the claims literary critics have made for years. One watermark of "modern" literature seems to be the expression of a restless and divided self. Fragmentation and division dominate modern experience. Jurgen Habermas suggests that an older form of ideological control, "false consciousness," required older ideological formations. In modern societies false consciousness has given way to a new structure called "fragmented consciousness."[25]

If fragmentation and ethical pluralism characterize modern culture and the modern self, we should examine how these features play a role in modern *ethos*. Traditional readings of Aristotle and other classical thinkers describe *ethos* as a fairly simple interaction among selves. *Ethos* presents itself as a clear voice of authority and a vigorously dominant force presiding over a curious background of silence. Effective rhetoric establishes authority, clearly communicates its meaning, and effectively silences its opposition. Such thinking may effectively describe the kind of self and society that Aristotle knew. But such a self and society is not our own.

Consider another less tidy model to describe the modern rhetorical context. In this option, effective rhetoric is not a clearly authoritative and all-powerful energy in discourse; instead, it is a force always in conflict with an opposition. Effective rhetoric indeed dominates other voices. It subdues the noise of other voices and is heard above them. But in modern culture, effective rhetoric never completely silences other voices. Modern selves, it seems, suffer a certain failure of repression and can always, when they listen carefully, hear other competing noises, or voices of opposition, in the background. Modern texts, when paid some attention by modern selves, always deconstruct. A model for modern *ethos* should reflect this character of the modern condition described here. It should acknowledge the multiplicity of modern culture, the divided nature of the self, and the contingency of truth claims.

It is not easy, however, to redefine modern ethos in terms of textual multiplicity. If *ethos* is, as defined here, an argument in which rhetorical force derives not from "logical" support for what is said, but from the perceived personality of the agent behind what is said, then a modern *ethos* may appear theoretically inconceivable. An "author's" voice heard in a text by a reader seems to generate many different messages, and thus never appears singular or securely "itself." Increasingly, authors appear to be very unstable entities. Their characters become a function of readers' projections and their meanings become the result of ideological effects. If texts really have multiple voices, then authors disappear.

It often seems we can't have both at the same time: a theory that explains the rhetor's presence in a text and a theory that fully describes the plural disseminations of textual codes. Contemporary critical theory seems to require us to choose between two theoretical alternatives. If we embrace the multiplicity of discourse, we must abandon any notion of authorial presence and intention. If, on the other hand, we believe in the efficacy of rhetorical presence and intention, we must abandon a belief in the plurality of textual meaning.

I think we can have—at the same time—a theory of textual multiplicity and a modified theory of authorial intention. *Ethos*, in fact, is best understood as an interplay of two features: first an author's voice in a text and, second, that voice rhetorically manipulated by the plural nature of self, text, and context. I want to consider *ethos* as an externalization of various aspects of the rhetor's self-structure (present as "voice") affecting—that is, contributing to the internalization of—the reader's self-structure. I also want to consider *ethos* as something energized precisely by the plural, self-oppositional, and divided nature of both the self and conflictual cultural ideologies. I discuss this last assertion in more detail later. Let us now concentrate on the earlier, more simple assertion.

In seeking to understand *ethos*, we should examine relationships among three things: the structure of the argument, the self-structure of the speaker, and the self-structure of the addressee. What we see and talk about in this triangular relationship will always be determined by culture, history, and personal projection. Nonetheless, we will always be able to see something in a text, and in most cases we will imagine the "real" voice of an author in relation to the rhetorical effects produced by a text. When we feel rhetorical effects, we will always tend to attribute them to the agency of another personality outside us, working the rhetorical effects of language on us.

There should be nothing objectionable in this. If we construct a more complicated notion of texts and selves, we can legitimately imagine relationships this way. If culture, through language, provides devices that structure selves, there must be links between the self-structuring effects of rhetoric on readers and the self-structures (reflective of ideological forces working through them) left in texts (and, in some marginal sense of the term, intended) by rhetoricians. Cultures, we may say, structure selves. But cultures do not speak by themselves. They speak through the selves they construct. In speaking through selves, they construct selves. Texts, thus, must contain devices that connect the self-structure of authors with the self-structure of readers.

We can imagine these issues in a more concrete way by considering relationships between the concept of *ethos* developed by rhetoricians and the concept of charisma developed by sociologists. Think of charisma as both an aspect of self-structure and as an agency for rhetorical force. Studies of charisma provide clear, almost empirical, descriptions of strong personalities making effective rhetorical use of self-structure.

In *Wirtschaft und Gesellschaft*, Max Weber sought to explain how new values and institutions are introduced and supported in society. In short, he sought to explain change. He began with an analysis of the sources of a culture's authority, and maintained that leadership derives from three major sources of power: traditional, rational, and charismatic. Traditional and rational authority, he argued, have a certain permanence and are both "institutions of daily routine." Charismatic authority is a different mode of authority. Its legitimacy comes neither from special knowledge nor from the leader's special place in a social hierarchy of power. Charismatic authority is held by people who "have been neither office-holders nor incumbents of an occupation . . . that is men who have acquired expert knowledge and who serve for remuneration."[26] Such authority derives, Weber argued, purely from the personal qualities of the leader. By virtue of their personality, charismatic leaders are "set apart from ordinary men [women] and treated as endowed with either supernatural, or superhuman, or at least specifically exceptional powers."[27] Weber's emphasis on the persuasive role of personality in charisma is analogous to *ethos* as I have defined the term: an argument in which rhetorical force derives not from the logic of what is said, but from the perceived personality of the agent behind what is said. Considered from this perspective, the power of charisma is precisely the power of *ethos*. In both charisma and ethical argument, power stems directly from the personality of the speaker.

Whereas sociologists have documented the widespread occurrence of charismatic leadership, psychoanalysts and psychoanalytically trained sociologists and anthropologists have tried to explain its mode of operation. W. LaBarre argues that the charismatic leader's message is "not new information of the structure of the world, but only of new inner emotional structuring in people's culture-personality."[28] Theorists argue that the self-structure of the charismatic leader plays two roles in social interaction. First, and this is all too obvious, these leaders have a particular structure of personality that appeals to their followers. Second (and this is more interesting), charismatic leaders know how to "elaborate" their personality-structure symbolically for followers to emulate. In this "elaboration," leaders activate many messages within the more literal message of their speech. Charismatic leaders often outline a "mission" for their followers to follow. This mission may require the performance of real actions, but also encourages followers to develop a structure of defenses, desires, and repressions—a self-structure—similar to that of the leader. It is as if charismatic leaders rely on and draw rhetorical power from a certain (usually unconscious) control of the plural voices of their own text. A key component of the charismatic leader's power, then, lies not simply in the structure of personality, but in the ability to communicate, and especially to communicate oneself (and all the various linguistic layers of oneself), in all the various layers of one's message. As Winer, Jobe, and Ferrono point out, the charismatic leader "must have extraordinary powers of communication, usually oratorical as well as written."[29]

How do the mechanisms of charisma operate within the field of discourse? Two dimensions of psychoanalytic speculation seem to offer answers. First, numerous thinkers have linked charisma to speakers' ability to "share" and "elaborate" an unconscious fantasy within the more obvious material of their message. Second, charisma has been linked to speakers' power to depict, for others, their own mastery of a conflict analogous to the conflicts experienced by listeners. Charismatic leaders' power to elaborate their fantasy might be understood in relation to Ernest Borman's work on group decision making. Borman argues that the unconscious sharing of group fantasy often directs the path of group decisions. If group decisions are manipulated by the sharing of fantasy, then charismatic figures may be leaders who are especially adept at unconscious (and perhaps conscious) communication and elaboration of fantasy. In another context, Jean Wyatt claims that literary texts can contribute to the production of politically consequential fantasy as they invite readers to participate in their own politically relevant fantasies.[30] Clearly, relationships between politics and fantasy are important and require more research. Here, however, I want to subordinate concerns for particular fantasies and focus sharply on the relation between charisma and the mastery of psychological conflict.

Recall the claim I made earlier: *Ethos* links the self-structure of the reader to the self-structure of the author. Winer, Jobe, and Ferrono suggest that people who respond to charismatic leaders (that is, to masters of *ethos*) respond especially to a fantasy about the mastery of conflict.[31] However, what may be most important here is not the nature of a particular conflict, but the general structure of conflict itself. Consider this generalized human experience, the mastery of conflict, as something not present in a text in the form of a subject or content, but as a structuring device. This device indeed "structures" the language of the text, but it is able to work rhetorically because it "reflects" the linguistic structure of the author and "affects" the linguistic self-structure of the reader.

There are many ways to talk about the elements of a text. We talk about some elements as present in a literal way—for example, things an author literally names, such as places, objects, and people. Other elements we talk about are not present literally but symbolically. Psychologists, for example, analyze how literal events may represent unconscious fantasy material. I want to discuss something more primitive, not so much an entity as an event that seeks not to represent selves but to structure selves. When texts structure the mastery of conflict as a rhetorical strategy, this event is not a "what" that the text talks about, but a "how" that structures the reader's response to the subject of a text's discussion.

Consider a particular aspect of a rhetor's personality—an experience of conflict, self-opposition, and mastery of conflict. This theme of conflict can be considered as simply another fantasy theme, or as a structural principle—a principle both within texts and within selves. Imagine, first, that texts "elaborate" and "master" conflict (self-opposition) in various complex ways and, second, that textual "forms" for the mastery of conflict are at the same time "forms" for human experience that "inform" self-structure. Readers experience the conflictual nature of self-structure as they participate in the effects of conflict that they find elaborated and organized for them in texts. Authors, through the conflictual language of a text, leave traces of self-structuring devices that organize in particular ways the content of their own selves. These devices affect readers— that is, they work on the self-structure of readers—not all in the same way, but in a multitude of recognizable patterns.

A text's rhetorical power is related to the effect it produces through its particular organization and elaboration of conflict. Certain relationships between psychological conflict and argument are obvious: An argument always participates in a conflict, because there are no arguments when there is absolute agreement. When an argument shows real power, that is, when it triggers change or increased commitment, it does two things. First, it engages a conflict. Second, it overcomes some opposition.

For example, perhaps when we read an article we agree with, we say that it is a good argument. But if the article merely restates what we already believe, it has not overcome an opposition and thus has not yet shown true argumentative force. If the self is to be changed by a piece of writing, it must participate in a conflict and be moved by argumentative force to overcome its own inner opposition, or resistance to change.

I have located the resistances to change within the structure of the self. The self resists change because self-structure tends toward homeostasis. But if self-structure explains the self's resistance to rhetoric, it also explains the self's seduction by rhetoric. I want to suggest that the unique psychological "torque" of modern rhetorical power can be explained as a mechanism "funded" by the divided character of modern self-structure. Modern forms of *ethos* can "divide" us from our habitual values because, as moderns, we are always, in advance, at a deeper level, divided, self-conflicted selves.

It may be that the central power of "modern" *ethos* derives not so much from a rhetor's ability to develop unconscious fantasies and gratify unconscious needs of the self, but more primordially from the rhetor's ability to activate the inner dynamics of self-division—to liberate repressed voices, to activate self-conflict, to reshape the linguistic form of self-components. The work of Martin Fishbein and Icek Ajzen suggests that self-persuasion may be the most effective form of persuasion. Self-persuasion, they argue, creates intrapersonal discrepancy as it challenges beliefs and value premises. It unbalances fixed cognitions that preserve dominant values. In self-persuasion individuals are not given an opportunity to mobilize ego defenses that easily resist the assaults of other voices. Instead, individuals are placed in a position that changes the structure of their inner self-components as they listen to their own inner voices in new ways. Self-persuasion does not come from the outside as an external "authority" goading people to accept certain values; it comes from the inside as an internal voice (both an agent and an expression of self-change) reorganizing relationships among self-components.

Fishbein and Ajzen suggest that effective persuasion creates a conflict within the self.[32] But it may be that, given the nature of the modern self, the task of rhetoric is not to create conflict in the self, but first to bypass ego defenses that normally maintain a stable character, and then to mobilize, at a deep level of self-structure, the inherently conflictual nature of the self.

Modern theories of the self see it as, in various degrees, divided. Freud, Kohut, and Lacan see the self, not as a unified master of its actions, but as a more compromised structure presiding over negotiations among conflictual inner forces. In Freud's early topographic model of mind, behavior is explained as the result of compromises between the unconscious push of drives and the preconscious restraining structure of the ego.[33] As Freud's theory evolved, three structures—id, ego, and superego—are seen in conflict within the self. In the later work of ego psychologists, psychic "structure" becomes a term that describes the relatively stable organization of the self's restlessly unstable and conflictual inner components.[34]

The ego would seem to be the rhetorical center of the self. Its task is to organize, synthesize, reconcile, or otherwise repress divisive and conflictual self-components so that individuals can effectively (or somewhat effectively) pursue their needs and desires. We normally think of the ego as a structure that manages the conflicts of self-components clearly "inside" the self. In a certain sense this is true, but it is also misleading. Psychoanalytic theorists have more than a little difficulty distinguishing between those representations of people (often in the form of memories) inside the self that serve to represent the outside world, and those representations of people inside the self that structure the self's inner organization. Freud, for example, argued that a person's superego often develops from an internalized image of the father. Extrapolating from this principle, we might say that all internal self-components are in various degrees modeled after the self-structures of external others. A person's "internal world" is always something brought into the inside from the outside world (although the act of taking in also involves a degree of reshaping).

Psychoanalytic theory thus provides a model for understanding *ethos* as the effect of a specific fluidity within self-structure being affected by the flow of social discourse. This has implications for argument, writing, and pedagogy. When students hear the speech of others, this speech always has the potential to become part of their own "inner speech." Consider how students respond to classroom discussion. Some discussion is boring, some is highly engaging. Some of the engaging classroom speech may be remembered. Some remembered speech may be internalized and, furthermore, some of the internalized speech may be so durable as to become part of the student's self-structure. However, not all speech becomes internalized; what is internalized always reflects the particular dynamics of a student's self-structure. We cannot know in advance what sort of discourse engages self-structure and what does not, but we can say that when students confront through response to outer voices the conflicts within their own inner voices, they are doing ego work; they are reworking the inner organization of self-components. They are, at once, doing the work that contributes to the formation of a self, and doing the work of rhetoric. Indeed, when rhetoric "works," it works in a literal sense to construct a self.

There are further implications. When conflictual voices within the self are heard speaking through the voices of real people outside the self, such argument taps the deepest powers of rhetoric. Such persuasiveness is simultaneously very public and very private. It is, like the "hypnotic" effect of highly charismatic leaders, a form of communication erasing boundaries between speaker and listener and exposing "inner" self-structure to the reformulating power of "public" rhetoric.

In summary, if the modern self is highly divided, and if reconciling the self's inner voices of opposition is the task of both rhetoric and self-building, then texts that activate and direct these oppositions and reconciliations embody the key principles of modern *ethos*. More precisely, if rhetoric is always at the scene of conflict, and if the divided nature of the self participates in this conflict—and, indeed, facilitates rhetorical action—then it follows that a particular kind of representation of self-conflict (an "aesthetic manipulation," that is, of self-divisive conflict) provides an effective formula for *ethos*. In short, a distinctly "modern" *ethos* may well be grasped as an aesthetic manipulation of self-division.

It would be instructive to illustrate this claim in a writer like Bertrand Russell, who, with his ebullient confidence in argument, seems precisely the opposite of a divided self. But I defer this more complicated case of self-division in order to focus on the more simple case of George Orwell's "Shooting an Elephant." Orwell does not reflect all the variations in the structural principles of self-division I have tried to describe. The ethical and argumentative strategies of his essay are a bit too obvious. Nonetheless these all-too-obvious strategies may effectively support the more controversial aspects of my description of modern *ethos*.

Orwell's Ethos *as an Aesthetic Manipulation of Self-Division*

Eric Blair was not a great social leader, but as "George Orwell" Blair became a highly visible and "charismatic" journalist. Orwell's charisma is very much a function of his writing style, one that still serves as a model for many teachers of writing. T. R. Fyvel, a later friend of Orwell, describes the effect Orwell's writing had on him:

I had spent the nineteen-thirties for the most part abroad, but already in that decade I had come to admire Orwell's first novels and his journalism, and I thought of him as the English writer whom upon my return to England I would above all love to meet.[35]

A number of critics have commented on a sense of personal presence, the presence of the living writer, experienced while reading Orwell. George Woodcock observes:

What makes almost all of Orwell's essays still so fresh and fascinating, long after the occasion for their writing has lost its original interest, is the informality, the sense of linear development, which gives one the feeling of being inside the author's mind as he is developing his thoughts.[36]

Alok Rai argues that the sense of honesty that Orwell's writing conveys stems in part from an "aesthetic of acknowledged self-division," which provides a kind of "all-purpose verification principle" making Orwell "in every position, the most dependable of witnesses, an 'unwilling' one."[37] Repeatedly Orwell's persona represents the experience of a thinker in the process of balancing various opposing positions in particular acts of observation and judgment.

Orwell's own self-divisions are many, various, and fully documented. Early in life he suffered as a middle-class boy trying to be part of the Eton elite. Some writers argue that this sense of class division tormented Orwell all his life. He was a police officer in Burma who admired the Burmese. Later, he was an Eton graduate living as a bum in France and England, an Englishman fighting for socialism in Spain, a socialist fighting for the nationalism of England. As a writer, Orwell uses his dual perspectives on life to give depth and immediacy to his reporting. Rai observes that Orwell's persona, charged with self-division, is "valuable not so much for the individual findings, which are often commonplace, but rather because the persona is, in itself, a living record . . . of the process of finding out, of the difficulties of knowledge and commitment."[38] Eric Blair, dramatizing himself in the persona of George Orwell, uses writing as a strategy for expressing and seeking a kind of intellectual mastery over his own many internal conflicts. Rai argues that Orwell writes by "working through, and simultaneously towards a mythical persona which is constituted precisely through the stress between contending elements, between contradictory yearnings and divided loyalties."[39]

In the latter part of his life Orwell was both popular and widely read. However, many critics question his stature as a literary figure. The "aesthetics of self-division" that served Orwell well as a journalist and essayist did not work terribly well in his novels. Repeatedly, Orwell's central characters are passive and self-destructive. Rai describes these characters as having a sensibility "wastefully but also innocently at war with itself."[40] Raymond Williams describes Orwell not as a great artist but as a vigorous thinker, in effect, a powerful rhetorician.[41] But he is not a dated rhetorician. "We have been using him, since his death," Williams says, "as the ground for a general argument."[42] Orwell's essays demonstrate remarkable power in prodding others to take action or rethink positions. This power has waned little over the last forty years.

"Shooting an Elephant" continues to be very popular for teachers of freshman English. The piece has many of the qualities of "great literature," and at least one of the virtues of strong propaganda: a clear and powerful argument. Orwell wrote the essay with a political purpose. He was at the time a socialist solidly identified with anti-imperialist politics. But the essay does not sound like anti-imperialist propaganda because powerfully self-divided feelings characterize the *ethos* of the author.

The essay does not begin with a clear position statement. Instead, it begins with a confession:

In Moulmein, in Lower Burma, I was hated by large numbers of people—the only time in my life that I have been important enough for this to happen to me. I was subdivisional police officer of the town and in an aimless, petty kind of way anti-European feeling was very bitter. As a police officer I was an obvious target [when playing soccer] and was baited whenever it seemed safe to do so. When a Burman tripped me up, the referee looked the other way and the crowd yelled with hideous laughter. This happened more than once. In the end the sneering yellow faces of young men . . . the insults hooted after me . . . got badly on my nerves.

All this was perplexing and upsetting. For at that time I had already made up my mind that imperialism was an evil thing and the sooner I chucked up my job and got out of it the better.

I was all for the Burmese and all against their oppressors, the British. As for the job I was doing, I hated it more bitterly than I can perhaps make clear.[43]

This principle of self-division is repeated many times and in many ways. Much of this internal division is obvious:

With one part of my mind I thought of the British Raj as an unbreakable tyranny, as something clamped down, in saecula saeculorum, upon the will of prostrate peoples; with another part I thought that the greatest joy in the world would be to drive a bayonet into a Buddhist priest's guts.[44]

But much of the "message" of self-division is not so obvious: the irony of the essay's tone; the sharp division between the present "speaker" of the essay and the actor of the unfolding narrative; Orwell's powerful conclusion that curiously imagines the "scene" of the elephant's death as vastly "distant" from the actual scene of the elephant's bleeding body—

all of these elements and many others that I do not have the space to invoke press on the reader with subtle if undeniable rhetorical pressure.

Orwell's expression of self-division serves a strong rhetorical function in the text's ethical argument. The text does not begin by identifying with one pole of the political argument, so both sides of the issue can identify with the story. The essay does not attack the values of a reader and does not force a reader into a rigidly reactive and self-protective response; instead, the essay invites projection, sympathy, and identification. The essay has, indeed, some of the virtues of a Rogerian argument, insofar as Orwell is sympathetic to his opposition. Though anti-imperialist himself, he concedes certain virtues to the British Empire. "I did not know," the persona says, "that the British Empire is dying, still less that it is a great deal better than the younger empires that are going to supplant it."[45] But Orwell's essay is more complicated than a Rogerian argument. The author is not a person who "listens" sympathetically and nonjudgmentally to an argument of an "other." Instead the position of the other is an aspect balanced within the author's own position. And just as the author balances the two perspectives in conflict, the reader is invited to do the same.

As the story develops, the author's self-division participates in an action that sharply reveals its own inner struggle and seeks to attain a kind of mastery over the various values in opposition. Readers of the essay may initially read merely for the plot, that is, to find out what happens to the author. But when readers become engaged in the plot they begin to participate in the unique nature of Orwell's experiences. As the suspense of the plot increases, the reader's feelings about the action become more intense, and this promotes an increasingly intense identification with the conflict experienced by the central character. In reading about an external conflict that produces an internal conflict, the reader's internal self-components become responsive to the textual shape of the conflict represented through many textual strategies—plot, character, irony, symbol, imagery.

The text encourages the reader to identify closely with the character and scene, thus readers soon become identified with much more than a particular character in a particular circumstance. One possible result will be that a political position—one perhaps initially excluded from the reader's own values—will receive increased personal attention. But there are several plausible developments. For example, a reader may have never been fully conscious of two sides to the political issue and will, only through the essay, come to "see" and appreciate an opposing position. The rhetoric of Orwell's essay, moreover, encourages this new seeing to be a highly charged emotional event. The reader may not "think" about a logical argument, but the principle of an "other side" becomes embedded within and amplified by the reader's vicarious experience of self-division. In another outcome, a reader already experiencing two sides to the issue finds that the essay intensifies the conflict and pushes toward a rhetorically manipulated resolution.

In *The Road to Wigan Pier*, Orwell says that "every Anglo-Indian is haunted by a sense of guilt which he usually conceals . . . because there is no freedom of speech" in his or her society.[46] "Shooting an Elephant" is an attempt to free speech from concealment and repression, thereby putting rhetorical pressure on self-structure. Every self contains two kinds of voices: those stifled and repressed, and those heard and idealized. Orwell's essay seeks to empower marginalized voices within the self, to give them a hearing and then to idealize, for self-structure, those repressed voices that are heard. When marginalized voices within the self are thus empowered, they exert power over the thoughts and actions taken by the self; they "speak" in such a way that the ego can identify with them. In Orwell's text, feelings of entertainment, suspense, and aesthetic pleasure appeal to the id's desire for pleasure; attending to this pleasure, however, has consequences for the ego. A curtain of repression that normally suppresses anti-imperialist thought and feeling is lifted. A reader, reading for pleasure, gets "involved" in the story and wants to know more about what is happening "in" the text. But in so doing, readers hear (as their own "inner voice") voices they have not fully heard before. Wanting to know what happens "in" the text, readers become attentive to what is happening "in" themselves. Rhetorical effects are thus achieved by the pursuit of pleasure and concomitant venting (and entitling) of repressed voices.

The resolution of the plot—the shooting of the elephant—rebalances the rhetorical forces in conflict within the narrator's "inner" self. The story, while representing external events, also at some level "expresses" the rebalancing activity that is at work within the self. Orwell comes to recognize that it is not only the natives who are betrayed by imperialism; imperialism betrays the people it is supposed to serve. Thus motives of self-interest, and not altruism, contribute to the strength of anti-imperialist feeling: "I perceived in this moment that when the white man turns tyrant it is his own freedom that he destroys."[47] The essay represents an ironic experience where a literal example of brute mastery expresses, paradoxically, a loss of mastery. Conversely, however, the recognition of loss of mastery contributes to a rhetoric of self-understanding: "I perceived in this moment that when the white man turns tyrant it is his own freedom that he destroys." It is hard not to see in this moment of self-recognition a fantasy of mastery that captures the ego much as in Lacan's account of the mirror stage an image captures and situates the agency of the ego.

Orwell's idealization of this moment of recognition, his capturing, recovering, and verbally masterying this moment through the act of writing the narrative, becomes a creative act that reshapes various organizations of feeling and value within the speaker. The author begins to formulate what he now begins to experience as his "real" feelings about imperialism, and he vigorously labels this enterprise as morally wrong. The essay ends with an extended description of a dying elephant, and there is a curiously intense identification between Orwell and the elephant. In some remote and overdetermined symbolic overlay, it seems to me, it is not an elephant that Orwell has killed in the essay, but an older version of the self. The experience of shooting the elephant and the experience of thinking and writing about it change the "shape" of the author's self.

The text presents the reader with a curious argument. It does not tell the reader what to think. There is not, as in the case of an Aristotelian ethos, a character of intelligence and good will presenting a clear case for his side. The *ethos* of the text does not say: "Trust me. Do this." Instead the *ethos* says: "This is what happened to me." And through a kind of plotted intricacy, the instability of the text's initial political position promotes its rhetorical effectiveness.

I am suggesting, by way of this discussion of Orwell, that self-division can provide a rhetorically effective form of argument. I am also suggesting that most modern arguments (and perhaps also more traditional arguments), when closely examined, reveal particular structures, and particular styles, of self-division. But I should emphasize that structures of self-division are not all equivalent, not all variations on the same theme. The mere expression of self-division, for example, is not always rhetorically effective. Often a reader responds to a representation of self-division with confusion; either readers are confused themselves (and feel no rhetorical pressure), or they feel sure that the writer is. Many composition teachers, for example, find that students identify with one belief on the first page of their paper and identify with an opposing belief on the third. When asked what they really believe, they commonly reply that they are, indeed, confused. The teacher replies, "Well, if you are confused yourself, how do expect others to be convinced by your argument?" It is one thing to experience self-division and another to develop a rhetorically effective strategy for activating a reader's self-division. Consequently, teachers often instruct students to avoid expression of self-divisive feelings. But this may be the worst advice we can give. The point is not to avoid self-division, but to make rhetorical use of it and to develop a "style" or an apparently unified "voice" that "moves" a reader's self-structure. Self-division, if it is to work effectively, must be present as an *ethos*. It must speak as a recognizable voice, a voice that has "worked through" and crafted a sense—or a "fantasy"—of mastery over the pain of inner conflict.

I will further elaborate on my argument about *ethos* and mastery in chapter 4. This brief analysis of Orwell's essay cannot entirely prove the claims made in this chapter. My arguments have been broadly historical and deeply theoretical. Nonetheless, my analysis of Orwell should clarify aspects of the theoretical position I have described. Orwell's voice speaks with a particular rhetorical style—one might say a confessional style—of self-division. This self-division has powerful rhetorical effects because it reflects a particular dynamic of self-structure that "moves" us. Rhetorical effect is related to self-structure because both are organized psychological processes that direct attention, orchestrate affect, and provide form for human experience. Rhetorical effect and self-structure are best understood, then, not as language or representation, but as dynamic forces that give form to the various contents—cultural, biological, textual, psychological—that they work on. In turn, in working on these various contents, they change them. Change, after all, is what rhetoric is about.

Notes

1. Aristotle, *Rhetoric*, in *The Basic Works of Aristotle*, ed. Richard McKeon (New York: Random House, 1941), line 1356a.

2. Burke, *A Rhetoric of Motives*, 55.
3. Quintilian, *Institutio oratoria*, trans. H. E. Butler (Cambridge: Harvard University Press, 1960), line 1.9.
4. Michael S. Halloran, "Aristotle's Concept of *Ethos*, or If Not His Somebody Else's," *Rhetoric Review* 1 (1982): 61.
5. Paul Smith, *Discerning the Subject* (Minneapolis: University of Minnesota Press, 1988), 32.
6. Amelie Oksenberg Rorty, "A Literary Postscript: Characters, Persons, Selves, Individuals," in *The Identities of Persons*, ed. by Amelie Oksenberg Rorty (Berkeley and Los Angeles: University of California Press, 1976), 303–7.
7. Ibid., 304–5.
8. Ibid., 309–11.
9. Ibid., 309.
10. Aristotle, *Rhetoric*, line 1356.
11. Rorty, "A Literary Postscript," 312–15.
12. Ibid., 313.
13. Ibid., 315–17
14. Ibid., 302.
15. Johnathan Culler, "In Pursuit of Signs," *Daedalus* 106 (1977): 104.
16. Ben Johnson, "Poetaster," in *The Complete Plays of Ben Jonson*, ed. G. A. Wilkes (Oxford: Clarendon Press, 1981), line 5.1.
17. Paul Valéry, *Aesthetics*, vol. 13 of *The Collected Works of Paul Valéry*, ed. Jackson Mathews, trans. Ralph Manheim (New York: Pantheon, 1964), 183.
18. Jane Gallop, *Reading Lacan* (Ithaca, N.Y.: Cornell University Press, 1985.
19. Terry Eagleton, *Against the Grain* (London: Verso, 1986), 60.
20. Burke, *A Rhetoric of Motives*, 55.
21. Clifford Geertz, *The Interpretation of Cultures* (New York: Basic Books, 1973), 49.
22. Clifford Geertz, *Local Knowledge* (New York: Basic Books, 1983), 161.
23. Ihab Hassan, "Pluralism in Postmodern Perspective," *Critical Inquiry* 12 (1986): 503.
24. Heinz Kohut, "The Self in History," in *Self Psychology and the Humanities: Reflections on a New Psychoanalytic Approach*, ed. Charles B. Strozier (New York: Norton, 1985), 168–69.
25. Jurgen Habermas, *Theorie des kommunikativen Handelns*, vol. 2 (Frankfurt: Suhrkamp, 1981), 522; quoted by Dominick La Capra, "Culture and Ideology: From Geertz to Marx," *Poetics Today* 9, no. 2 (1988): 380.
26. Max Weber, *On Charisma and Institution Building*, ed. S. N. Eisenstadt (Chicago: University of Chicago Press, 1968), 18–19.
27. Ibid., 48.
28. W. LaBarre, *The Ghost Dance: Origins of Religion* (New York: Delta, 1972), 360.
29. Jerome A. Winer, Thomas Jobe, and Carlton Ferrono, "Toward a Psychoanalytic Theory of the Charismatic Relationship," *The Annual of Psychoanalysis* 22–23 (1984–85): 173.
30. Wyatt, *Reconstructing Desire*.

31. Winer, Jobe, and Ferrono, "Toward a Psychoanalytic Theory," 155–77.
32. Martin Fishbein and Icek Ajzen, *Belief, Attitude, Intention, and Behavior* (Reading, Mass.: Addison-Wesley, 1975).
33. Mark Levey, "The Concept of Structure in Psychoanalysis," *Annual of Psychoanalysis* 22–23 (1984–85): 138.
34. Ibid., 150.
35. T. R. Fyvel, *George Orwell: A Personal Memoir* (London: Hutchinson, 1983), 4.
36. George Woodcock, *The Crystal Spirit: A Study of George Orwell* (Boston: Little Brown, 1966), 332.
37. Alok Rai, *Orwell and the Politics of Despair* (Cambridge: Cambridge University Press, 1990), 45–46.
38. Ibid., 42.
39. Ibid., 45.
40. Ibid., 44.
41. Raymond Williams, *Culture and Society: 1780–1950* (New York: Columbia University Press, 1983), 285.
42. Ibid.
43. George Orwell, "Shooting an Elephant," in *The Orwell Reader: Fiction, Essays, and Reportage by George Orwell* (New York: Harcourt Brace, 1949), 57.
44. Ibid., 58.
45. Ibid., 58.
46. George Orwell, *The Road to Wigan Pier* (New York: Medallion Books, 1961), 125.
47. Orwell, "Shooting an Elephant," 60.

Projection and the Resistance of the Signifier: A Reader-Response Theory of Textual Presence

There is more to a mirror
than you looking at

your full-length body
flawless but reversed.

    Margaret Atwood, "Tricks with Mirrors"

Reader-response theory can be useful for explaining the mechanisms of textual rhetoric. But the present theoretical positions that define reader response generally undermine the rhetorical complexity of interactions between the text and the subject. Because reader response is most often represented in either emphatically psychoanalytic terms or in emphatically poststructuralist terms, reader-response theories either underestimate the status of the text (as in psychoanalytic perspectives) or underestimate the status of the subject (as in poststructuralist perspectives).

Rhetoric, in order to function as rhetoric, has to assume that language in and of itself can affect a reader's response. This assumption is generally denied by the psychoanalytic reader-response theories that emphasize the reader's role in creating the text by projecting meaning on it. The early work of Norman Holland, Stanley Fish, and David Bleich, for example, insists that a text has little power to guide, direct, or determine the response of readers. Considered in these terms, the text does not really exist apart from readers. Readers construct their own different texts as they construct different meanings; there is no "objective" text, no real, stable, and controlling textual entity that directs textual response and exercises the power rhetoricians imagine.

In this account of textual response, the multiplicity of meanings found by readers becomes a problem for rhetorical theory: readers produce their own text and there can be no pressure exerted by the text on the reader. Rhetoric can occur as an accident of response, but the text itself exerts no rhetorical pressure. Psychoanalytic reader-response theory may understand people, but it does not understand texts.

Poststructuralist perspectives on reader response also make the idea of rhetoric impossible, though for a different reason. Deconstruction imagines the multiplicity of textual meaning not as a function of different subjective responses to a text, but as a function of a textuality itself: a text's collection of indeterminate signifiers. The text is never "iterable," that is, never the same text twice. Similarly, readers are—like the text itself—collections of indeterminate texts. Poststructuralist theory may understand something about texts, but it does not understand people. The rhetoric conceived by poststructuralist thought is described in terms of a reader's subjectivity effortlessly configured by the signifiers of the text. Such a rhetoric is not worthy of the name; it is not fully possible because both the signifiers of a text have no stability and the interior "textuality" of the reader has no constancy. Rhetoric is a largely inconsequential effect of subjectivity being temporarily subjected to particular signifiers. Poststructuralist and psychoanalytic accounts of reader-response theory have been helpful in broadening our notion of how texts operate. But these theories misrepresent the relationship between texts and selves and fail to account for the operations of textual rhetoric.

These theoretical positions generally misrepresent relationships between texts and selves because they are unable to fully imagine the differences between texts and selves. Texts are made up of signifiers that, in themselves, bear little resemblance to subjectivity. Although, in a limited sense, it is true that people are a collection of signifiers, collections of signifiers are not people. Signifiers do not contain emotion, but people do. Signifiers do not in themselves organize emotion, but people do. Signifiers in themselves have no libidinal charge, no libidinal organizations or relationships. Signifiers are not like subjects. They are in themselves flat coding devices, useful to both humans and computers for a variety of purposes.

Subjects, unlike computers, *use* signification to construct subjectivity. Because signifiers can signify *for* a subject, texts can affect the subjectivity of a reader. Signifiers do this, not because of what they are in themselves—ink marks on a page—but because of subject functions that animate signification. Signification participates in a larger social universe of discourse manipulation and reflects the rhetorical strategies used by both people and cultures to "position" subjects. Texts affect subjectivity because texts echo rhetorical messages left by others; they contain rhetorical traces left by an author, an author's unconscious, and a cultural unconscious working through an author.

When we respond to texts, the messages we perceive are not determined exclusively by our subjectivity, and, conversely, our subjectivity is not controlled by the libidinal messages coded by others. When we respond to texts, we respond to a scene of complex social interaction; we associate texts with people talking and sharing all the conscious and unconscious messages that people share. When we respond to texts, we can be attentive to a clear, "objectively" present sequence of signifiers. These signifiers, while they may evoke private meanings for us, also connect our response to a wider world of social and verbal interaction. There is an enormous variety of messages latent in any discourse sample, consequently reading engages us in many possible and many different meaning arrangements.

Rhetoric is a complicated verbal art because, to be effective, it must use verbal strategies to manipulate self-components. Textual rhetoric, as I envision it, uses verbal structures not simply (and not always) to define and advocate a particular libidinal organization. It also uses them to amplify the experience of conflict, multiply textual meaning, and encourage readers to *identify with* various and often mutually exclusive libidinal organizations of value judgment and subject positionings. Through this interaction between the multiple and polyvocal formal structures of rhetoric and the multiple polyvocal internal structures of the self, a text can loosen the usual rigidity in terms of which readers maintain habitual values.

Chapter 2 formulated a description of *ethos* at work in the verbal structure of a text. This chapter shows, first, how a text is an entity resistant to the individual reading strategies that create meaning from it, and second, how a conflictual signification serves rhetorical purposes.

Poststructuralist and traditional psychoanalytic reader-response theories oversimplify the rhetorical mechanisms of the text by being insufficiently attentive to the essential otherness that distinguishes a text from its reader. A text is not essentially the reflection of a reader, and a reader is not essentially the reflection of a text. A text, in and of itself, possesses an otherness that plays a role in rhetorical interactions. Rhetoric, in fact, is funded by interactions between the subjective projections of readers and objective significations of texts. Textual rhetoric is powerful because projection "projects" the material of self-structure and then introjects the material of text structure. Rhetoric works as components of text structure become organized into components of self-structure. In order for a text to function as a rhetorical device, the reader must encounter in it something "other"; my purpose here is to describe how texts exist independently of readers.

The Status of the Text

Traditional psychoanalytic and poststructuralist perspectives on the text, despite their many differences, obscure the differences between texts and selves. Major works produced by both theoretical camps frequently argue that it is not possible to assume the presence of an objective text. The text cannot be objective because if it is considered as the encoding of an author's message, the text cannot remain tied to the integrity of its originating or controlling purpose. It loses its message as it is violated by reading strategies. If one dismisses the importance of the author and thinks of the text as an autonomous linguistic artifact, the text still cannot exist as an objective entity, because it cannot control or deliver univocal meaning. As a verbally autonomous entity, the text cannot be autonomous; it is always on the point of dissolving. It is unable to enclose the boundaries of its subject, unable to limit the pluralities of its signification. These discoveries of linguistic unfaithfulness changed the attitudes of many prominent critics. Stanley Fish, for example, observes that in his early years "the integrity of the text was as basic to my position as it was to the position of the New Critics."[1] Later in his career, however, Fish came to recognize a disquieting arbitrariness in what had been called with reverence, the "text." The text does not exist as a stable objective entity. It *becomes* differentially present and "objective" through any one of the many interpretive methods of responding critics. The text "in itself," Fish argues, possesses "objectivity" only as black ink stains upon paper.

Fish insists that "there isn't a text . . . if one means . . . [what Hirsch means] 'an entity which always remains the same from one moment to the next.' "[2] But Fish and other critics who dismiss the objective text nonetheless insist on an interpretive vigilance in any act of interpretation. Paul de Man asserts that "literature as well as criticism—the difference between them being delusive—is condemned (or privileged) to be forever the most rigorous and, consequently, the most unreliable language in terms of which man [woman] names and transforms [her-] himself."[3] Barbara Johnson, who quotes de Man on this issue, explains that deconstruction "involves a reversal of values, a revaluation of the signifying function of everything that, in a sign-based theory of meaning, would constitute noise."[4] As "noise" becomes seriously examined for its signifying function, it calls into question the stability of the text's more apparent "intention" or "meaning." The perception of a textual content (noise), which is "at war" with the text's more obvious rhetorical intent, should be important for any theory of rhetoric because rhetoric derives its power precisely from its ability to overcome the noise of its resistance. But this description of deconstructive practice should also have important implications for understanding the nature of the text. The presence of noise in a text implies, first, that the notion of a clearly dominant authorial intention disappears. Second, the "unstable" text offers, through the medium of noise, clear, convincing, and verifiable (one might say "objective") evidence of its inner incoherence.

Poststructural methodology is on the one hand more relativistic or, from a traditional perspective, more "subjective" than traditional criticism. Yet on the other hand it is also more rigorous, farsighted, and attentive to signifiers than traditional criticism. This paradoxical avowal of interpretive rigor and denial of textual presence is worth examination. If poststructural methodology is shunned by many critics, it is not because it lacks clarity, method, and rigor (properties in fact usually allied with objectivity). It is shunned because it somehow *seems* more irresponsible. In a word, it seems narcissistic, and narcissistic modes of reading seem to deny objective texts. In actuality poststructuralist thought, although it reveals a degree of narcissism involved in reading, does not go far enough in understanding the narcissistic nature of textual production and response.

Poststructuralist theory seems narcissistic in the negative sense because it makes emphatic claims about the importance of the reader's role in interpreting or constituting the text. Signifiers in the text do not disappear, but the thing signified by the signifiers becomes a product of reading strategies. Michel Foucault, for example, asserts that those "aspects of an individual which we designate as an author . . . are projections . . . of our way of handling texts."[5] Roland Barthes argues that "the birth of the reader must be at the cost of the death of the author."[6] Traditional critics recoil from these claims, arguing that they overemphasize the subjective aspects of interpretation. George Steiner compares Derrida's *Glas* to the mirrors that "make up the autistic sovereignty of Narcissus," and argues that Derrida's reading of Rousseau "is 'irresponsibility' in the exact, concrete sense of an inhibition of vital response, of a ruin in the arts of reciprocity and felt dialogue between text and reader."[7] In a similar fashion, Hayden White complains that much current critical theory serves as mystification, and "mystification of the text results in the fetishism of writing and the narcissism of the reader."[8]

Critical reactions to contemporary theory frequently, either descriptively or pejoratively, circle about a set of concepts deriving their rhetorical force from the root adjective, "narcissistic." The concept of "narcissism" may be used explicitly in seemingly descriptive accounts of deconstructive or reader-response methodology; or it may be used with full pejorative intention to describe other critics and their methodologies; and finally, it may be "bootlegged" into critical commentary, hidden beneath other terms associated with errant subjectivity.[9] Yet however the term appears, it works determinedly for its author to distinguish one mode of aberrant subjectivity from another mode of enlightened subjectivity.

Writers who employ the notion of narcissism, however, normally ignore the complex psychoanalytic theories (and paradoxical modes of subjectivity) implied by their concept. The term *narcissism* thus functions rhetorically and not analytically in contemporary critical practice. Whether used to pronounce judgment on other critical practices or simply to describe or explain them, narcissism implies a great deal but has no clear or concrete meaning. It distinguishes "good" subjectivity from "bad" subjectivity, but it does not in fact reveal how one mode of subjectivity differs from another.

As a rhetorical term, narcissism implies a kind of self-indulgent, irresponsible, and insidiously imaginary domination over any "other" posited in discourse. But critical theory has no clear taxonomy or hierarchy that names the variety and plenitude of all the others of discourse. Every instance of discourse is selective, so every example of discourse always excludes some other. Certainly it is true that poststructuralist theory dominates and subjugates one kind of other—the author's apparent intention. But another other, the signifier itself, is not dominated or subverted by the new methodology. Thus it would seem that whereas poststructuralist theory is narcissistic in one sense, it is, in its respect for the signifier, not narcissistic. Yet again, because the poststructuralist signifier functions as an empty term (a term whose presence is only the consequence of a particular reading context and a particular reader's will to meaning), poststructural practice might seem more narcissistic or solipsistically self indulgent than traditional practices. Such reasoning only reveals the circularity of our confusion over the meaning of narcissism. For the traditional critic's assumption of a meaning exterior to the signifier (in an author's intention perhaps), which he or she has securely (we should say narcissistically) discovered by defeating a confusing abundance of conflictual evidence, is certainly as narcissistic and self-indulgent as poststructural assumptions. These observations, then, suggest that as yet we have no clear model for rigor in critical response. And this confusion is the consequence of our more covert confusion over what we really mean or want to mean by narcissistic (or errant) forces of subjectivity.

As long as we are unable to understand the function of narcissistic subjectivity, we will be unable to formulate criteria for accountability in reading. Narcissistic activity is an especially intricate, paradoxical, and complicated phenomenon; critical theory has used the term generically and has failed to understand an important subset of narcissistic activities essential to the reading process. A more thorough understanding of these activities may help to disentangle some incompatible assumptions embodied in various critical perspectives. A fuller understanding of particular narcissistic processes—narcissistic projection, idealization, and the role of language in narcissistic functions—offers theoretical tools for defining a poststructuralist notion of textual rhetoric and "objectivity."

Projection and Narcissism

The Narcissus myth is always a useful starting point for reflecting on narcissistic phenomena. For the Western world, the history of the concept of narcissism is securely bound to the image of Narcissus looking at himself in the river. Freud's 1914 essay on narcissism implicitly alludes to the myth when commenting on the doting self-admiration of the narcissist.[10] More recent analysts have used the myth to explore subjects of particular interest to complex psychoanalytic theories of narcissism—subjects such as the narcissist's fear of self-loss in the beloved object and the narcissist's libidinal "cathexis" of her- or himself. The myth of Narcissus continues to be a useful narrative for reflecting on the complexity and confusion of narcissistic behavior, despite the fact that most readers oversimplify the myth by remembering it as a general explanation of narcissism.[11]

Most of us, I suspect, have a narcissistic understanding of narcissism. We understand the concept by means of the myth, but the intelligibility we achieve is vitiated by assumptions we project into the most "apparent" of narcissistic mechanisms, that is, narcissistic projection. We oversimplify the Narcissus myth when we use it to abstract what I call a "visual overlay" model for understanding the narcissistic gaze. The visual overlay model suggests that narcissism is a state of perception in which an image in the "real" world is covered up by an image projected on it from the self's imaginary inner world. According to this model, the narcissistic gaze functions to substitute, in a highly imperialistic manner, one image for another. A "real" image available for all to see in the "external world" is unconsciously hidden and "covered up" by an unreal image, that is, an image manufactured by a wayward and undisciplined (narcissistic) subjectivity. With this understanding of the narcissistic gaze, an understanding only too effectively dramatized by the Narcissus myth, highly distorting modes of perception have become synonymous with projection and have come to characterize the quintessential act of a narcissistic subject.

Freud's work lends analytic rigor to the relationships outlined here and provides an almost unquestioned authority for establishing an emphatic link between projection and narcissism. In projection, an image is "projected" from the mind just as an image is "projected" by a mechanical illuminating machine. One image is covered up in a purely arbitrary way by another. The objects that are visible on the visual screen do not in any significant way determine or influence the character of the images projected on the screen. This analogy was highly suitable for Freud's emphasis on the subjective force of distortion. A "real" image—one that is real, public, and available for all to see—is covered up, and the image that is superimposed on the public image is a private one, an image idiosyncratically manufactured by the mind. Projection involves, as Freud points out, a loss of reality. It occurs when "the original reality-ego, which distinguished internal and external by means of a sound objective criterion, changes into a purified pleasure-ego, which places the characteristic of pleasure above all others."[12] Projection is thus a gesture of narcissistic self-indulgence; the narcissistic self does not want to see a reality that is potentially painful.

The Freudian theory of projection is more complicated than is outlined here, and it diverges sharply at many points from the understanding of projection in the work of critics like Norman Holland.[13] Nonetheless, the term *projection* has become popular and influential. For many reader-response theorists, projection of this sort seems to define the essential mechanism of reading. Reading, thus characterized, seems to be a process whereby a reader's fantasies are substituted for the words in the book. Many advocates of reader-response criticism assert that readers project their personal stories on literature just as a projection machine projects movies on a blank screen. The text, thus characterized, does not really exist. Fish argues that there are no real differences between different texts, because the words of the text, despite our painstaking attention to them, do not guide or direct our experience.[14] Instead, words are empty and passive: blank space victimized by the reader's imperialistic will to meaning. The "pictures" the reader "sees" in the text are determined not by words, but solely by the film inside the projection machine, which contains the fantasies animating the reader. Reading thus seems to be a narrowly narcissistic, or even solipsistic, activity.

Such generalizations oversimplify the more recent work of critics like Fish, Bleich, and Holland. But psychoanalytic accounts of reader-response theory that focus most closely on the reader identify the role of the reader with projective activities. Even Derrida's concern for the supplement, the slippage of signifiers, and the infective nature of reading contexts has sometimes been read by American critics as descriptions of projection. On the whole, Fish's claim that "the formal patterns" of literature "are themselves constituted by an interpretive act," Bleich's refutation of the "objective paradigm," and Holland's rejection of a "biactive theory of text-reader interaction" has had the effect of supporting deconstructive ideas and has lent credibility to the view of the text as a blank screen animated by the meanings projected on it by readers.[15]

Norman Holland, like Stanley Fish, is another prominent critic whose best-known work disavows any notion of textual objectivity. In a relatively recent essay on the "transactive process" of reading, Holland disputes New Critical assumptions about the sovereignty of the text. According to these assumptions, words in the text somehow limit or direct the response of the reader. Words do not direct meaning, Holland argues, because words have no real meaning in themselves. Words *mean* only in so far as they are consumed by projective processes. Holland's early articles on the reading process explicitly characterize reading as an essentially projective activity. In "Unity Identity Text Self," Holland argues that the "overarching principle" of interpretation is that "identity re-creates itself. . . . All of us, as we read, use the literary work to symbolize and finally to replicate ourselves."[16] The form and unity of the text, Holland suggests, are a function of the reader's highly arbitrary subjectivity.

Holland originally believed in the myth of the objectivity of the text, but was saved from his folly by empirical research. Through careful empirical investigation of how readers actually read, he discovered that the variety of response to a text was enormous. The words in the text did not limit meaning, but instead seemed to multiply meaning. In his empirical sampling of student response, Holland discovered that response to literary works was so varied that meaning could not be explained by the "objective" nature of the literary work. "If you actually collect people's free responses to texts," Holland observes, "they simply do not show a uniform core (from the text) and individual variation (from the people). The responses have practically nothing in common."[17]

Holland's early work in reader-response theory was highly influenced by David Bleich. Bleich's arguments led Holland to conclude that "stories do not have defense mechanisms and plays do not sublimate—but people do."[18] Bleich's work, especially his chapter "Epistemological Assumptions in the Study of Response," seems especially thoughtful in its discussion of the epistemological ground of perception. For many readers, the work succeeds in making projection synonymous with aesthetic perception. For Bleich, interpretation is understood as "motivated resymbolization."[19] Signifiers, Bleich argues, do not announce meanings that exist before reading acts. Instead, signifiers take on meaning through the motives of readers. Because the motives for this "resymbolization" are characteristically unconscious, interpretation serves to express the unconscious motives of the reader. In effect, reading reads projection; it does not read anything distinctive in texts. "The object of attention," he argues, "is not the item itself but is the response of those who observe it."[20] Bleich's description of aesthetic perception thus resembles what I term a "visual overlay" model of projection. "Motivated resymboliza-tion" serves as Bleich's substitute term for projection.

Unfortunately, Bleich's theory, however engaging, ignores issues cru-cial for an understanding of textual objectivity and conflates two differ-ent claims. Bleich correctly asserts that all images are subjective. But he is led too hastily from this assertion to another: All images are equally subjective. This latter claim requires careful consideration because it suggests that no "common denominator" bears witness to a common source informing different readings of the same text. It suggests that no "family resemblance" exists among different readings of the same text. Furthermore, it suggests that aesthetic perception cannot be "improved" by referring back to the original source of the perception, the text. It also suggests that perception cannot (in Lacan's terms) asymptotically recover the shared social features of the text's discourse. Responses to texts instead proliferate endlessly and arbitrarily, and differences among readings of the same text are no different from those among readings of disparate texts.

Projection and the Materiality of the Signifier

The conceptual failure in many reader-response theories lies in their tendency to see all subjective "distortions" in perception as equal in degree and effect. This failure is the consequence of another larger failure to grasp important distinctions in subjective processes. Texts are not blank screens reflecting the projections of a reader; textual signifiers manipulate projection. Readers who fail to encounter the signifiers of a text fail to encounter the rhetorical facilitators of the text. Reader-re-sponse theory frequently assumes that because there can be no "correct" reading of signifiers, there can be no sense of accountability in reading. However, such an assumption is naive. The "material" signifier does not guarantee a stable referential event, but does guarantee a stable perceptual event that plays an important role in conscious, unconscious, and narcis-sistic reading processes. The material signifier offers itself as a criterion for accountability in textual response. Readings that fail to encounter the actual signifiers of a text are failures in reading.

A judgment about objectivity in reading reflects a judgment made about a reader's encounter with the material signifiers, or sequence of signifiers of a text. It does not reflect any judgment whatever over the complex and compelling systems of meanings readers discover through those signifiers.[21] No critic really disputes the fact that *signifiers* are objectively present in the text. Holland grants that there is text in so far as there are "words-on-the-page," and even Fish grants that signifiers are material objects ("marks on the page") that are materially present, thus objectively present for reading.[22] Nonetheless, poststructuralist theorists often insist, like Fish, that "there isn't a text that remains the same from one moment to the next." Yet poststructural theory requires something in the text—the signifier—to remain the same. Thus, paradoxically, poststructural practice denies the iterability of the text, but requires the iterability of signifiers. The text disappears, but the letters and words of the text stand out ruggedly (in the form of noise) as unflinching witnesses to the betrayal of meaning. The objectivity of the text disappears in one sense, but it reappears again with unmistakable insistence in another sense. It reappears in the materiality of the signifiers that constitute the text.

The signifier is clearly materially present, and "reading" is distinct from hallucination in so far as it describes a sequential encounter with signifiers. But the objectivity of text, as it is understood in these terms, is generally dismissed as theoretically inconsequential. Bleich, for example, denies the importance of the material signifier and the "nominal meanings of words" because these things cannot "mean" anything except themselves, and this "meaning" can never be transferred from one person to another except by repetition of mere dumb signifiers.[23] This argument would seem to imply that one could legitimately "read" a text without ever encountering the material signifiers that compose a text. Such an assumption is absurd.

This dismissal of "dumb" signifiers is ill-considered. Most teachers would agree that there is a style of reading that fails to see the text, and therefore fails to register the material presence of the signifier and the sequence of signifiers that comprise a text. Many readings of texts fail to recognize major events in narrative and to register the particularity of vocabulary that describes these events. Clearly these readings are failures in perception and failures to respond to the objective text. The repetitive encounter with dumb signifiers is not, then, as Bleich would have it, theoretically inconsequential. It is time to give the signifier its due. We must recognize that an encounter with the dumb signifier is essential to reading.

To appreciate the importance of the dumb signifier (that can mean nothing because it can mean anything), we must review some recent psychoanalytic observations about language. There is an increasing recognition among psychoanalytic theorists that language is somehow central to what is called the psychoanalytic process. Marshall Edelson suggests that "perhaps only a theory of language can begin to account adequately for the complex phenomena embraced by psychoanalysis."[24] Edelson's own book carefully probes relationships between forms of literary language and forms of psychoanalytic exchange. Meredith Skura, a literary critic trained in psychoanalysis, explores similarities between literary experience and psychoanalytic experience. She argues that the "complex ways in which literary texts elaborate and call attention to the play of consciousness . . . have a parallel in the way that these phenomena are handled in analysis—in the moments of integration and insight."[25] The most widely influential theorist of the relations between language and psychoanalysis, however, is Jacques Lacan. Lacan, more rigorously than anyone else, argues that the crucial function of the psychoanalytic cure is the linguistic function.

Lacan's theory postulates a self "anchored" by certain signifiers but also "split" and divided as it is drawn toward other signifiers. Lacan's concept of linguistic anchoring points defining the self-system explains "the dominance of the letter in the dramatic transformation that dialogue can effect in the subject."[26] In many ways, Lacan's claim simply formalizes something all analysts take for granted: Transformations of the self occur because of transformations in ways of speaking.

Critical theory must recognize that the *materiality* and the *particularity* of the signifier are crucial in the self's anchoring and its splitting—and in its transformations. Lacan's examples of the role of language in the unconscious repeatedly call attention to punning, homophony, and lexical allusion. More generally, Lacan argues that "the slightest alteration between man and the signifier changes the whole course of history by modifying the moorings that anchor his being."[27] For Lacan, rhetorical pressure is a consequence of the self's being tethered to the particularity of words. Lacanian theory would support the generalization that close reading of particular signifiers *matters* because the particularity of the signifier exerts an inexorable rhetorical pressure on the *matter* of the self.

For Lacan, words and networks of words in their particularity serve self-functions something like the bones of a skeletal system. They enable certain possibilities, and they disable others. In a certain sense, words are evasive and immaterial. In another, they are quite material, and they constitute nothing less than the true *body* of the self. "Language is not immaterial," he says, "it is a subtle body, but body it is. Words are trapped in all the corporeal images that captivate the subject; they may make the hysteric 'pregnant.' "[28] The symptoms manifest in psychological disorders, symptoms that bind, restrict, or paralyze parts of the body and mind (thus preventing certain thoughts and actions), have their ground in the airy substance of words. Words, it is clear, can exert a biological control over the body. Words, precisely in their apparent casual and random nature, can cause paralysis, hysteria, hallucination, false pregnancy. Words can control the body because they organize the libidinal structures of bodily experience.

Moreover, it is not simply that words govern biological functions, but that this control is maintained by an unnerving particularity in words. The unconscious seems to admit to no paraphrase and no synonyms. Words matter in their particular material signifying substance—both as marks and as sounds. Lacan's own writing and speech bristles with homophony, idiosyncratic syntax, phonemic allusions, and a wide variety of tropes. Such acute consciousness of verbal particularity is important for Lacan because words function in psychoanalytic discourse by exploiting a distinctly literary function. "Poetry," Lacan writes, "is the creation of a subject assuming a new order of symbolic relation to the world."[29] Because the linguistic creativity of poetry reflects the creative remaking of the self, Lacan argues that "psychoanalysis manipulates the poetic function."[30] But Lacan is not the only psychoanalytic theorist to emphasize the importance of the material aspect of language. Edelson, for example, observes, "Words are the object through which one seeks for a way to handle the unconscious. Not even the meaning of the words, but words in their flesh, in their material aspect."[31] Human subjects, it seems, are strangely "attached" (libidinally invested) in particular signifiers and particular collections of signification. Ask a lover to curse his beloved's name; ask a patriot to curse her country's name.

If it is clear that the material presence of words matters enormously to the functions of the self, and especially to the unconscious functions of the self, then it should also be clear that critical theory needs to examine how projective activities are animated by the signifier's materiality. If texts are not blank screens for projections, and instead projections are filtered or deflected by the libidinal charges we perceive in signifiers, then we must carefully attend to this process.

Projection, Rhetoric, Idealization

Unfortunately, the term *projection* can refer to two distinctly different kinds of activity. On the one hand, projection can refer to a subjective replacing or deleting of an objectively present signifier (an avoidance of the perceptible features of the object).[32] On the other hand, projection can refer to the subjective interpreting and contextualizing of signifiers actually encountered. For clarity, I term the projective covering up of the text *projective denial,* and the reworking of signification *projective attentiveness.*

The projective denial of the text is not the same as the "projective attentiveness" of the text. From a psychoanalytic perspective, a question about objectivity is answered by a fairly easy analytical act: Does one ignore publicly verifiable signifiers in order to project meaning into the text in an arbitrary and imperialistic manner, or does one use the associations of textual materiality as a stimulus for deriving personal significance? Both modes of response can occur in reading or perception. But the two events that can occur (and are often confused with each other) are not the same event.

Projective denial is not a personal reworking of signifiers already present in the text. It is an avoidance of signifiers, especially an avoidance of signifiers charged with associated meaning that challenge one's values and sense of self. Projective attentiveness, on the other hand, responds to textual materiality and uses associative meaning as a context for building a reading experience. It builds on the material signification of the text, quotes the text, becomes libidinally "attached" to the verbal particularity of a text, and delights in the verbal formulations of a text. Projective denial ignores the particular matter of the text, denying the potential meaning latent in signifiers. Moreover, projective denial is not equal among all readers and in all interpretations; it is a true misreading of the text. It is inattentiveness due to a variety of possible causes:

fatigue, haste, distraction, and psychological defensiveness. As a defense, projective denial is characterized by avoidance, denial, memory loss, and wholesale, arbitrary, and unconscious replacements of one signifier or set of signifiers for another.

We should acknowledge that the unconscious replacement of signifiers is a component in everyone's reading. But it is a component we test by dialogue and attempt to subdue by rereading. Although rereading cannot recover a "correct" interpretive reading, it can encounter more fully the particularity of signifiers and bring them into the purview of consciousness, reworking them and creatively organizing their effect. Rereading hence makes reading a discipline, not an opportunity for hallucination or visual slips of perception.

As a teacher involved with the freshman English program, I frequently find myself teaching Baldwin's "Sonny's Blues" to students lacking experience with close reading. Often when I discuss the story, I discover responses that seem in the old sense of the term "incorrect" readings. For example, I often focus on the theme of guilt in the story because it helps me to bring attention to some of the psychological conflicts at issue in the story. When I ask the class if the narrator feels guilty about his neglect of his brother Sonny (who has become a heroin addict), a great majority of the class will sometimes answer: "No, he does not feel guilty."

Normally it takes me only a few minutes to suggest that the narrator *seems* to feel very guilty. First I read a letter that Sonny writes to his brother:

Dear brother,
   You don't know how much I needed to hear from you. I wanted to write you many a time but I dug how much I must have hurt you and so I didn't write.[33]

I point out an earlier section of the text where the brother has made a vow to his mother always to "be there" for Sonny. And then I read the section where the narrator describes how he feels when he gets the letter: "He wrote me back a letter" the narrator says, "which made me feel like a bastard."[34]

I read these lines, first showing Sonny's clear expression of his neediness to hear from his brother; second, the narrator's promise to be there for Sonny; and third, the narrator's clear confession that, when he hears about Sonny's desperate need to hear from him, he "feels like a bastard."

After all this, the class changes its answer. The narrator's use of the word, "bastard," directed at himself, implies self-blame, a distinct and heavy sense of guilt. This matter now suddenly seems very straightforward. When first asked if the narrator feels guilt, the class said, "No." When I asked the same question after reading the sentence where the narrator says he feels like a bastard, the class agreed, "Yes, the narrator does feel guilt."

I could, of course, imagine an intelligent critical essay exploring the narrator's sense of guilt and arguing that the narrator, though expressing guilt, actually feels little of it. And perhaps some students really sense this argument and this is the ground of their "forgetting" this dimension of the text. It is always possible that students not attending to certain textual "facts" are at the same time unconsciously responding to other clues that suggest the presence of arguments that would minimize the importance of such "facts." The complexity of textual meaning makes it seem irrefutable that all of the "facts" of a text can always be disputed. But no good essay that argues the meaning of a text can ignore the existence of compelling evidence that, for a large group of readers, seems to formulate and clarify the various critical issues of a text. As Fish points out, every reading needs to participate in the meaning constructions formulated by a larger community of readers. Thus no critical essay would be published on the subject of Sonny's guilt if the author ignored the narrator's own sense of guilt when it was recognized by a community of other readers. When the narrator says that he feels like a bastard, this does not prove that the narrator feels guilty. However, it is evidence that a close reading of the text, concerned with these issues, must consider.

Professional critics are required to be careful readers of texts. For many students the reading experience is simply a series of perceptions that do not add up to anything, or else it is the perception of a clear moral that is not carefully tied to the language, plot, or characters of a texts. Students, unlike most professional critics, are often largely unaware of the evidence related to those arguments about a text that they themselves are interested in developing. Such data simply have not been noticed.

In my experience teaching "Sonny's Blues," it seems that the reasons for missing such data sometimes can be explained as a result of specific psychological projections. Students defend themselves from their own inner feelings of guilt by seeing none in the narrator. For example, when

I show students that the narrator seems to express a sense of guilt, they sometimes respond by first acknowledging the validity of the evidence I give, but insist subsequently that although the narrator may feel some guilt, he has no reason to feel it. He is being too hard on himself, they say, if he feels he so responsible for someone else. In this case, an ideal important to the students is being used to minimize precisely the conflict that the text structures as part of its rhetoric, that is, its *experience* of meaning.

When the reading of a text proceeds in this way, with a subjectively organized commitment to suppress key themes linked to stress-creating emotions, it becomes an activity of projective denial. Rather than participating in an aesthetic of self-conflict, reading instead suppresses data that for other similar readers richly augment the depth and feeling associated with a story. Reading of this sort, when certain discourse possibilities within the vocabulary of readers are systematically excluded from thought in order to minimize conflict, is an example of projective denial. The reading self is selectively inattentive to issues that for other similar social groups are precisely those devices providing a useful focus on the story. The reader (in the example of "Sonny's Blues") seeking to deny feelings of guilt and responsibility, selectively denies data suggesting that others do and should feel such guilt and responsibility. Such recognition, because it can produce uncomfortable psychological conflict, is avoided. To this end certain signifiers are not registered.

My point here is not to insist that we must read the "correct" text. Instead, I want to reflect on what we seek to accomplish in teaching reading. We can always endlessly debate what a text means, or whether or not in "Sonny's Blues" the narrator actually does or should feel guilt. We can debate the most important themes in the text requiring attention. We can point out that every example of reading is an example of selective inattention. But when we read a text well, we are both attentive and responsive to an extended range of conflictual signification. Good reading engages a reflective appreciation of the various conflictual and rhetorical powers of a text—even when the specific nature of such subjects is something we do not admire.

In contrast to projective denial, projective attentiveness acknowledges and, more importantly, "feeds on" the presence of conflict linked to the sequence of material signifiers constituting the text. Rather than ignoring the signifier in deference to its own fantasies, it uses the conflictual interaction of signifiers to grasp, visualize, or master the latent conflict. It may seek to clarify, articulate, elaborate, and perhaps just reflect on this complex image of values. Projective attentiveness, in short, suffers conflictual narcissistic investments in the conflictual interactions of signification.

When my discussions of "Sonny's Blues" go well, my classes often circle about a center of rich reflective silence as they slowly bring forth statements that they find "insightful." Different classes focus on different themes for attention. But as they focus on these themes, students begin to more clearly understand their own conflicts. Their speaking and listening is shaped by their participation in both the story and their own experience of life. If for the moment they find their own speech unusually engrossing, it is because it is in some way new for them, suggesting, I think, that a certain reshaping of perception and libidinal investment has occurred.

Literature can act like a mirror to reflect the arbitrary fantasies of the reader's mind; but most of us do not see only our own fantasies in literature. We use literature to embody or articulate in particular ways our values or "idealizations" (even if our idealization requires the deconstruction of idealizations). Every careful reading of the text makes narcissistic investments in signifiers in order to formulate what might be called a *projective idealization*. When we respond fully to the material signifiers of the text, we use them to embody our partly conscious and partly unconscious values. Further, we gain satisfaction from this process because the idealization is made more concrete (and more representable) by passing through what Lacan calls the "defiles of the signifier."[35] Projective idealization of the text refers to the manner in which the often inchoate ideals of the self are "defiled" by concrete particularities suggested by signifiers of the text. (I want to convey by this awkward pun the sense of both human desire passing through a channel or filter and being changed or alienated by this process.)

Projective idealization refers to the process by which material from the internal world encounters material in the external world and becomes modified by it. Reading, of course, is too complex a process to allow one to formulate easy generalizations about how particular signifiers influence readers. Signifiers have meaning because, as subjects, we are constantly participating in the meaning constructs—the libidinal positionings—generated by the signifying activities of a larger social world.

At their most primitive level these meanings are intuitive and associative. They are the ground of our ongoing self-definition through social interaction. Dictionaries represent institutional attempts to regulate and police these meanings, and these regulating activities have had important effects. But the meaning we derive from signification is immensely complex; it is regulated by the needs of social communication and disrupted by personal association and libidinal investments.

In the future perhaps we may be able to classify recognizable and generalized patterns of fantasy, idealization, and mourning that are socially shared and thus generally predict responses to specific signifying chains. Jean Wyatt and Claudia Tate, for example, demonstrate how textual signification can trigger socially shared patterns of fantasy in order to generate social change.[36] Attention to historically significant social fantasies offers particularly rich opportunities for rhetorical analysis. When we understand how fantasies are socially shared as well as individually calibered, and how we share communal libidinal investments, we will be in a better position to understand the unconscious rhetoric of fantasy generation and its link to the "objectively" present signifiers that allow us to share feelings and perceptions.

When texts are used to generate fantasies or ideals, narcissistic mechanisms operate through signifiers to reorient the self toward themes or values that signifiers, because they participate in a social world, suggest. This is projective idealization. The particularity that material signifiers lend to this event is crucial because this rhetorical effect, this projective idealization, however creative it may be, depends on an encounter with the material presence of signification. The material presence of the signifier resists, defiles, and manipulates the personal content of a particular reader's projection. In this way reading exerts pressure on the core of the self and general linguistic field that defines, for any particular reader, self-image and "reality."

An appreciation of the importance of the material signifier in "defiling" projective mechanisms can benefit critical theory in a variety of ways. First, the material presence of the signifier serves as a necessary theoretical postulate for explaining what readers negotiate when they work together to seek meaning. The rules of reading demand attention to the materiality of the text, thus the text's materiality becomes both the means and the scene for sharing interpretive discourse. We might think of a text's signifiers as sites of intersection, or places where the pathways of various language codes converge as they pursue other purposes.

In addition, specific material signifiers often serve to anchor a set of libidinal relationships important for cultures and for people composing, in their libidinal relationships, the form of a culture. James Kinneavy points out that "a social personality probably does not emerge until it has its own subdialect. Jargon, therefore . . . is a sign of a forming social personality."[37] As signifiers come to define new libidinal organizations, they define new social relationships and new personalities. Frequently, in fact, libidinally charged signification is socially contested and disputed by warring interpretive perspectives. Often different discourse strategies are used to appropriate and employ key signifiers in cultural conflict. Kinneavy quotes Cassirer's observation that after the Nazis came to power "he found that the German words which he had known had taken on entirely new meanings; he found new words, and he found new emotional charges injected into formerly neutral terms."[38]

Words, by their material presence and by the shared social meanings linked to their material presence, color and influence the content of projection. The materiality of words, the associative meanings linked to words, and the literary effects made possible by this materiality (sounds, rhythm, puns, phonemic allusions, indeterminate meanings, onomatopoeia, visual patterns, etc.) make reading more like social dialogue, and less like private hallucination. Because the reader must encounter and meaningfully "process" the signifier, critical theory must claim responsibility to an "objective text."

Let me offer a range of examples showing how signifiers resist and direct projection. I start with a simple example and build to more complex generalizations.

If we assume that a text contains the signifier "mother," we might allow that the word "mother" will mean many different things to different people. All of us have different images of "mother," and different readers will project their own private meanings and associations on this term. Signifiers, thus, seem to legitimize an infinite number of responses. Such a generalization, however, oversimplifies the complexity of reading. Signifiers legitimize many different responses for different readers, but repeated signifiers, as they are repeated in different contexts, call forth again and again a reader's particular web of projections in many very different contexts. Thus any particular reader's response to the signifier "mother" is called forth in different meaning contexts as the text places the signifier in different contexts. The different placings of a projective content will either juxtapose a projective content with another different projective content and thus exert rhetorical pressure, or will juxtapose a projective content with a social context and thus also exert pressure on projective content.

The objective nature of the signifier plays an important role in this transaction. The first occurrence of the signifier "mother" is objectively the same as the second signifier "mother." A reader's projections are not likely to be exactly the same in each response, but there is a limited range of personal meanings—formed through memory, fantasy, daydream. The signifier, though it appears in a different context, manipulates experience. Thus, some of projective material linked to the first signifier "mother" will be again tapped in the second occurrence of the word "mother." But in drawing forth again the projective material linked to the first occurrence of the word, the text will exert pressure on this projection by placing it in a different context. It is of course true that any context will itself be shaped by projection, but nonetheless this context, because it is plotted by the signifiers (and plotted as well through repeated signifiers), is another example of a text manipulating the content of personal projection.

Reading is not determined entirely by the purely random desires and projections of the reader. Signifiers orchestrate (much like musical signifiers orchestrate noise) projections. My initial discussion of the word "mother" oversimplifies the role signifiers play in textuality; let me now give this example a larger scope. We should imagine much larger verbal structures—character, setting, key words—exerting meaning effects by making use of particular repeated material signifiers. Consider how often, for example, character and place names are repeated. Consider how often the word "he" or "she" or "it" becomes a substitute for a character name or place name. Consider how our experience of vast collections of particular signifiers are "summed" up by abstract signifiers that remind us of our experiences with these elements and carry us through various contexts where these meaning references take up new meaning associations. In the *American Heritage Dictionary*, Henry Kucera points out that frequency of particular words is a partial but interesting determinant of writing style.[39] Style is, in part, a subjective repetition of signifiers, even though it is "bad" style to repeat a word. Kucera also points out that in a mammoth collection of representative American texts, the *Standard Corpus of Present-Day Edited American English*, containing 1,014,232 words, there are only 50,406 *different* words.[40] This shows that in the average text there is a tremendous repetition of signifiers. Meaning, which depends partly on the choice of a signifier, is also very much determined by the repetitive positioning of a signifier. To make sense of a message we must grasp and make sense of a network of repetitive positionings.

I do not believe that language in and of itself creates "positions" that human subjects are fated and determined to occupy; I do think social discourse—the language of social interaction—loosely positions selves in relation to experience. Social participation in language generates for subjects socially induced meaning experiences apparently "produced" by language. Stable patterns of libidinally charged social discourse (which dictionaries in part maintain) help keep these meaning effects stable. For example, political words like "freedom" and "democracy" and even more psychological words like "love" and "sex" are repeated "key" terms for our culture.

However, because texts are constructed by conflictual subjects, they characteristically express conflicts between different usages of signifying terms. Often repeated key words or thematically related sets of words are mechanisms for focusing attention on this conflict. If we look at the verbal density of a text we might imagine various hierarchies of socially constructed meaning working to make sense of a single key word. At times single words, like "divorce," (and its equivalents) in Hardy's *Jude the Obscure* can become the scene for overt conscious conflict. At other times a single word seems dominated by one cultural coding. This single word, however, with its controlling cultural coding, can participate in a larger grouping of words that the text uses to create a different meaning effect. Literature characteristically makes fertile use of the conflicts between different layers of meanings created by signifiers. In this way particular signifiers whose meaning effect has been co-opted by dominant cultural codes can come to have conflictual meaning as they participate in different layers of meaning effects found in texts.

In *Heart of Darkness*, the larger "meaning" of the book's narrative about exploration comes to seem very different from early usages of the term *exploration*, an activity admired by Marlow and represented by Kurtz's bold return by canoe to the heart of the continent. In this conflict between our response to a particular "heroic" event and our response to the larger despair of the novel, our libidinal response to the signifier "exploration" or perhaps "adventure" can be restructured by a narrative that "explains" exploration. In this conflict between an ideological coding for exploration, which has captured our projections, and Conrad's own personal narrative coding for exploration, which has also caught our projections, literature generates a meaning that can be used in social discourse to restructure the ideological libidinal bindings of language. If ideologies are bad because they make us suffer, we can unmask them only when we create or discover narrative texts that expose the suffering and conflict of our libidinal investments.

In considering the rhetorical role of the signifier in discourse, we must also pay attention to more primitive experiences of signification. Signifiers can use their own verbal properties—sound and rhythm—to intensify our attention to them. Freud and others noted how the mind takes delight in puns, alliteration, and verbal condensation. For example, the phrase, "I'd rather have a bottle in front of me than a frontal lobotomy," usually produces a humorous response. This humor seems to rest entirely on the verbal condensation and reconstruction of "bottle in front of me" to "frontal lobotomy." The meaning here is relatively banal, and yet when it is concentrated by the punning of language, it is experienced differently, with more intensity. Poetry is especially likely to take delight in the weight, heft, and resonances of particular words, but other genres also utilize such practice to direct the attention that readers bring to texts.

In novels, key words (and a host of other sets of repeated words related to theme and authorial style) are repeated signifiers that focus attention on important themes and, as they connect or fail to connect to other meaning networks, suggest possibilities for conceptual defamiliarization. Jonathan Swift's use of "gentlemen" in "A Modest Proposal" is one example of how a repeated ideologically pleasing signifier can be wrenched into a defamiliarizing position by a carefully constructed text. We are encouraged to admire "gentlemen," but not when they are eager to eat babies. After reading Swift's essay, the word "gentlemen" begins to sound heavy and sinister.

Swift's "Modest Proposal" is a good example of a literary undoing of libidinal investments. Most readers have positive feelings for signifiers like "gentlemen" and "infants." We have these positive feelings because culture has done its job (for most of us) in structuring our emotions in relation to these two words. Swift's essay achieves tremendous rhetorical leverage by simply signifying a particular relationship between gentlemen and infants: "gentlemen" "eat" "infants." Each of these three signifiers (or their equivalents) is repeated many times in the course of the essay, and this simple relationship structures in general terms other relationships among the other more varied signifiers that populate the text. Different readers get different meanings from the text, but for most readers it generates a libidinal withdrawal from signification, either from the text itself, or from heedless participation in a social discourse that blithely labels eager consumers as "gentlemen."

These examples demonstrate that texts are powerfully defined by our projections. But these examples also show that texts are not blank screens supporting all possible projections. Texts are meaningful compositions created by a temporal succession of signifiers orchestrating successive projections. Like complex algebraic formulas or musical scores, texts are notations for innumerable meaningful constructions. We can compose many different texts from a sequence of signifiers, but we cannot compose *all* possible texts from the same signifiers. We can compose many different versions of *Heart of Darkness,* but we cannot compose *Midsummer Night's Dream* from *Heart of Darkness.* The construction of meaning is not something we can do independent of the signifiers; our interpretations must be fixed at various points to the signifiers they interpret. They must be anchored to the signifiers that constitute a publicly verifiable text—the text editors want to get "right" when they examine various "good" manuscripts.

Texts, therefore, are not purely the product of a reader's projection. They have particular properties and particular structures of their own. These properties may not be universally shared or defined in terms of referential meaning, but they can be considered in terms of something we might call rhetoric, or the conflictual interaction between text and reader.

Our discussion of the linguistic structure of the self encourages us to hypothesize a relation between the projective forces brought to bear on the text by the reader and the rhetorical forces brought to bear on the reader by the text. Projection has a boomerang effect in reading: Projective moments become introjective moments as the self invests itself narcissistically in the conflictual particularity of the signification it discovers. Words in their particular material presence assume certain energies from the projective forces working on them, but in doing so they "defile" those energies by entrapping them in a larger network of signification. In this context, words absorb projective forces and deflect them, thereby exerting "rhetorical" pressure on self-functions.

Rhetoric is a force empowered by projection. The rhetorical power released by projection derives from the self-divided linguistic ground of the self's own being. If the self is a warring system within which various smaller self-components vie for control of thought, feeling, and behavior, then we must examine how the libidinal organization of signification produced by a self in reading resembles and reassembles the particular libidinal organization of language that is a self.

What kind of force within a self forces some examples of discourse to be repressed and other kinds of discourse to be idealized? What kind of force avoids certain forms of discourse and incorporates others? Clearly, this force is termed many things by the different disciplines that feel a need to account for its functioning. But in the area of critical theory a good name for this force is rhetoric. Rhetoric is concerned, not with the meaning of language, but with the way language orchestrates emotion, the way self-experience is structured by language. Rhetoric reflects the libidinal investments that selves make in language.

The concept of rhetoric is a theoretical juncture where literary theory, rhetorical theory, and psychoanalytic theory should converge. We normally assume that rhetoric is a force in language that manipulates emotion in humans. But in a technical sense this force can never be *in* language; language (from a purely "objective" position) is only a collection of dumb signifiers. Rhetoric, then, is not *in* language. It is in subjectivity. More precisely, it is a force in the linguistic constitution of the self. Rhetoric, as we discover it in texts, always bears witness to the social and psychological forces whereby language "positions" selves in relation to affect.

Rhetoric is always the umbilicus of a text. It is the point at which a meaning that *matters for* the self emerges as the structuring *matter of* the self. Rhetoric designates particular sites of textual signification where readers consciously and unconsciously make choices about the interpretive codes they choose to follow. Through such complex decisions (compromises between conscious and unconscious investments), words assume rhetorical power. Also through these decisions, words attain particular "meaning" and by acquiring this particular meaning, words give particular being (Lacan might say "body") to the self.

When we encounter rhetoric in texts, we encounter the libidinal forces attached to words that generate, employ, or "bind" emotion. This manipulation of emotion amounts to nothing less than a manipulation of the components of the self. Rhetoric designates the forces in the linguistic construction of the self that structure affect. In reading, these forces transform projective energies by verbally recontextualizing them. Through such verbal recontextualization, affect itself becomes susceptible to restructuralization. Further, because the unconscious structuring of the self is built on a particularity of words, rhetoric also depends on verbal particularity for its restructuring power. Words in the particularity of their visual and phonemic properties (punning, homophony, onomatopoeia, phonemic allusion, visual metaphoricity), in their sheer dumb repetition of the same (mother and mother, for example), and in their associative and referential possibilities become "rhetorical performers" for selves. As particular words and particular signifying chains of words become animated by projective forces, words manipulate affect. But words work (just as ad writers and poets insist) precisely in their particularity.

It follows, then, that readings attentive to the particularity of words, and attentive to words as rhetorical performers, can be especially rewarding.[41] I do not want to insist that referential approximations are nonfunctional; I merely want to emphasize what English teachers have always claimed—attention to the concrete text matters. Through such an attentiveness, a reader may encounter new possibilities for perceiving and reorganizing the restless nature of verbal self-components.[42]

Rhetoric as a Social and Private Force

A broad understanding of the rhetorical role of the signifier in interpretation should embrace both psychological and sociological considerations. Of course, sociological critics have long claimed that selves are products of the same processes that produce texts. From a sociological perspective, words, in the particularity of their effects on consciousness, are cultural artifacts that constitute selves around systems of culturally sanctified value. Generally speaking, however, sociological critics have avoided the complexities of psychoanalytic issues and denied personal, creative, and adversarial relations between texts and readers. Fish speaks for many sociological critics:

If selves are constituted by the ways of thinking and seeing that inhere in social organizations, and if these constituted selves in turn constitute texts according to these same ways, then there can be no adversary relationship between text and self because they are necessarily related products of the same cognitive possibilities.[43]

It may indeed be true that both "selves and texts are produced by ways of thinking and seeing that inhere in social organization." But such productions should not rule out adversarial relations. Sociological critical theory, by ruling out the presence of adversarial relations, oversimplifies relationships between texts and selves.

If texts are always conflictually heterogeneous (both in terms of abstract meaning and libidinal codings) and the social constitution of the self is also always heterogeneous, then rhetoric of texts should be examined in terms of an interaction between these differing unstable codings. Idealizing projection explains how the social strands of conflict suggested by textual signifiers and articulated by critical disagreements reflect, but also *work on*, components in conflict within the inner network of the self.

When considering the conflicts in texts, we must consider the conflicts within readers. Such conflict (present both in selves and in cultures) is not merely a fracture point in the structure of language; it is often an agonizing point of tension and turbulence within a self. Such conflict can encourage something that, from another critical perspective, is called *interiority*. Interiority describes a sensed connection between the inner life of a reader and the inner life of a writer. Such an experience of connection will always be a fantasy of some sort—we never have transparent access to the inner life of a writer—but there is usually some ground for this fantasy. Because authors speak a public language of libidinal investment at the same time as they speak a private one, a text usually contains codes that facilitate the production of new structures of libidinal investments. In this manner, the self-conflicts experienced by writers can contribute to particular forms of self-conflict and libidinal organization experienced by readers.

Interiority, considered in this sense, can be a socially constructive mode of suffering. It can be "productive" in the Marxist sense of the term. Through the material signifiers it produces, such interior conflict changes our perceptions of ideological codes and offers an impetus for change.

For various reasons, professional readers are usually more comfortable talking about conflict within a text rather than conflict within a reader. But—to paraphrase Norman Holland—texts don't have conflict; people do. The experience of conflict betrays narcissistic discomfort and reveals a textual interface where self cannot be comfortably composed. Conflict is in a certain sense the raison d'etre of critical theory. Many schools of criticism, however, attempt to deal with conflict by outlawing certain possibilities of meaning. As a consequence, meaning becomes a function of repression. An adequate theory of rhetoric should avoid repression and privilege conflict (on both the social and the intrapersonal level) as the seminal principle of the hermeneutic endeavor.

A psychoanalytic attention to the materiality and particularity of words as rhetorical performers offers this possibility. For the psychoanalyst, hermeneutic conflict betrays the struggle of overdetermined meanings. Overdetermined meanings frequently mark a point where the subsystems of the self, as they conflictually interact, produce an unacknowledged experience of suffering. Particular words, charged with overdetermined meaning, can reveal the combat of avowed and disavowed values. These particular words often draw attention to themselves in "literary" ways and betray unconscious values that oppose the dominant values of the self's discourse. This betrayal may surface under standard interpretive procedures as simply a logical contradiction, and appear quite puzzling. From a psychoanalytic perspective, however, this evidence of conflict and overdetermination can mark the beginning of useful realizations about self-construction —a struggle between opposing motives and values.

Furthermore, these considerations show that the psychoanalytic perspective on the text offers another strategy for using words: Words can probe and reveal the knots of conflict and contradiction within the self; words can lift experience from inarticulate suffering to conscious political expression; words bring into the purview of consciousness the ragged seams of linguistic self-constitution. Like psychoanalytic experience, reading can enable the registering in consciousness of multideterminate but particularized systems of signifiers exerting their inexorable pressure on another overdetermined system of signifiers—the self. In one textual "message," reading can register multiple and conflictual rhetorical intent. More importantly, reading attentive to the plurality of possible rhetorical organizations inherent in systems of signification can produce a frictional sliding in consciousness between disparate and unsynthesized units of rhetoric and intelligibility within the self.

In texts, as well as in selves, unsynthesized units of intelligibility or "meanings" normally find their proper subordination in relation to dominant master terms that exert their various, conflictual, overdetermined, often repressive, but nonetheless ordering, force across a variety of subordinated symbolic networks. These master terms normally anchor the reader and the text, thus subduing an otherwise chaotic struggle between dominant and adversarial cultural ideology, and dominant and adversarial personal idiolects. But an encounter with the conflictual seams (hitherto unnoticed) in the unsynthesized units of meaning in texts can dislodge the "meaning" of repression and liberate value from ideological denial.

The materiality and particularity of words therefore not only constitute the self, but offer themselves in their particularity as tools (best used in moments when a breadth of vision has been achieved by an accumulation of reference) for redefining and renegotiating self-constitution. On this basis, we should postulate that "good" readings of texts productively reshape a reader's projections by appreciating the rhetoric linked to the materiality of textual signifiers. Readers respond actively to the objective and material signifiers of the text seeking to rework the content of their projection. This activity is possible because, although we do always perceive through the decoding effects of our own personal reading strategies, we also refer to material signifiers of the text in all their particular polyvalent qualities (and especially in their polyvalent qualities), seeking to modify, enlarge, and if necessary, reorganize the habitual decoding strategies that normally allow us to "consume" and dispose of signifiers. Even if Holland is right that our reading strategies tend to be univocal and ideological as a result of defensive identity themes, it remains true that the discipline of textual study traditionally demands, in the response to signifiers, more subtlety than the mechanical application of univocal decoding systems. We are encouraged to read reflectively. We are encouraged to recover from repression signifying codes that are latent and not dominant in ourselves and in the texts we read. Of course, this ethics of reading is not always successful, but it is outspokenly idealized.

This idealization defines the humanistic promise of reading. It assumes that reading is not a simple process whereby the unity of a subject responds to the unity of the text; nor is reading a simple process whereby the text constitutes the reader along the lines of a simple ideological principle. Instead, reading reflects the rhetorical friction produced as the self (the organizing process behind a plurality of linguistic codes) suffers the disorienting "orders" of a different plurality of codes (the text), which it must in some manner order.

If the signifiers of a text are "rhetorical performers," manipulators of the libido binding selves to systems of value (and not merely representations of a writer's experience or a reader's experience), some traditional literary endeavors assume a more restricted, yet still legitimate role. First, literary canons (in all their arbitrariness) can be seen as collections of systems of signifiers situated in historical moments that have had, for particular groups of people, significant rhetorical effect. Some texts, for certain people in certain contexts, are better rhetorical "performers" than others. We need to understand the mechanisms that enable these texts to perform. Second, to develop a student's rhetorical expertise and facility with language, it would be profitable to seek to know the various verbal strategies of any epoch's rhetoric. Third, it will be useful to seek to know an author's apparent intention—not in order to know the meaning of the text as equivalent to the intention—but to understand more fully what relation rhetorical effects have to professed intentions.

Projection and the "Objective" Text

A reader who has found my extended discussion of projective idealization plausible might at this point pause, reflect, and object that my original claims about the existence of an objective text must be illusory. Each person, after all, perceives the text differently in his or her idealization. Because texts come into being through the perceptions of readers, there can be no objective text.

However, this objection can be overcome if we make two distinctions. We must distinguish, first, between the *perception* of signifiers and the *interpretation* of the text. The signifiers of a text are not perceived differently; the meanings are perceived differently. But even while these meanings are perceived differently, the meanings perceived are limited by the set of signifiers perceived. Consider the distinction between (a) an infinite and unlimited set of interpretive possibilities and (b) an infinite but nonetheless limiting and excluding set of interpretive gestures.

An imprecise understanding of infinity has suggested that interpretation is the effect of an unlimited set of interpretive possibilities. A clearer understanding of infinity can remedy this mistake. The objectivity of the text is an objective perceptual event that produces an infinite but limited set of possible interpretations. The existence of an infinite number of correct readings for a text does not mean that the text can mean anything. It means that the text offers an infinite set of reading permutations defined by a limiting set of signifying rules.

The concept of a limited infinity may, at first, be puzzling. But it should not be. In mathematics, there are a variety of formulas that can designate a variety of infinite sets of numbers. The elements within each set of numbers designated by a particular formula are infinite in number. But two different formulas produce rules that can define two very different, mutually exclusive, sets of elements. The set of odd numbers, for example, is infinite. Yet this same set of infinite numbers is also limited because it does not contain the infinite set of even numbers. The elements within both sets (odd numbers and even numbers) are infinite in number, but each set of numbers contains different particular characters. It is therefore possible to describe a set of elements that is infinite in number but limited in terms of what it contains. Thus, the set is both infinite and limited.

The text, like a particular formula in math, offers infinite possibilities for meaning, but it also limits and excludes other possibilities. There are a variety of ways to talk about how interpretive possibilities are limited. Although words can in principle refer to anything (and seem to legitimize an absolute infinity of possibility), words (and systems of words) cannot mobilize and organize affect in unlimited ways. Each language, in order to function as a language, must provide a limited and not infinite code linking words to ideas, images, and feelings. Additionally, each cultural system legitimizes and offers support for a relatively limited set of personality paradigms. Each culture offers distinct models for organizing affect and distinctive style for manipulating that organization. Each cultural system, in other words, possesses its own unique repertoire of rhetoric.[44] It authorizes and endows with potency its own system of metaphors and thereby limits and preconditions certain possibilities for the constitution of the self. Thus, although there are new and "creative" organizations of affect emerging in most cultures, affect is itself limited by the biological constitution of the organism and the signifying structures of affect made available by a culture.

The ability of projections and associations to be meaningful for other readers functions as another limitation on meaning. Usually the reader's power of association is taken as evidence for the impossibility of defining an objective text. One could easily argue the opposite. Although it seems possible to free associate infinitely in relation to any one word of the text, it is quite a different matter to tie clusters of free associations into a meaningful system that first makes sense of a sequence of signifiers and second meaningfully serves others as a possible interpretation of that sequence of signifiers. The ability of free association to produce meaning does not make the text disappear. Instead it limits the meanings the text can produce.

An interpretation intended for a rhetorical purpose would, however individualistic, require a rhetorically effective contextual placing of individualistic responses into communal patterns of discourse. This communal contextualization would be necessary for the rhetoric of the interpretive performance to have its effect. It would vouchsafe the possibility of something that might be termed "intersubjective textual transactions": the potency of textual codes to modify the affective organization of another textual code, the self. Thus, the need for "intersubjectively transactive" patterns of discourse would restrain what might otherwise be a chaos of projection and free association.

Fish and Culler are partially correct in insisting on the limiting and directive effects of interpretive competence. Readers are constrained in their interpretations by the interpretive conventions of their culture. Clearly, meaning *is* meaningful only in a social and cultural context. But a responsible reader-response theory should acknowledge that both readers and authors, though limited with respect to certain semiotic operations, can transcend the signifying horizons of their culture and community. Indeed, an original and idiosyncratic discovery of meaning on the part of an aberrantly signifying author can be so rhetorically forceful as to assume a dominant role in culture. Many critics (e.g., Iser) assume that a prime function of the artist is to recover the repressed that has been excluded by conventional meaning. If an author can invent a meaningful yet "aberrant" signification, a reader can do likewise, sometimes transforming a neglected text into a useful rhetorical tool.

Reading, like writing, can produce "private" or idiosyncratic meaning, but an acknowledgment and appreciation of this idiosyncratic generation of meaning does not mean there is no objective text. Returning to the analogy with mathematics, we might compare a text to an algebraic formula. There are infinite ways of substituting numbers for the formula. But the formula's "objective" structure controls the meaningfulness of the calculations derived from it. The formula, objectively considered, may mean something by itself, but this meaning is flat and empty. The "objective" formula is only a pure expression of a structure of relations. The full meaning of the formula becomes practically significant only when certain numbers are fed into it to derive useful calculations.

Like algebraic formulas, texts "work" only when they are processed by another level of signification. Texts are not objectively present as units of meaning. By themselves, texts are only notations for potential relationships for signifiers. However, texts are objectively present as complex codes stimulating complex rhetorical relationships between chains of material signifiers.

The point of all this is that an infinity of different readers can produce an infinity of different readings of *Othello*, but such an infinite set of interpretations would exclude the infinite number of interpretations produced by readings of *Moby Dick*. Anyone who doubts such a claim should write a good, close thirty-page interpretation of *Othello*, change all the names to reflect names in *Moby Dick*, and try to teach or publish such an interpretation of *Othello* as an interpretation of *Moby Dick*. The result would be a failure to communicate. Of course there is always a level of abstraction at which one text resembles any other text. Both *Othello* and *Moby Dick* reflect quests for "truth." But such similarity does not make the texts equivalent. High levels of textual abstraction should not be equated with textual rhetoric, for they ignore or suppress the minute verbal particularity and temporal sequence of subjective experiences in terms of which texts are meaningful—and rhetorical—for us.

Often, texts are not distinguished from the meanings or rhetorical performances that they produce. Arguments about what a text is are conflated with arguments over what system of meaning should be used to process the text. Fortunately, however, there are repeated attempts to counter these assumptions. Hallet Smith's "Introduction" to the *Twentieth Century Interpretations of the Tempest*, for example, compares the play to a kaleidoscope and laments attempts to freeze its many-faceted signifying potency:

Because the plot is so simple and the characters so far from complex, the critics find it difficult to account for the great effect the play has upon them. In desperation they turn to biographical, allegorical, religious, philosophical, or psychological interpretations of the play.[45]

Biographical, allegorical, religious, philosophical, or psychological interpretations are systems of explanation fed into the mill wheel of the play's signifying structure, or algebraic formula. Through such signifying transformations, broad and general explanatory abstractions become illustrated by particular elements found in the work. The results of these signifying conversions fulfill idealizing projections and provide stuffing for the pages of countless journals and books. But as Smith's metaphor implies, none of these productions (and we can imagine an infinite number of them reflecting an infinite number of theoretical positions) should be equated with the text.

All of these productions are the effects of projective idealizations. Projective idealization is a meaning effect, a rhetorical effect, produced by an angle of vision. Projective idealization uses an angle of vision to produce a personal organization of the rhetorical effects of signifiers. Projective idealization, further, can rework the particular givens of cultural signifiers in an infinite number of ways. Reading and interpretation thus offer infinite possibilities for difference, and Holland is indeed correct in suggesting that the words of the text do not limit meaning— they proliferate meaning. But if a text offers infinite possibilities for interpretation, this does not mean that the words do not limit, inform, or direct meaning.

Smith's metaphor of the text as a kaleidoscope might be improved on by a comparison of the text to a crystal, which is a mechanism that diffracts the focus of light. (I apologize to readers who find the metaphorical implications of this analogy too idealistic.) The crystal, unlike the kaleidoscope, has three dimensions. There is always a particularity in its depth we cannot see that influences, by its manipulation of light, the surface we do see. There is a curious depth to a text that enriches what we do see by suggesting the presence of things we do not see, just as there is a rich depth to a crystal that enriches the surface we see by making use of the reflective depth we do not see.

Because of the limitations of mental representation the angular faces of a three-dimensional crystal are best observed by being viewed from many different angles of perspective. The crystal will authorize a different sketch when seen as two-dimensional from any of a variety of perspectives. Yet all the infinitely different, two-dimensional patterns produced by infinitely small changes in rotations of the viewing angle have their ground in a particular three-dimensional structure. This is also true with criticism: To insure the systematic unity in argumentation, writers can only write from a two-dimensional perspective; otherwise central concepts lose their clarity as they shift around the rotation of changing angles of vision. Nevertheless most critics can appreciate the beauty of things they discuss from three dimensions. They can see how other people get the ideas they do when they look at something from a "different angle." Critics can even appreciate the "depth" perspective of the art object: They can appreciate the beauty of it precisely in its ability to produce multiple, intricate, and compelling effects from multiple angles of vision.

The signifiers of a text allow an infinity of different perspectives and different rhetorical performances, but this does not mean that the text has no distinctive qualities of its own. A good interpretation of a text offers other readers a persuasive "network of projections" stimulated and rhetorically sustained by close attention to the particular properties of a referentially unstable, but not a perceptually unstable, verbal artifact. Fish's refutation of the objective text, then, is misguided. There is an objective text that "remains the same from one moment to the next." We cannot say "objectively" what the text means, but the objective text, like a mathematical formula, can be used to assess the propriety of the things we do with it. It can be used to evaluate the amount of projective denials and gratuitous free association present in any interpretation. The language of a text, precisely in all its imaginable possibilities, conditions and influences the set of associations the text can legitimately support. If words are rhetorical performers, the meaning of texts may be the reader's creation. But this creation cannot be legitimately produced if the reader fails to hear all the performers. Just as music can be performed in different keys and different tempos, texts can be read in different tones and from different perspectives. The differences in performance are often great, but the music performed must reflect a set of musical relationships suggested by the musical notes.

If both good and acceptable interpretations depend on a reader's organization of the force of rhetoric potentially present in texts and not on the recovery of truth, then the rewards of interpretation indeed lie in the attainment of "narcissistic" gratification. Many people see this as a "sad" state of affairs and as characteristic of the "whole problem" of humanistic study. I would argue that this is not so much the whole problem of humanistic study as the "whole point" of humanistic study. For this means that interpretive activity is involved not simply with the gratification of suppressed wishes, but with a communal attempt to rework a culture's terms of idealization from within a deep structure of unconscious aspiration. Furthermore, this reworking of aspiration circles about the textual materiality of language, that is, the socially shared units of expression we use to talk to each other. To claim that reading always re-explores ideals and terms for value through participation in textual materiality is but another way to state my central argument: Reading engages projective idealization. Reading thus is always narcissistic. Reading, in fact, should be narcissistic. But reading should not be solipsistic. It must reach beyond solipsism to recover the social ground of dialogue that signification participates in and reflects. When reading carefully recovers the vitality of signification, "narcissistic" activity does not destroy a text, and it does not deny the knowledge that can be gained from texts. It, instead, appropriates signifiers for human purposes.

Notes

1. Stanley Fish, *Is There a Text in This Class?* (Cambridge: Harvard University Press, 1980), 7.
2. Ibid., vii.
3. Paul de Man, *Allegories of Reading* (New Haven, Conn.: Yale University Press, 1979), 19.
4. Barbara Johnson, "Rigorous Unreliability," *Critical Inquiry* 11 (1984): 279.
5. Michel Foucault, "What Is an Author?" in *Language, Counter Memory, Practice* (Ithaca, N.Y.: Cornell University Press, 1977), 127.
6. Roland Barthes, *Image, Music, Text* (New York: Hill, 1977), 148
7. George Steiner, "Narcissus and Echo," *American Journal of Semiotics* 1 (1980): 8.
8. Hayden White, *Tropics of Discourse* (Baltimore: Johns Hopkins University Press, 1978), 265.
9. See, for example, John Brenkman, "Narcissus in the Text," *Georgia Review* 30 (1976): 293–327.
10. Sigmund Freud, "On Narcissism, An Introduction," 73.
11. Jeffrey Berman's *Narcissism and the Novel* offers a useful reading of the Narcissus myth in relation to clinical findings.
12. Sigmund Freud, "Instincts and Their Vicissitudes" (1915), *Standard Edition* 14: 136.
13. In everyday speech, projection is a kind of externalization of inner mental

phenomena. Projection and identification are thus similar forms of perception in so far as they represent conditions in which objects in the outside world are subsumed in terms of equivalences to figurations of the inside world of the self.

In the strictest sense, however, projection is the opposite of identification. It is a more paranoic mechanism. It is a means of disowning identity, not of appropriating it. As Laplanche and Pontalis (*The Language of Psychoanalysis*, trans. Donald Nicholson-Smith [New York: Norton, 1973]) point out, "The relationship between identification and projection is highly confused, owing in part to sloppy linguistic usage. The hysteric, for instance, is sometimes described interchangeably as projecting [her-] himself on to or identifying [her-] himself with such and such a character" (355). Laplanche and Pontalis want to insist on a distinction between the terms. Identification involves an imaginary self-recognition. In identification, people recognize themselves in another. Projection also invests the external world with the qualities of the inner self. But unlike identification, projection is a refutation, not an acceptance, of those qualities. Projection, then, does not involve a self-recognition. Just the opposite: In investing the external world with the qualities of the self, individuals thereby refute those qualities, failing to recognize them as originating in their own mind. Projection, as Pontalis and Laplanche point out, is "always a matter of throwing out what one refuses either to recognize in oneself or to be oneself" (355).

Projection and identification, then, are completely opposite in effect. Identification makes the outside familiar, comfortable, and similar to what is inside, in consciousness. Projection, on the other hand, is an encounter with the unfamiliar. It is an encounter with disowned and rejected material repressed from consciousness.

In *Five Readers Reading* (New Haven, Conn.: Yale University Press, 1975), Holland acknowledges the technical sense of projection when he points out that "when the ego projects, it deals with a danger by seeing it as outside" (115). But in practice, Holland emphasizes that "projection may also be a way of empathizing with another person, seeing his point of view" (115). Thus, for Holland, projection works like identification or like a narcissistic alliance. This chapter follows Holland's lead in artificially conflating the two activities in order to draw attention to the larger implications of both of them.

14. Fish, *Is There a Text in This Class?* 170.
15. Ibid., 13; David Bleich, *Subjective Criticism* (Baltimore: Johns Hopkins University Press, 1978), 88; Norman Holland, "A Transactive Account of Transactive Criticism," *Poetics* 7 (1978): 177–89.
16. Norman Holland, "Unity Identity Text Self," *PMLA* 90 (1975): 813–22.
17. Holland, "Recovering the Purloined Letter," in *The Reader in the Text*, ed. Susan R. Suleiman and Inge Crosman (Princeton, N.J.: Princeton University Press, 1980), 366.
18. Holland, "A Transactive Account," 181.
19. Bleich, *Subjective Criticism*, 97.

20. Ibid., 98.
21. Bleich and others seem to feel that because words can mean anything, the text does not offer anything significant for acts of attention. Such a view conflates the issue of objectivity with the issue of acceptability. Certainly it is true that because words can mean many things, it is impossible to define a discrete number of "correct" textual interpretations. But concerns for objectivity are not equivalent to concerns for correct interpretations. Acceptable or correct readings of texts are measurements of the satisfactions and rewards of interpretations, and acceptable readings need not be exactingly responsible to objective texts. Editors, operating within the ideological context of their historical moment, will publish criticism they find rewarding and reject criticism they find unpersuasive, unoriginal, or uninspiring. Acceptable interpretations posit certain meanings as rewarding, so acceptability is always a function of ideological and rhetorical relevance. Objectivity is a different matter.
22. Holland, *Five Readers Reading*, 286; also Fish, *Is There a Text in This Class?* 173.
23. Bleich, *Subjective Criticism*, 111.
24. Marshall Edelson, *Language and Interpretation in Psychoanalysis* (Chicago. University of Chicago Press, 1975), 28.
25. Skura, *The Literary Use of the Psychoanalytic Process*, 11–12.
26. Jacques Lacan, *Ecrits*, trans. Alan Sheridan (New York: Norton, 1977), 154.
27. Ibid., 174.
28. Ibid., 87.
29. Lacan, "Les psychoses, 1955–56," in *Le séminaire de Jacques Lacan*, ed. Jacques-Alain Miller, Livre III (Paris: Edition du Seuil, 1975–81), 91. Quotations are translated by Mark Bracher.
30. Lacan, "Les écrits techniques de Freud, 1953–54," in *Le séminaire de Jacques Lacan*, Livre I (Paris: Edition du Seuil, 1975–81), 106.
31. Edelson, *Language and Interpretation*, 87.
32. These two possibilities, in part, reflect the two meanings of "projection" (the appropriating and refuting of identity) discussed earlier. Reading, thus considered, poses two threats: First, we can become *like* the alien other that we encounter when we read. But second, there is the possibility that we fail to recognize the unfamiliar aspects of ourselves in what we read. In this sense, reading erases our own strangeness to ourselves. It makes over what we read into something resembling our self-image.

    In commonplace usage, projection indicates a kind of identification. But even identification is an ambiguous term. From a technical perspective, identification can mean introjection, incorporation, or projective identification. Thus, there are many ways in which identification can respond to the otherness of people: Identification can mean a temporary mode of responding positively to qualities we admire, do not have, but want to have. It can mean incorporating within ourselves modes of behavior that we find and admire in another. It can mean incorporating from others attitudes and behavior so deeply influential that they slowly change our self-structure.

But identification can also mean failing to respond to the otherness of people. It can mean a mode of perception in which viewers impose their own self-images on the other. Viewers do not see an other as themselves. Here, identification means responding to another *purely* as if that person were an image of the self. The real other, then, is never seen and identification becomes a failure of perception.

33. James Baldwin, "Sonny's Blues" (1948), in *Norton Introduction to Literature*, 5th ed., Carl E. Bain, Jerome Beatty, and J. Paul Hunter (New York: Norton, 1991), 5th ed., 31.

34. Ibid.

35. Lacan, *Ecrits*, 255, 327.

36. See Wyatt, *Reconstructing Desire;* Claudia Tate, *Domestic Allegories of Political Desire: The Black Heroine's Text at the Turn of the Century* (New York: Oxford University Press, 1992).

37. James Kinneavy, *A Theory of Discourse* (Englewood Cliffs, N.J.: Prentice-Hall, 1971).

38. Ibid., 432.

39. Henry Kucera, "Computers in Language Analysis and Lexicography," in *The American Heritage Dictionary*, ed. William Morris (Boston: Houghton Mifflin, 1981), xxxix.

40. Ibid.

41. For a discussion of a Lacanian theory of reader response, see Ellie Ragland-Sullivan, "The Magnetism between Reader and Text: Prolegomena to a Lacanian Poetics," *Poetics* 13 (1984): 381–406. Ragland-Sullivan tries to show that "the magnetism between psychic and literary meaning derives from shared affinities at the levels of a linguistically material ego, an inherent symbolicity in the act of perception, and from analogous laws of cognitive function" (381).

42. This possibility may be presented in several ways. First, readers may encounter the particular signifiers that anchor their subjectivity, but encounter these same signifiers linked to different systems of affect and cognition. In this case, the reader's self-system may not change, but values held by the self-system may. The self extends its approval or understanding to new areas of experience. Second, however, a self-system may undergo radical change as deep stratas of affect and repression become evoked and then networked and anchored to new verbal systems. In this case, the self-structure may itself change. This change, indeed, may be experienced as a kind of "freedom." But critics believing in linguistic determinism might not call this freedom a choice, but an effect produced when consciousness is subjected to certain rhetorical pressures from the particularity of signifiers.

43. Fish, *Is There a Text in This Class?*, 27.

44. Norman Holland, *The I* (New Haven, Conn.: Yale University Press, 1985), 144–51, discusses relations between identity and society.

45. Hallet Smith, ed. *Twentieth Century Interpretations of The Tempest* (Englewood Cliffs, N.J.: Prentice-Hall, 1969), 9.

Character, Plot, and Imagery: Mechanisms That Shift Narcissistic Investments

In the beginning was the word and the word was with God and God saw that the word was good.

(handwritten) ?

John 1:1

(handwritten, right column) In the beginning was the word, and the Word was with God, and the Word was God.

God also made us sufficient as ministers of the new covenant, not of the letter but of the Spirit, for the letter kills, but the spirit gives life.

The spirit giveth life, but the letter killeth.

2 Corinthians 3:6

(handwritten, lower left) as in obeying the spirit of the law, not the letter, don't you suppose?

Professional critics normally imagine reading as a complex conscious attentiveness that moves toward interpretive understanding. Wolfgang Iser emphasizes that reading requires problem-solving tasks and complex syntheses of perception and recognition. Norman Holland emphasizes that the matter of reading is not so much conscious as unconscious: Reading engages identification and unconscious fantasy formation. All of these descriptions of reading, however, attempt to name a particular "content" that is given to consciousness, or the unconscious, through reading. To understand literary rhetoric, it will be useful to consider the unique nature of the reading process as more significant than the reading content. Victor Nell's work, for example, suggests that reading produces not simply a consciousness of something different, but a uniquely different state of consciousness.[1]

In his examination of the data of experimental research, Nell draws attention to what he terms a state of "absorption" induced by reading. Absorption offers, Nell suggests, a "heightened sense of the reality of the attentional object," an "imperviousness to normally distracting events," and an "altered sense of reality in general and of the self in particular."[2] Fully involved readers are reluctant to break away from a book, even

when other pleasures—eating, conversation with friends, outdoor play
—awaits them. This curious pleasure, absorption, which reading engenders, is worth examination because it draws attention to absorbing but
largely unconscious rhetorical events that take place during reading.

Many theorists suggest that during reading there is a temporary change
in the ego or in the relationships among the various self-components that
make up the self.[3] If, as analysts say, the self-system relies on various
defense mechanisms—repression, denial, "splitting"—to control consciousness, self-contradiction, and value perception, reading seems able
to relax the ego's control, to reposition relations among self-systems and
thus resituate and perhaps redefine the inner material of the self-system.
Meredith Skura suggests that the fantasies we discover in reading may
resemble the child's experience with transitional objects.[4] Children who
are fiercely attached to a teddy or bed sheet experience it as part of
themselves. The transitional space is a play space where usual perceptual
distinctions between subject and object do not apply. Reading, like
transitional objects, can release pleasure and blur boundaries between
self and other. It promotes a fluidity, not just in the libidinal structures
of the text, but a corresponding fluidity as well in the subject components—the many-layered consciousness—that responds to the text.

Norman Holland's work suggests that literary texts relax the rigidity
and vigilance of the ego as they encourage the ego to entertain wishes
and desires that in other contexts would be suppressed. According to
Holland, reading preserves the censorship of the desire (the id); but this
censorship of desire does not contain desire. Reading allows desire to
speak in "disguised form." Although the expression of desire "in disguised form" can operate as a control for desire, disguises for desire can
also operate as investments for desire. In this manner, reading can liberate desire from repression and attach it to the sublimating imagery of the
text.

As desire circulates around signification in the absorption of the reading process, our perception of objects can change. Nell draws attention
to research indicating that reading often allows us to see things differently, so differently that objects may, in the words of one researcher,
"acquire an importance and intimacy normally reserved for the self."[5]
When imaginative objects are transformed in this way and come to
appear to have the same value as the self, we should suspect that transformations in narcissistic libido have somehow occurred. Reading allows or

encourages libido that has been bound in a specific location to move temporarily to new locations. In this way, things that may not otherwise seem "interesting" can come to seem so—as interesting as the self itself —through the libidinal energies released by reading. In *Heart of Darkness*, for example, Kurtz becomes significantly interesting for Marlow when Marlow has an "image" of him as like himself, doing things that he would like to do, exploring the mysterious African continent. Kurtz becomes interesting because unbound libido, seeking terms for investment, becomes attached to him.

As reading promotes a fluidity of libido and the attachment of libido to new objects of perceptions, reading contributes to a state of absorption: Reading pulls us into a newly formed and utterly absorbing world. This book attempts to describe how we become "attached" to the elements of this fictional world. Chapter 2 discussed textual rhetoric as a response to identification. We respond to an author's *ethos* present in the text as a controlling subjectivity responding to multivocal structures of conflict. We are moved by a text because we become identified with and invested in an author's *ethos*. *Ethos* operates as a rhetorical force when texts generate patterns of identification that offer opportunities for perceiving and mastering conflict. Chapter 3 suggested that we become attached to texts when we project our narcissistic concerns on the signifiers of a text. Through our projections, textual conflicts become our conflict. These conflicts, however, are not solipsistic; in important ways they are not at all like dream work. Our conflicts become psychoanalytically "elaborated" by the signifier's resistance to our projections: As we experience our conflicts in signifiers, we also experience how these same signifiers participate in conflictual networks of social signification. In this manner signifiers link our conflicts to social conflicts and remind us that our conflicts usually originate in prior social conflicts.

This chapter focuses on other elements in a literary text that structure conflicts for readers. These elements are more complex units of intelligibility than signifiers, but the meaning these structures take on is informed by the particular signifiers that participate in and give particular form to these larger elements. These conflictual structures are very familiar to anyone who teaches literature. Plot, character, and imagery structure conflict, engage identification, and contribute to rhetorical effect.

Before I focus on these structures, however, I need to once again call attention to the drive for mastery that readers commonly display in their response to the conflicts of literature. Fredric Jameson asserts that the most common form of criticism is ethical criticism.[6] Geoffrey Harpham, who quotes Jameson on this issue, points out that Jameson complains about ethical criticism, only to offer his own brand of ethical criticism: "Always historicize."[7] In psychoanalytic terms, ethical criticism can be considered a form of idealization. Ethical criticism "reads" a text, but the purpose of this reading is to assert a value. The recurrent attempts on the part of critics to assert value when reading a text has all the attributes of the idealizing projections discovered by Heinz Kohut in his experiences with transference.

We can think of idealizations as libidinally cathected structures that define our values. Kohut points out that "it is from their idealization . . . that the specific and characteristic aura of absolute perfection of the values and standards of the superego are derived."[8] A strange characteristic of human beings is that we are prone to assert our values on others. We do not just have values; we see our values in terms of an "aura of absolute perfection," and we want others to share these values with us. When we "idealize" a text, we shape it so that it will represent our values and serve as a fitting image so that others will be drawn to us.

Heinz Kohut describes idealization in dialogic terms. And this is the best perspective for considering literary response. We often project idealizing qualities on an object in order to see it as we want. We also, however, modify our own self-images in order to conform to the "ideal" objects we encounter.[9]

This dialogic process suggests how we may use texts for developmental goals. Kohut describes the child's superego development as a process in which the child learns to withdraw "idealizing libido" from internal representations of the parents and in the process of maturation learns to "employ" these previously idealized parent figures for the construction of drive-controlling structures."[10] The child learns strategies for libidinal control (discipline for example) when it internalizes the properties of the objects it has idealized. Drive-controlling structures that regulate libido are structures that master the conflictual appeals of desire. When we develop the superego, and when we develop the ideals and idealizations appropriate to a superego or to an ego ideal, we are mastering conflict. It follows then that when we idealize a text, after our conflicted response to it, we are often also using it to master conflict.

The following pages describe how reading releases fantasies, or libidinally invested imaginative structures. In participating in the *multiple* fantasies released by reading, however, readers often feel conflict, and this experience of conflict has consequences that lead to idealization. Conflict motivates readers to regulate their libidinal investments, to formulate fantasized ideals or even stronger idealizations that synthesize their conflicting libidinal perceptions in a "satisfactory way." This processes gives readers a sense of both pleasure and control. It also exercises the basic structural components of the self, the id, and the superego. Such an exercise is rhetorical.

Pleasure is an important dimension of reading. It explains our powerfully rhetorical "absorption" in a book. But our experiences of pleasure are often ignored when we talk about a book. It is noteworthy that when we talk about our reading experiences to others (especially with strangers), we tend to idealize. We create meaning effects that reinforce, or in other cases reform, our customary values or ideal ego. Our private reading experiences are important and very complex psychological events, and we are often willing to "confess" these events to our close friends, but in our public discussions of literature—in an institutional setting—our representations of literary experience are more simple. They are largely ethical, and they tend to dwell on our assertion of customary or newly formed idealizations.

Idealization

Literature and literary interpretation have always gone hand in hand with idealization. Texts are frequently ideological structures idealizing the customs, virtues, and heroic achievements of a culture. Similarly, texts are used (and often consumed with little or no remaining residue) by idealizing processes. Too often, literary professionals encourage us to take value assertive interpretations of a text as something more or less equivalent to the text. This gesture masters conflict because the various conflicts of textual meaning are resolved on the basis of the value decisions imposed on the text by the interpreter. When value assertive criticism speaks in absolute terms, it idealizes repression and reduction as essential mechanisms of interpretive practice. It dismisses the underlying conflictual meaning and nature of the text. Even when we try consciously to avoid such assertions, however, we often replicate them. Too often our drive to make sense of experience—especially literature—in terms of idealizations (or moral summaries) prompts us to equate reading largely with idealizing interpretation and thus to be insufficiently attentive to a more primordial conflictual structure within literary textuality.

Much of this book is concerned with describing this more primordial conflictual structure of literature. But just as idealizing interpretations are not literature, a text's "more primordial conflict" is not literature either. Idealizing responses to literature always reduce the complexity of literary textuality, but we must understand why they operate and what they do for us. Texts are often useful to us precisely because they aid us in the construction of idealizations. It is always difficult to judge the value of idealizations, but we cannot really do without them, and we need to understand the role of literary response in the social formation of idealizations.

We are constantly seeking appropriate hierarchies of values that allow us to order our lives and efficiently pursue our goals. We are also always seeking new ways to consider and reflect on the hierarchies we formulate. For this reason, texts always participate in reading contexts that contain unfinishable arguments about questions of value.

We cannot do without an idealizing social context that situates every reading act. We must accept this fact and seek to understand how literature operates within this context. Idealizations, in the largest sense of the term, are "forms" for meaning. Readers try to force texts and other readers to conform to these forms. This is the basic interpretive procedure in Wayne Booth's *Rhetoric of Fiction*. As Susan R. Suleiman comments, "What matters primarily [for Booth] is the ethical and ideological content of the message."[11] Booth believes that a good text expresses a seamless commitment to a particular question of value. Similarly, a good interpretation of a text describes the text's unified vision of value. Good interpretations give us pleasure because they resolve and simplify the conflicts that reading typically generates. But Booth oversimplifies the nature of a literary text when he idealizes it as itself an achieved and perfected form of a complex idealization.

Holland's work has provided a much needed corrective to Booth's vision of literature. In *The Dynamics of Literary Response* and later in *Five Readers Reading,* Holland insists that the deepest powers of reading are best understood in relation to the *experience* of reading and not in relation to the *interpretation* of literature. Holland's work, with its insistence on the force of "instinctual urges" in literature, offends the professional ideals of many scholars. Holland argues that the reading experience is not what we think it is.[12] It is heavily informed by unconscious fantasy structures and not by the apparent content of the conscious experience of reading. Holland's ideas have struck many critics as narcissistic, regressive, and unseemly. This reaction to Holland, however, might be understood in terms of one of Kohut's observations: As the self constructs "drive-controlling structures," it finds it useful to idealize these structures to protect "the personality against the danger of narcissistic regression."[13] We can see in the dispute between Holland and Booth a conflict between narcissistic regression and superego assertion. At Modern Language Association meetings this conflict is social. In the psychological world of the individual reader this conflict is internal.

Rather than following Holland, who sees fantasy production as a better account of reading, we need to see it in relation to the idealizations that Booth and others so conscientiously labor to produce. Fantasy is important to reading, but we do not need books to fantasize. Books do not mirror our fantasies so much as extend them by developing textual forms for linking fantasy to idealization. A rhetoric of reading will seek to explain the relationship between fantasy and idealization. It will seek to understand how the libidinal structures of fantasy, linked to the projections generated by reading, contribute to the more conscious libidinally charged, but more emphatically libido-regulating structures of idealization.[14]

The change we seem to value most, the change most often associated with understanding and freedom, the change most beneficial for intelligent political action (and not mere rhetorical manipulation), is linked to a certain depth of reflection singular individuals experience in relation to newly formed idealizations.[15] Idealizations are often formulated when we perceive libidinal shifts in value and grasp these shifts as opportunities for the mastery of conflict. Our desire for mastery perhaps prompts us to experiment with shifts in libidinal investment. But it is probably the case as well that if the will to mastery is overcathected with libidinal investment, there is little energy left for an experimental "play" with the objects of reflection or perception. Thus literary texts characteristically demand a play of signification rather than a will to mastery as the proper role for an attentive reader.

Kohut draws particular attention to idealizations as fundamental tools of human change. Insisting that idealizations and identifications are extremely important in analysis, Kohut asserts that "it is only with their aid that many initial steps of inner exploration can be undertaken which would otherwise be prohibited."[16] Idealization and identification are important for analysis because they provide a unique "narcissistic" support for helping to free individuals from their conscription by particular self-defeating codings of desire and identity. Just as experiences of idealization and identification are important for psychoanalysis, they are equally important for the reading of literature. We might consider literature as a linguistic structure uniquely suited for encouraging new idealizations because it encourages new patterns of identification that can promote a resistance to habitual idealizations. The aesthetic category of literary reflection, in fact, might be considered a psychological space opened up in the gap between an old idealization, not yet abandoned, and a new idealization in the process of being formed. Literary texts can be imagined as a particular aesthetic "form" of self-division where such reflection is encouraged. As a special cognitive form of this sort, literary texts are linguistic strategies designed to express and aesthetically appreciate self-divided perceptions on questions of value.

Often "good" (that is to say literary) texts are precisely those texts passionately concerned with social and political issues, yet open to different interpretations. I believe it is the nature of literary texts (as opposed say to scientific texts) that some textual components (which are repressed or dismissed in the usual interpretive gesture) are constructed and thus uniquely fitted to resist submission to the synthesizing gesture of a larger idealized form. When we call a text "literary" as opposed to some other type, we are describing that text's ability to resist submission to idealization even as it appeals more strongly to our desire to idealize.

These claims about the rhetorical and self-divisive nature of literature clearly need more extended discussion. Concepts of "the literary" will always require endless debate, but Aristotle's interest in plot, character, language, and spectacle (four of his six major categories that distinguish "poetics" from other forms of writing) provides a useful schemata for developing my argument. Aristotle's categories are convenient tools for demonstrating in more detail my claim that the term *literary* defines a text that uses certain predictable linguistic strategies to amplify conflict and manipulate narcissistic libido. A more complete discussion of narcissistic libido would involve a discussion of many more categories than I have selected here. But Aristotle's concepts provide both a rough outline of the nature of the literary and a particularly rich set of terms for investigating conflict and libidinal fluidity.

Plot, character, and imagery (a substitution for spectacle) promote conflict, identification, and self-division. These elements, in themselves and as they work together, are uniquely suited to "elaborate" conflict and exacerbate self-divisions and prompt reconsiderations of value. Norman Holland describes the response of one of his readers (Sebastian) to Miss Emily Grierson in Faulkner's "A Rose for Miss Emily." This reader observes:

Even though I don't like *her*, I can feel more sympathetic with other old ladies because the story does serve the purpose of distilling the odium that's connected with her, with all old ladies with memorabilia.[17]

This reader testifies to a change in values, "I can feel more sympathetic with other old ladies." The reason given for this change in values is both curious and curiously worded. This reader (Sebastian) clearly feels a good deal of conflict about the story. He does not like Emily, "I don't like *her*," he says, and he feels there is an "odium" in the text connected with her. But this experience of not liking Emily has, curiously enough, helped him feel more sympathy for other old women. "I can feel more sympathetic with other old ladies," he says.

Why is this? "The story," he says, "does serve the purpose of distilling the odium that's connected with her." The word "distill" can mean to extract, purify, or refine. Distill can also mean to separate one thing from another. What does it mean to distill odium? It can mean that the odium connected to Miss Emily is separated from her. Her perversity is shown to be all too human. But Sebastian does not like Miss Emily; the odium connected to her has not been fully separated from her. If one "distills" odium, one also makes odium more pure, more refined. Miss Emily's perversity is indeed shown to be all too human, like that of other old ladies "with memorabilia," but it is also graphically *shown*. Its own unique "essence" is captured in the *image* of the decomposing body of her lover Homer, which is revealed as the *plot* brings the story to an end.

Sebastian's phrase "distilling the odium" suggests both these meanings of "distill." It reveals a sympathy he cannot fully accept and a dislike he cannot fully express. Yet in the midst of this double bind Sebastian feels toward Emily, there is an expression of a new sympathy for other, perhaps less perverse, old ladies. Sebastian's phrase "distilling the odium" reveals the conflicts he has suffered; this phrase is tied to a clear value formulation: "I can feel more sympathetic with other old ladies." Identification and conflict have led Sebastian to a value adjustment. His superego will not let him feel sympathy with Emily, but his fantasies (which Holland documents) have led him to recognize and formulate a new value; he can "identify" with old ladies and their memorabilia. He can respect them because of an understanding he has acquired of their unique suffering and experience. In other words, his values have changed. His values have changed because of his conflictual response to character, plot, imagery, and language.

Character

Desire is manipulated in a text in a complex manner as plot directs desire outward toward a potential world. Imagery directs desire through an inward circuit to recover the passion of deeper and more durable libidinal configurations within the self. Plot and imagery are uniquely structured, but these systems of signification do not develop isolated from each other. As plot directs desire outward to the objects of the world and imagery directs desire inward to draw from the power of repressed libido, character dialogically interacts with plot and imagery. Because our response to character calls on perhaps our deepest narcissistic desire —the desire to give a form, and especially an *ideal* form, to the self— character is often the focal point for complex adjustments in feeling and perception.

Our response to character expresses our love of our own ego. Holland argues that our concern for own identity is the most important force determining our reading of texts. His theory of reading helps support various claims made here. Clearly, our own sense of character determines our readings of other characters, and it may be that our desire to read others always in relation to ourselves is what we most want to do when we read.

Our response to character and our tendency to promote and reject identifications are extremely strong, and they betray our own need to have the perfect ego, to be as complete as we always want to be. Classroom discussion frequently demonstrates that our response to character expresses what we value, and reveals, also, how we intuit relationships between character and value. Our identifications reveal not only our values, but how we visualize a specific hierarchy of values operating within the larger structure of the self.

Any theory of rhetoric should explore the relationships among literary characters, human characters, and human values. When we respond to character, very frequently we respond to particular embodiments of ego-ideals. These ego-ideals represent an organization of idealizations that corresponds to an ideal self-image. Frequently, readers overtly imagine ego-ideals or ideal self-images in terms of fictional characters. Readers thus imagine themselves, not as complex syntheses of abstract values, but like James Bond or like Stephen Dedalus. This is how we commonly see students responding in the classroom, and frequently our response is to reverse this perspective so that being James Bond can be understood in terms of complex syntheses of abstract values and complex syntheses of libidinal attachments. Reading, thus, can serve rhetorical ends when it helps us see the larger form of our libidinal investments in relation to the multitude of specific investments that make up this form.

Fictional characters help us to understand what it means to live in the world with the values we embrace or want to embrace. Fictional characters enable us to visualize the consequences of using a specific structure of values. Often, however, our ego ideals change as we respond to fictional characters who embody traits that "interest" us. Changes in the intensity of identifications with characters often reveal the rhetorical operations of a text because they can indicate the changes in our values produced by our awareness of the consequences of our identifications.

A theory of rhetoric must trace how plot and imagery, as they work on readers, change their identifications with characters. Before I discuss this in detail, however, I should acknowledge that response to character does not always serve rhetorical ends. Often, the identification with a central character reinforces rather than divides the reader's ego. Identifications, in fact, can often encourage repression, dismiss change, and operate as fantasies that deny any awareness of conflict.

Quite frequently a reader's identification with a character is total and uncompromising. Popular literature especially (like popular movies) exults in strong heroines and heroes who evoke strong projective responses, gratify insecurities, and indulge clear and clearly enjoyed fantasies. Traditionally, however, we have believed that "serious" literature seldom encourages such unreflective admiration and enjoyment. When we find college freshmen reading serious literature as if it were an ego-fantasy, we traditionally respond by trying to teach them that serious literature values ambiguity and paradox. Texts, of course, do not of themselves value anything, but writers and teachers do.

Many of us no longer accept the distinction between serious literature and popular literature. But when we teach, most of us try to create problems for those students who respond to characters by means of wholesale, idealizing identification. We encourage students to recognize and reflect on aspects of the text that offer more critical perspectives on characters. I would hope that our goal is not to suppress the responses of students, but to make them more complex by putting them into conflict with opposing positions. We want them to experience conflict, not with us so much, but within themselves, to listen to those opposing voices that are part of their own subjectivity. We do this because we consider this discipline of response valuable.

Our responses to those of our students express the value system that most of us have chosen as scholars. This value system in part helps determine what texts we choose to teach as serious literature. (It is a value system that, apart from the various political forms it takes, is both rhetorical and ethical. It attempts to show how things that seem simple are more complex than they seem.) We should recognize that our own professional values operate in the classroom. We use our values to produce conflicts for students in identification where, initially, such conflicts might not be experienced. Our own values may also work in another way to promote conflictual identification: We choose as "literary" those texts that (because of the structures we find in them) help us divide and complicate the identifications of readers.

Strong identification with characters is an important and forceful trajectory of desire, even in sophisticated readers. But this desire is commonly held in tension by the discipline of reading academics characteristically embrace and teach. I do not think we express one response, critical reflection, and reject the other, forceful identification. Instead, we experience both poles of response—immediate identification and critical distance—and explore, by reflection, the space between them.

In describing *Tom Jones*, Wolfgang Iser argues that the reader comes to "acquire a sense of discernment" through a response to character. Discernment, Iser says, "requires the ability to abstract oneself from one's own attitudes—an ability brought about by stepping back from one's own governing norms of orientation."[18] Iser's discussion of "discernment" calls attention to an important psychological event instigated by the reader's conflictual participation in both immediate identification and critical distance. Iser argues that abstract thought is encouraged as readers respond to the complex dynamics of story. Readers want to identify with a "good" character, but they often discover that "good" people do things that do not seem good. In *Tom Jones*, the good man, appropriately named Allworthy, is deceived by Captain Blifil. Readers, feeling empathy for Allworthy, suffer a sense of loss as they experience the consequences of Allworthy's deception. In this manner they can recognize somewhat painfully that people thought to be "good" have flaws. The text can thus encourage readers to formulate a more complex formula for goodness in human character. Here a reader's identification with a character, rather than offering a useful screen for unrestricted self-indulgent fantasy, promotes self-division. Readers are forced to make changes in themselves because they are prompted to formulate a more adequate model for the effective expression of human goodness.

Part of the meaning of aesthetic contemplation is the pleasure we get from experiencing the tension between these two poles of response— immediate identification and critical distance. We have been trained to respond this way, and we have been generally convinced that the aesthetic pleasure gained from this discipline of response is worthwhile. It is important to recognize, however, that this pleasure can be appreciated only by participating in the *conflictual tensions* of response. If our awareness of either pole of the structured conflict is diminished, so is the intensity of aesthetic pleasure.

Let me emphasize for a moment the importance of immediate identification. Hans Robert Jauss argues that, embarrassing as it may be for literary scholars to admit, "the literary hero is indispensable."[19] Identification guarantees that our experience of reading literature is different from our experience of reading philosophy. Identification usually fosters empathy, and empathy prompts us to experience a set of relationships rather than merely think about them.[20] Our empathy with central characters draws from us memories of our own analogous experiences. Identification encourages us to blur the boundary between our experience of the text and our own experience of the world. Literature, unlike philosophy, puts us in communication with, not only how we think about the world, but how we *live* it. It reminds us of our own libidinal attachments to the objects of the world. One of Norman Holland's readers (Sandra) gives the following response to Homer Barron: "[He's] something out of a musical comedy . . . barrel chested. Um—Howard Keel. I would be more drawn to him, his open nature, and he's described as always the center of a laughing group."[21] This recovery of our own experience of living in the world, our responding through identifications to an "open nature," and to "the center of laughing groups" is crucial for the rhetorical forces literature can bring to bear on us. Sandra's assertion reveals that readers often experience the representations of literature as if they were their own representations of the world.

It is interesting that earlier in Holland's book Sebastian expressed his understanding of Emily in relation to his perception of her "attachment" to memorabilia. Our identifications with characters indicate our attachments to them, but they indicate as well our attachments to the worldly objects to which they are attached. The totality of this attachment response to text and character makes literary response curiously alive, and for that reason powerfully rhetorical.

Strong identification makes literature literary. Strong patterns of identification (either overt or covert) often seem simple and necessary gestures of literary response, but they are complicated psychological events. Jauss describes an "aesthetic attitude" of serious reading and calls attention to the fact that identification, as it operates through such an attitude, is less an unmediated fantasy (as Holland often characterizes it) than a complex pulling together of experience, recognition, and cognition. Through identification the reader is encouraged to pass through a "sequence of attitudes":

Astonishment, admiration, being shaken or touched, sympathetic tears and laughter, or estrangement constitute the scale of such primary levels of aesthetic experience which the performance or the reading of a text brings with it.[22]

Our identification with characters encourages us to unify into a larger form diverse varieties of experience. Identification also encourages us to unify different perceptions and different aspects of experience. The signifiers that name characters gather into one network a complex of perceptions and associations that make sense of character. Through this process, we are encouraged to both experience and think about experience in vacillating and conflicting moments of time. Through identification we are also drawn to experience imaginatively things we might not want to experience, and we are often encouraged to make judgments about experiences that we might not like to judge.

If the ego is itself a kind of compromise formation between the id's desire for pleasure and the superego's desire for moral approval, then our identification with character probably encourages similar compromises. The conflicts of a text often prompt us to soften the harshness of our superego, or regulate the libidinal expression of our id.

In reading we move back and forth between pleasures of and critical judgments about experience. Literature gives power and freedom to our id when it encourages us to admire pleasures we might in other situations feel more critical about. But if literature encourages us to participate in pleasure, it also encourages us to judge it. Just as literature can provide us with powerful images of what we want, it can provide us with powerful incentives to judge what we want. Literature gives strength to our superego when it prompts us to be critical of pleasures we might in other contexts simply enjoy.

In literary texts, our narcissistic attachments to characters are constantly manipulated by what we learn about them. At the most fundamental level we might say that characters can be fully realized as *real* characters rather than mere fantasies only when our narcissistic fantasies in relation to these characters are deformed in unexpected ways. A basic freshman text introducing students to literature argues:

Major characters can grow and change, as Macomber does [in Hemingway's "The Short Happy Life of Francis Macomber"] and as Judith does in Doris Lessings's "Our Friend Judith"; by the end of these stories both protagonists have acted in a way not predictable from what we learned about them and their past actions earlier in the story. Characters who can thus "surprise convincingly" . . . are round characters.[23]

Round characters, it seems, owe their life to the surprise readers feel in imagining them. This surprise can only come when our inner imagined model of this character, with its narcissistic attachments, is modified by the text's ability to express to us things we now believe, but have not been apt to imagine earlier.

Another way in which our values and narcissistic attachments to characters are manipulated is through the text's development of paired characters or in some cases obvious "doubles" who compete for our approval. Maynard Mack discusses the importance of the mirroring situation in Shakespearean tragedy in which "the hero will be confronted with a version of his own situation."[24] In *Hamlet,* both Fortinbras and Laertes have different ego-ideals from Hamlet, and Hamlet is self-divided because of his partial identification with these characters who are so much like him, yet different. Like Hamlet, readers are frequently self-divided in their attachments by the various characters the play offers for identification.

In other works, characters who are not at all similar may be in conflict, and readers, who detect something admirable in both very different characters, may find their values held in tension by conflicting orders of value and identification. Even eighteenth-century texts, which so often seem to have clear commitments to certain characters as heroic, often, almost in spite of themselves, seem to offer support for conflictual identification. In a recent essay in *College English,* for example, a critic complains of William Beatty Warner's reading of Richardson's *Clarissa:*

As a tactical move, in opposition to Richardson who upsets the balance of his text by siding with Clarissa, Warner takes the side of Lovelace and argues his case. But that is not where he belongs.[25]

This case is particularly interesting because it shows that even when authors (here Richardson) themselves print their own unambiguous endorsement of a particular character, the text seems to offer enough material for a critic like Warner to take up and publish an oppositional perspective. We might assume that Beatty once read Clarissa "properly" as Richardson wanted his readers to read it. But due both to ideological commitments outside the text and to psychological complexities within it, Beatty's values shifted from sympathy with one character to sympathy for another. Beatty's values may seem, from various perspectives, outrageous, but they should not be surprising. It is in the nature of literature to accommodate the sort of value changes offered by Beatty's criticism.

Why is it that in literary texts, conflicts between "good" and "bad" are so often fluid, with each side contaminated by a measure of its opposite? The work of Greenacre suggests that the "identity" of the artist may be more fluid or multiple than the identity of others. Gilbert Rose summarizes:

The intensity of all experience of the child of potentially great talent means that all the early libidinal phases tend to remain more lively, to overlap and communicate with each other more readily. The unconscious mechanism of splitting has in part become developed as a conscious ego device. The gifted person, while knowing the conventional sense of reality, is thus also able to hold it in abeyance in order to explore and concentrate full powers of integration on imaginative possibilities.

The artist's selfhood is not unitary: there are two or more selves. There is a lively if often adversarial *two-way conscious* communication between the self-organizations—both between the conventional and creative identity as well as within the private world where the reality sense is held in temporary abeyance until it is reinstated.[26]

Greenacre's work provides a sophisticated understanding of the personality of the artist. It suggests that literature is especially effective at developing self-division because the work itself emerges from the fluid and conflictual, but nonetheless interactive self-divisions of the artist's self. The text supports conflictual perspectives on value because the text emerges from a site of conflictual perspectives.

The conflicts of a text express the author's grasp of character as well as the author's use of plot, imagery, and language. These conflicts are present as libidinal organizations of affects. Authors project these organizations on texts because they themselves establish transference relationships to them. Meredith Skura points out that, for Freud, the poet's position in society evolved from "transference exchanges." "The poet made repetition of the original patricidal crime unnecessary by inventing slaughter on an epic scale and presenting it to the group."[27] Poets project and express their own libidinal urges, and they repeat these structures in their text. In this projective expression, however, the poet creates imaginative forms that organize and displace libidinally charged perceptions for others. Although the signifiers of a text, in themselves, have no libidinal organization, the readers do.

To the extent that readers and authors share signifiers and share the libidinal organizations communicated by such signification, the conflicts created in the text by an author can be perceived by a reader. And to the extent that readers do not share the libidinal organizations attached to signification, reading becomes a more complicated social transaction. Readers can libidinally edit and organize signification spontaneously without regard for historical scholarship. Or readers can seek to recover historical data suggesting the libidinal organizations linked to cultural signification.

Characters are a powerful organizing structure for libidinal investments. And characters are not just "something" in a text that we read about; characters are something we are. Characters always reflect organizations of affect that define our own characters; and just as texts are plotted relationships among multiple characters, so are we. Characters, plots, and images are elements in a text that reflect our own self-components. Plots and images are things we are, not just things we read about. We are plots for desire, we are conflicted characters, and we are sequences of imagery igniting around the conflicts of plot and character. The categories of the self defined by psychoanalysis—id, superego, and ego—are no more basic to the essential nature of self-structure than the literary categories I have been discussing. Id, ego, and superego are arbitrary classifications of self-components useful to the work of analysts. For the average individual, however, categories such as character, plot, and image, are equally useful to the work of planning life tasks.

Narrations that employ plots, characters, and images help individuals organize self-components in an effective manner for pursuing particular goals. Fictional narratives compose much of our interior life. As Burke argues, they are "equipment for living." They allow individuals to develop effective strategies for pursuing their goals.[28] When we engage the plots, characters, and images of a text as experiments in libidinal organization, and not just as structures of signification, we are organizing the components of the self into strategic positions for particular purposes. This is why reading can be such a powerful rhetorical experience. It generates strategies for responding to life tasks. On this basis one might argue that literature is a term that designates a discourse structure especially responsive to the rhetorical potential inherent in self-structure.

Plot

Aristotle argues that plot is the "soul" and first principle of tragedy. Recent interest in narratology would seem to support Aristotle's evaluation of plot and reverse much of early modern and Romantic criticism centering on characters. If plot is the soul of literature, we might also say that conflict is the soul of literature. It is common to argue in freshman courses that plot is always about conflict. There can be no plot without conflict.

Hayden White argues that in order for a subject to be *narratable* at all, a certain conflict must be experienced about the events that compose the narrative. Thus it is not simply that plots are about conflict, but that the narratives themselves spring from an experience of conflict. For White, true narratives do not become possible until there is a conflict or "contest" in the authority whereby events become selected for reporting. "Unless at least two versions of the same set of events can be imagined, there is no reason for the historian to take upon [her-] himself the authority of giving the true account of what really happened."[29] White's work suggests that narratives, in order to be true narratives, must emerge from subjects who imagine divided perspectives on an event, and want to claim greater authority for one version as opposed to another. Considered in light of my claims about literature as a site of conflict, it should not be surprising to reflect that some modern novels emphasize this narrative conflict by not choosing one version over another, and instead offer two different narrative versions of the same event.

White finds Hegel's analysis of historical narrative useful, and suggests that narratives emerge from conflicts between "law" and "desire":

The reality which lends itself to narrative representation is the conflict between desire, on the one side, and the law, on the other. Where there is no rule of law, there can be neither a subject nor the kind of event which lends itself to narrative representation.[30]

White's description of a conflict necessary for the generation of narrative describes the state of subjectivity from which narrative emerges. It suggests how deeply the theme of conflict—especially the conflict between desires connected to the id and the controlling principles of the superego, or law—infects the structure of narrative. Conflict is both the subject of a narrative and the enabling condition that makes the perception of narrative possible. White's discussion reminds us that beneath our interpretive arguments responding to a particular theme of a plot, narratives are deeply implicated in conflict as they consciously and unconsciously specify material for narration.

If White helps explain the conflictual state of narrative, Peter Brooks helps explain the conflictual nature of plot. Brooks argues that plot is a mode of textuality particularly successful at engaging desire. We might consider "the reading of plot," he says, "as a form of desire that carries us forward, onward, through the text."[31] Plot divides us from ourselves and carries us into the pleasures of conflict as it carries us past the limits that normally define us by naming and containing our desire.

Brooks begins with one of the most apparent of observations about literary response: Narratives engage our interest. But Brooks shows how this mobilization of desire infects signification. "Narratives," Brooks says, "both tell of desire and arouse and make use of desire as dynamic of signification."[32] This emphasis on desire as a "dynamic of signification" is astute. Plots *mean*, Brooks claims, by virtue of our *projection* of desire into them. Consequently, the kind of meaning we find in literature is always of a special sort because it is determined and formed by a projection of desire.

Brooks's work seems to suggest that the prose genre we call the novel may be uniquely characterized by the dynamic energy it generates through forming links between plots and projections of desire. Plots are projects for projection.

Plots interest us by revealing how our particular interests, projected onto the themes of a novel, become transformed by textual signification. Textuality, as it responds to plot, does not simply signify desire. It makes us more aware of the "plot" of desire. Plots reveal how desire suffers the vicissitudes of temporal change. They can also express totalizing configurations of particular projective themes. According to Brooks, "One could no doubt analyze the opening paragraph of most novels and emerge in each case with the image of a desire taking on shape, beginning to seek its objects, beginning to develop a textual energetics."[33] Plots thus lure readers into texts by stimulating them to create a world revealed in terms of desire. When readers, in this manner, engage the promissory signification of books, they begin the process of libidinal binding that produces the "absorption" symptoms described by Nells. The world inside the text becomes more "interesting" than the world outside it because we are more "attached" to it.

Brooks argues that the engagement of desire is a basic strategy manipulated by an author to elicit and entangle forces fundamental to literature's nature and meaning:

Narratives portray the motors of desire that drive and consume their plots, and they also lay bare the nature of narration as a form of human desire: the need to tell as a primary human drive that seeks to seduce and to subjugate the listener, to implicate him [her] in the thrust of a desire that never can quite speak its name —never can quite come to the point—but insists on speaking over and over again its movement toward that name.[34]

An author's need (and we must call this a narcissistic need) for a listening reader is as fundamental as the reader's need for a plot. Both needs fund the libidinal economy of the text's promissory signification, and both needs meet at the level of plot, where author and reader share the concern for the meaning and outcome of human conflict.

Desire is an energy that enables readers and authors to share a concern for the meaning of a text. But although this sharing means that desire is a *bond* between authors and readers, it is not, strictly speaking, a *meaning*. Readers, of course, always find meanings in texts, but Brooks is careful to suggest that the meaning of plot can never be adequately grasped in terms of representation or signification of desire. For Brooks, desire itself is the meaning of narrative. Narratives are "motors" of desire. Desire indeed "means," but it "means" precisely by failing to finally and authoritatively refer to anything other than itself. This paradox, however, describes precisely the rhetorical power of narrative. Desire is the meaning of narrative because desire, both the reader's and the author's, comes to narrative seeking to take up residence in signification. But because desire, always following the lead of signification, easily turns elsewhere to better, more promising signification, desire cannot be finally welded to a representative signification. Narrative satisfaction, thus, is achieved more by the turnings of desire it performs than by the signifiers it reveals.

Stories engage human desire by promising to fulfill it, but stories never quite make good on their promise, never imagine final meaning in terms of a final fulfillment of desire. Even when they achieve clear endings, stories merely turn the motor of plot in another direction. Stories, therefore, are not as we often imagine them—significations of desire. They are processes for turning the directions of desire. Readers invest signification in light of their own desire, and plots turn the illuminated theme of desire. This is the implication I attempt to develop in some detail: Narratives are rhetorical because they turn the direction of desire.

Brooks argues that the signifiers of plot that initially engage desire are revealed at the end of the narrative to be much different than originally thought. When plot achieves completion, desire comes back to the signifiers that initially engage it to judge or "re-cognize" the signification that originally engaged desire.

Narration, then, is a process whereby the signifiers that begin a story change their meaning as a result of the story they tell. But these signifiers do not do this by themselves. We animate signifiers by becoming libidinally invested in them. Signifiers, as we inhabit them, position us in relation to what and how we feel. If the signifiers that initiate plot change their meaning, this change is performed, in part, by our shifting of libidinal investment in them.

Authors may not participate in, or even be aware of, the transformations plotted by the text they create. But the libidinal transformation of the reader can repay an author for the labor of writing. As I argued earlier, an author markets "something that matters to the self"—a certain "commodity of being" in the text of fiction. Fiction implicitly promises to give somebody "something." Plot, working with character and imagery, performs the transfer of this "something." As we respond to plot, we become different from ourselves. In this differing, this splitting of our being from the initial signification of our desire, we perform the ends of narrative closure—and recoup in new terms a surplus of our own desire as this material has been reshaped by our own particular investment in the text.

In this sense all plots are narcissistic: We look into them seeking to recover the engendered surplus of ourselves (as other) on the "other" side of the mirror of narrative. In this sense all plots are also rhetorical. They divide us from ourselves but persuade us that we can be happier if we imagine ourselves as a new product achieved by imaginatively experienced self-divisions.

Imagery

Rhetoric is performed as texts reformulate desire and restructure those components of the superego that decree some desires to be lawful and others unlawful. Both plot and imagery manipulate the formations of desire. Plot carries desire outward along metonymic pathways. Imagery, as I argue here, characteristically recovers repressed desire and introduces it into new structures of signification.

Plot offers readers global and generalized perspectives on desire. As a reader follows a plot, the text first offers opportunities for investing desire and later offers opportunities to compare different forms of invested desire. In this manner, a text provides structures for shifting investments of desire from one signifying structure to another. A text's rhetoric thus does not command a change in value, it envisions a change in value as ultimately desirable. Literary rhetoric thus uses desire (and not the force of authority) as a mechanism to shift desire. In this manner, desire can contribute to the development of self-structures that may seem unrelated to desire.

Geoffrey Harpham argues that systems of *desire* and systems of *law* are not mutually opposed, but part of a "'peculiar system,' inside the horizon of an expanded and complicated desire." Developing his case, Harpham argues that many thinkers misrepresent the nature of desire:

The problems in both Kant and de Man . . . stem from a fundamental misconception of the self and of desire. Both posit on the one hand a "free" subject who would, if not coerced, follow its desires, and on the other, some utter and external rebuke to those desires, whether in the law or in the text. We behave ethically, both argue, by choosing that which we cannot desire. A more fertile and suggestive argument would proceed from the premise that the subject itself has a self-interfering, self-resisting, self-overcoming ethical thickness, and that the moral law of the inhumanity of the text is no more external to the subject than are its "desires." Both the law and the subject take on complexity and depth if we think of the law standing, perhaps as a "peculiar system," inside the horizon of an expanded and complicated desire.[35]

Harpham's notion of the self's own self-resisting ethical thickness" helps explain the social and psychological products that produce literary rhetoric. Literary rhetoric emerges from a self-divided complexity in the textual representation of desire. Responding to the text, the reader becomes caught in many and conflicting desires, which encourages a new desire: the formation of syntheses, ideals, and idealizations that resolve the conflicts experienced.

Idealizations are typically self-conscious structures influencing value judgments. Idealizations are the discourse systems of law and the superego. In the technical sense of the term, however, idealizations are not simply values. Kohut speaks of idealizations as values that have been given special energy by being charged with libido. This energetic attachment of libido to value positions is often beneficial.[36] It helps us to keep values alive in memory and at hand for ethical thinking. Idealizations are especially interesting because, whereas they are the discourse of law (reflecting the desire controlling power of the superego) they are themselves investments of desire. Many of our idealizations come from others; we take them because we become "attached" to them. We also form many idealizations ourselves simply because we want to. Idealizations are desired investments of desire, and we often change when we no longer desire the idealizations that define our characters.

Like abstractions, idealizations organize and define a complex network of elements. But unlike pure abstractions, idealizations organize libidinally invested elements. They summarize a particular form of libidinal investment. Often, in fact, this organization is represented by a few signifiers that are also libidinally invested. Words like "radical," "liberal," or "conservative," for example, summarize a multitude of more specific value judgments and self-definitions and by themselves evoke gut-level emotions for politicians.

If fantasies are essentially signifying systems of precariously bound libido, reading transforms us by helping us to generate many of these structures, and to respond to this production, often with fantasized ideals. The testimony of Holland's five readers indicates that the fantasies and fantasized ideals generated by reading develop often from images that particular readers feel drawn toward. Holland, for example, describes a reader's perception of Emily's father in "A Rose for Miss Emily." She (Sandra) was able, he observes, "to see a feature not even the professional critics pointed out."[37] As Sandra speaks of this image she produces, the image soon develops a fantasy narrative:

I think he's wearing black. Well, he's really an ominous presence. His face is there looking down at her from the crayon portrait when she's on her deathbed, I believe, and that's really chilling, very effective.[38]

Holland argues that Sandra "used the story to create a set of pleasurable unconscious fantasies personal to her."[39] But if we look closely at Sandra's response, we can see an example of a response to a text producing an image, and this image, in turn leading to a fantasy, and this fantasy in turn (still responding to the general structure of the text) leading to a primitive value assertion.

Lisa's threatening image of the father—"he's really an ominous presence"—expresses or perhaps releases emotions that she has within her. Fears that are part of Lisa's character are visualized in her seeing the image of Emily's father. This visualization of the father is not, however, a random and aberrant event isolated both from Lisa's general personality and from her total experience of reading. Instead this visualization expresses (as Holland documents) Lisa's inner subjectivity as it also plays a role in the larger experience she forms as she reads. After Sandra imagines the father and senses the threat he poses, she is prompted to imagine other fantasies that contain or control this threat.

Holland points out that Sandra, in another personal response, imagines Emily's relation to Homer (though it turns out badly) as a useful alliance. Sandra has fearfully fantasized about Emily's father, and this threatens her. Sandra has also (as I mentioned earlier) generated a fantasy about her attraction to Homer. In response to these variously assembled fantasies, Sandra forms judgments about relationships among them. Holland points out that Sandra's response to Homer and Emily shows a positive judgment of the relationship "In effect, she was saying, [Holland remarks] getting close to Homer gave Emily the strength to defy her father."[40]

Sandra does not say this overtly, but she moves toward this ideal because she desires it. And she desires it because it helps her manage both her attraction to Homer and her fear of her father. We should recognize here that Sandra, in moving toward her primitive idealization of human relationships, is formulating a model for investing and regulating the investment of libidinal investment. She is prompted to structure these investments in particular ways because she is responding to a particular text in her own way.

There are signifiers in the text attached to characters who play certain "signified" roles in conflictual relationships. As Sandra responds to these characters, projecting her emotions on them, they come alive for her in particular ways. The figures in the text function much like her own internal representations of people, and just as those internal representations structure her emotions, her projected grasp of character in the text contributes to her structuring of emotion.

Holland's representation of Sandra's inner feelings—"In effect, she was saying, getting close to Homer gave Emily the strength to defy her father"—is not something that Sandra quite says. But if she were to say it, and it is easy to imagine the logic that would lead her to his claim, this claim would be an example of an ideal produced by an interaction with a literary text. It is an ideal very much like the one made by Sebastian, who concludes, "I can feel more sympathetic with other old ladies." And an ideal produced in this manner would be a powerful instance of rhetoric. It will be sensed as true and important because it helps Sandra manage her own fears and fantasies—not fears someone else has told her about, but fears that she herself lives, and senses diminishment in—precisely because her formulation of the ideal helps her to diminish them. The text contributes to her forming of this ideal, but it does not give it to her as a packaged "knowledge," insisting that she must believe in it. Lisa, through her libidinal projections in the text, and her configuring of libidinal organizations by means of the text, herself formulates this ideal in the form of a statement that promises to satisfactorily regulate libidinal investments. This ideal is rhetorically produced "knowledge" that Lisa creates in response to the text.

According to Holland, Sandra "liked the story 'very much.'" Sandra focused on particular images, generated fantasies, and on the basis of these fantasies and her understanding of the conflicts involved in the story, moves toward the generation of a primitive ideal: "Getting close to Homer gave Emily the strength to defy her father." Holland quotes Sandra saying somewhat cryptically about her response to the text, "I got that much in it for me as a piece of literature, besides having a strong impact. I admire so much the way it all hangs together."[41]

There is no way of knowing if the valuation Sandra puts on alliance and intimacy is something new or something old for her. Thus it is hard to know if Sandra's experience of the text is as "rhetorical" as Sebastian's. Holland's examination of his five readers in *Five Readers Reading* relentlessly seeks to prove that identity repeats itself in any reading act. Holland ignores Sebastian's new discovery, "I can feel more sympathetic with other old ladies," and is not concerned with documenting new ideals or idealizations that students produce.

Holland argues that Sandra's positive valuation of Homer and Emily's relationship is nothing new, but simply a reflection of Sandra's abiding, "characteristic" identity theme. Holland may be correct in his judgment of Sandra's response. But it is nonetheless the case that students often change their values. And often this change is facilitated by an intense reflection on the subjects of literary texts.

In classrooms students seem (I think) to take more pleasure in the discovery of new idealizations than in the repetition of old idealizations. But in general this analysis of the rhetoric of new and old idealizations needs more clarity. A psychoanalytic perspective would suggest that there are two processes of ideal formation corresponding to two different rhetorics. These two rhetorics produce different idealizations and different changes in desire.

One mechanism, and the idealization corresponding to it, would shift desire from one signifying structure to another compatible signifying structure that offers additional or more powerful narcissistic support.[42]

This might be a metonymic shift in desire, which could contribute to idealization because in a limited sense it would formulate a new "formula" for desire. Sandra, for example, seems to make a value judgment about the relationship between Emily and Homer. But an idealization of this sort would be relatively easy to make if it involves very little change in invested values or self-structure. It might be termed an "egoistic idealization," because it requires no real change in basic values. It extends the self's values to a structure very compatible with the self's general theme of values. It might involve a change in the particular object of desire, but very little change in the larger structure of desire defined by the self-system.

A more consequential idealization, a "sublimating ideal," derives from a more revolutionary shift in desire. This more revolutionary—that is, more powerfully rhetorical—shift in desire seems closely tied to sublimation. Sublimation involves changes in repression and achieves, not a change in the object of desire, but a change in the nature of desire.[43] The experience of sublimation transforms, not a particular object, but an entire spectrum of possible objects. Sublimation changes our view of the world. These changes, however, are more difficult to make, and they are often painful because they require changes not just in what we desire, but in ourselves.

The sublimating process is not well understood. But the effects of sublimation are important to analysts concerned with character change. Laplanche and Pontalis state that an "instinct is said to be sublimated in so far as it is diverted towards a new, non-sexual aim and in so far as its objects are socially valued."[44] Sublimation, like idealization, as Laplanche and Pontalis point out, seems to "depend to a high degree upon the narcissistic dimension of the ego." This is because "the object of sublimated activity may be expected to display the same appearance of a beautiful whole which Freud . . . assigns to the ego."[45] Although sublimation requires a narcissistic response, it would paradoxically be less "narcissistic" (in the negative sense) than an idealization that merely affirmed and extended (thus narcissistically reinforcing) the dominant priorities of a rigid self-structure.

These observations suggest that the strongest forms of rhetoric would be those achieving "sublime" affects (as Longinus argues). Sublime affects are achieved not by simple changes in the object of desire, but in larger transformations of the structure of desire. The sublime is a mechanism operating on the more durable libidinal systems within the self-system and not merely on the representations the self characteristically entertains when imagining desire. A sublimating ideal releases repressed desire, directs its energy toward a newly discovered satisfactory object, and contributes to self-structure.

The process of formulating an egoistic idealization is quite different from the process of formulating a sublimating ideal. People are eager to form egoistic idealizations. Such structures happily and quickly satisfy desire and provide comforting narcissistic support. Sublimating ideals, however, are formed through a more difficult encounter with repression and resistance. We are not quickly drawn to sublimating ideals; we have to work through repression and resistance. We have to loosen our defenses and give up habitual self-images. Sublimating ideals require more demanding psychological work to formulate, but they are also more durable, and more closely linked to the more lasting components of self-structure. Kohut claims that in a successful analysis such ideals become a rich source of meaning for patients: "The patient's values now occupy a position of greater psychological importance, have become integrated with his ego's realistic goal structure, and quietly give meaning to his life."[46] Ideals that have drawn power from sublimating processes are deep features of our character, and not mere significations or empty idealizations to which we are temporarily attached. They have more power in influencing our behavior. They are harder to achieve, but more powerfully rhetorical.

Repression and Imagistic Thought

Freud argued that sublimation works as "higher level" values are achieved through desires abandoned at "lower levels." In order to understand the sublime affects of literature, we must, following Freud, understand literature's ability to make use of more primitive "lower level" structures of desire in the formation of higher level structures of idealization. We must also more fully understand the forces of repression that operate in the reception and expression of value judgments.

We can better understand the forces of repression and resistance operating in the response of an individual reader to a text when we better understand how readers construct and respond to imagery. Imagery, often triggered in specific ways by plot and character identification, speaks the language of Freud's primary processes and Lacan's "Imaginary." Because imagery speaks from repressed or unacknowledged desire, it can place deep structures of desire in conflictual relation to habitual patterns of repression and denial maintained by the ego. In this manner, imagery can release new possibilities for desire, self-definition, cognition, and sublimating idealization.

Literature engages a productive conflict between various structures of desire and cognition. Psychoanalysts call higher order cognitive patterns of thought *secondary processes*. These processes are modes of thinking further removed from an immediacy of desire and closer to a "reality principle." Lower order patterns of cognition are *primary processes*. These processes refer to stratas of thought and feeling further from the reality principle and closer to desire's unconscious insistent attachment to imaginary objects. Primary processes express repressed libidinal attachments to objects (parents, parental traits) that structure both perception and self-organization.

Language that taps the energy of primary processes can both elicit desire and attach it in different relations to the ideas and ideologies dispensed to subjects by language. The narcissistic forces activated by language in this manner are productive—in the Marxist sense of the term. These forces engender new relations among signifiers, experiment with new formulations of value, and release new signifieds for perception and imaginative testing. In short, language that taps the energy of primary processes can be especially rhetorical because it manipulates not simply a reader's representations of the world, but a reader's most durable, and repressed, internal patterns of desire.

A theory of rhetoric should show how "regressive" patterns of imagery serve as experimental forms or structures for more sophisticated and durable patterns of perception and cognition. My reading of Conrad's *Heart of Darkness* in chapter 4 describes how imagery taps the power of primary process desire, how the presence of such imagery produces shifts in higher level cognition, and how narcissistically invested imagery, as it undergoes textual development, produces idealizations and affects cognitive models of reality. As we shall see, such a process shows few of the features of pure ego-fantasy. Instead it shows the features of struggle as repression and resistance are suffered, repeated, and displaced in the process of signification.

Freud emphasized the relation of art to fantasy. More recent theories see more complex structures in literature. Heinz Kohut differs from Freud in his understanding of art and culture, not as symptoms of human fragmentation, but as exploratory expressions of an emerging wholeness of the self.[47] Art can be an experiment in resolving libidinal conflict. Gilbert J. Rose argues that art can contribute to what he calls "mastery": an "ongoing process of integration and reintegration endless in extent and variety."[48] Meredith Skura suggests that we consider art "not as neurosis or symptom or dream but as the dynamic movement toward self-conscious wholeness."[49]

For Skura, the imagistic distortions accomplished by artistic forms can serve as experimental modes of cognition. Traditional psychoanalytic views on imagery allow no such optimism. Art is simply a release of primary process thought. Primary processes express thinking manipulated or generated by the id. As a childish and repressed component of the self, the id ignores the reality principle and sustains desire in opposition to it. Freud's various speculations about the artist, especially as they are formulated in "The Relation of the Poet to Day Dreaming," suggest that the primitive thinking of creativity is analogous to the primitive thinking of schizophrenia. The artist, like the schizophrenic, regresses to unrealistic modes of thought. This implies a parallel between the artist's attainment of satisfaction through art and the schizophrenic's attainment of satisfaction through fantasy. Both modes of satisfaction involve a loss of the reality principle and a return to early narcissistic and regressive "ego cathexis."

Like Freud, I believe primary processes are central to creativity. Like Freud, I view the artist as a person who "cannot come to terms with the demand for the renunciation of instinctual satisfaction."[50] Unlike Freud, however, I believe primary process expression, especially the sort of expression found in "art," is not only, as Freud conceded, intermixed with higher levels of thought, but also essential to the development of higher levels of thought and self-organization.[51] In expressing or evoking primitive desire, primary processes indeed unleash psychological forces that distort cognitive processes. This distortion, of course, may be regressive. But it can also be progressive.[52] It can liberate thought and language from habitual but ineffective fictions of perception. In fact, it may be the easiest way to liberate language from strongly cathected but ineffective fictions of reality.

As I develop my argument, I appropriate traditional theoretical terms like idealization and primary processes, and also make use of Lacan's theory of the Imaginary. Lacanian theory is useful because Lacan has attempted to understand the relationships between socially communicative signifiers and the more private and primitive world of the Imaginary that animates them. Textual signifiers, Lacan teaches us, do not simply refer to things; they are social objects haunted by both personal and social currents of desire. Language, thus, operates in accordance to both a "Symbolic" and an "Imaginary" logic.

Lacan follows the general lead of many Marxist theorists who argue that language and the social forces built into language channel emotion and position selves in relation to terms of value. Language offers programs for the binding of libido. Unlike Marxists, however, Lacan argues that the socially coercive positioning effects created by language can be deflected and deformed by Imaginary idiosyncratic narcissistic processes operating in and through language. Language, especially the experimental language developed by the artist, can combat and resist the larger envelope of language and value into which selves are born and develop. This resistance is possible because of the libidinal "push" excited by Imaginary processes.

In subsequent pages I discuss two examples of the "push" of Imaginary thinking. One example is Lisa Erdman in D. M. Thomas's *White Hotel*. Lisa enters analysis because of hallucinatory images she fears and uncontrollably visualizes. A second example comes from the work of John Fowles. He describes how one of his novels began with a persistently recurring image. Because of the insistence of this image, Fowles decided to explore its meaning in a novel. It seems to me that both of these examples of images "pushing" their way into consciousness are not terribly unlike the images that readers often experience as they make sense of a text. We must make more effort to understand these images, not in order to understand what they mean about the text, nor to understand what they mean about readers, but to understand what they mean about the meaning we construct from texts.

Consider Lacan's Imaginary. The Imaginary has been notoriously difficult to define, but there is some agreement that it relates to images, and to the early childhood experiences that employ such images in thought. Ellie Ragland-Sullivan explains that "the first images imposed on infant perception are totalities or primary unities with which the infant merges in fantasy, these images setting up the originary matrices to which all other images become attached in hallucinatory networks of meaning."[53] The earliest images, then, are relatively undifferentiated perceptions, "totalities or primary unities," and these images help the child form its own identity. These images are libidinally charged structures that are the umbilicus for a network of affect, meaning, and cognition. This system of imagery operates parallel to, but sometimes also conflictually intermeshed with, language.

Ragland-Sullivan observes that the "the Imaginary dimension in being announces itself by inferring [implying] an immediacy in behavior, or a lack of individuation in identity."[54] Lacan's theories first explain why language so often does not say what it seems to say; and second, they explain why language so often effectively communicates what it does not say. Language can evoke a sense of immediacy when a word offers the reader a fetishistic representation of reality. In this case, the word (or perhaps more commonly a configuration of words) impresses the mind by seeming to announce something important, something lacking, something significant. As a representational fetish, the word presents itself to us in the context of both a profound yearning and an urgency that the word itself ameliorates by its presence. In such a scenario, the word confers immediacy by means of the complex linguistic and psychoanalytic mechanisms that govern the self's inner structure. Immediacy here is not a truth event, but a narcissistic event: Something the self counts as "being" comes into presence through language, and often this experience is an imagistic event, a "vision" of some sort.

The forces of the Imaginary are narcissistic and preside over experiences where the self is lacking in presence. Often the Imaginary works deceptively to imply the presence of something absent or nonexistent. But the Imaginary should not be conceptualized merely as a mechanism of deception. Ragland-Sullivan's discussion of Lacan's Imaginary stresses that Imaginary perception does not oppose perception of the "real." The Imaginary is a different mode of perception, and it may in many cases be "unrealistic," but it is not a cognitive process working on some "opposite side" of reality. Because the Imaginary expresses primary drives, and because the Imaginary may, in some cases, trigger perceptions more realistic than many fictions supported by language, the Imaginary can play a central role in innovative and revolutionary thought. Ragland-Sullivan explains:

Lacan's Imaginary order places the potential for revolution in man by making the drive toward fusion and agreement—the impossible one . . .—fundamental to perception and action. The Imaginary consequently seeks to circumvent the Symbolic order, which places the shackles of laws and norms on the absolutism of narcissistic goals.[55]

Lacan's theory of the Imaginary thus links primitive, imagistic, and repressive psychic forces to progressive developmental forces.

Lacan's discussion of the Imaginary and Freud's discussion of primary processes help explain how imagery affects our representation of ourselves, our world, and our desires. Lacanian Imaginary is not equivalent to Freud's primary processes, but the two are similar forces. The Imaginary is a "style" of experience very similar to the nonlogical style of primary process thought. It is imagistic, emotional, and linked to early childhood experience. Gabriele Schwab describes the imagistic, irrational, and emotional insistence of primary processes as

the fusion of or the absence of distinction among objects, overdeterminations, the pictorial character of experience, nonlogical connections without hierarchy or polarity, the coexistence of opposites, a disposition to invest things and ideas with imaginary meanings and affective contents, the interchangeability of part and whole, and the absence of categorization.[56]

According to analysts, primary processes develop during childhood and diminish as the child attains a firmer grasp of the reality principle. Primary process thinking reflects the energy of the child's infinitely grandiose ambitions and desires. Thinking influenced by primary processes, for example, is often associated with narcissistic illusions of omnipotence and magical powers. As the child grows, however, and primary process thinking encounters the limits of reality, it undergoes modification. Primary processes do not end, but they are pushed into the unconscious. In normal adult life, primary process thinking is held in check by the ego and the reality principle. But for each individual certain characteristic aspects of experience receive influence from primary processes: projections, fantasies, dreams, and daydreams become distinctly colored or instigated by primary processes. In many contexts of development these mental characteristics hinder development; they impede clear perception and provide false notions of what is real or possible. In other contexts primary processes facilitate development.

Gabriele Schwab describes how primary processes aid cognition.[57] As the self develops, Schwab argues, it learns to distinguish and differentiate itself from its fostering environment. This learning, however, is frequently a process of establishing fictional boundaries for social purposes.

As children name the space outside themselves, and name the space inside, they borrow terms from their environment. But these terms do not always designate real things. The language the child learns always embodies various social and cultural fictions. These fictions operate as children learn both "what is," and also who they are expected to be. In learning these things, children exclude certain possibilities from their development. Schwab observes that as the child develops,

everything must be excluded that does not comply with the norms transmitted by others, of the symbolic order of society. Only by way of exclusions can the subject become what he is to be; but they separate him from essential parts of his self."[58]

As the ego develops, it excludes from itself possible images of self-definition. But it also excludes something more—certain aspects of reality and certain possibilities for its own growth and satisfaction that will not "fit" into the system that dominates the method of self-definition.

Such exclusion can cause problems at later stages of life, and it is here that primary processes can be helpful. Repressed unfulfilled satisfactions continually exert pressure on language and perception through primary processes. In many cases such pressure distorts perception of the "real." But in other cases, when the real is under exclusion or repression already, primary processes can serve to reintegrate aspects of the real into the domain of language and consciousness. Because the self wants what it lacks, primary process thinking points to a lack that language and the self have not yet named. Under these conditions, as Schwab argues, language can serve in "expressing or even communicating what is excluded from the symbolic order."[59] Primary processes produce new signifieds by deforming and reforming signifiers. In this manner primary processes, seeking to name an absent lack, can generate categories of perception that help to name or visualize aspects of reality hitherto excluded from representation.

Lacan and other recent theorists encourage us to remember that when we consider the function of language in expressing "what is excluded from the symbolic order" (expressing knowledge of the real excluded from consciousness), we must be careful about our terms. We often confuse what we understand as reality, which is really an inner map we have constructed, with the "Real." The Real is not available for direct perception or linguistic reference. It is in Jameson's sense an absent cause. We do not know it in any pure way; we infer its presence from our ability to manipulate the world for satisfaction.

Our imagined reality, the one we talk about in language, is a map of human possibility imagined by the ego. It is indeed influenced by the Real, but it is also influenced by all the learned beliefs and social codes (fictions) arbitrarily manufactured by culture and the idiosyncrasies of personal development. Because the ego is formed as an interaction between the Real and social reality, it is allied not only to the Real, but also to the fictional components of social reality.

This has important theoretical consequences. In being allied to the fictional components of social reality, the ego will often, against its own self-interest, seek to deny the Real and affirm the fictional truth of an idealization—of a purely imagined reality—even when such "truth" is a fiction that blocks its ability to gain satisfaction from the Real.

In this case, all possible representation for the Real suffers repression. Under repression, however, aspects of the Real can be brought forward into consciousness through the distorting power of primary process thinking. The Real thus becomes paradoxically linked to processes traditionally seen as the epitome of "unrealistic forces." Through the expressive power of restless narcissistic forces seeking to name something that is needed and missing, the Real can achieve provisional or fragmentary modes of experimental representation—but only through opposition to the functions that ideally "map" and represent it.

Through a deformation of ego-approved representational structures, primary processes can give rise to imagery that can provide new categories for conceiving new signifieds. Often enough, however, this process can be enormously disorienting for the self. This is true because the ego finds its own map of reality very secure and comfortable. From such a perspective, any changes proposed for "reality" (the imagery of repressed cognition) can seem hallucinatory, fictional, and disorienting. In addition, because the Real is partially disclosed as a potential signified through narcissistic forces already closely associated with projection, hallucination, and disorientation, its provisional signifieds (signifieds frequently present, as I have suggested earlier, in the form of "images") may seen especially unhealthy and surreal.

D. M. Thomas's *White Hotel* offers a fitting illustration of these events. In the novel Lisa Erdman comes to Sigmund Freud suffering from severe pains in her left breast and pelvic region and a chronic respiratory condition. Lisa's promising musical career was interrupted by her illness. She would like to be happier, and she would like to be successful in her career, but health problems (she insists) hold her back. As Freud gains Lisa's trust he comes to learn of two recurring hallucinations—images of fires and storms—that plague Lisa's mental life and weaken her health. Lisa typically experiences these visions when she and her husband are sexually intimate. Lisa is not eager to talk about these problems, but her life has become so tortured that she is desperate for relief. Lisa has excluded much of importance from her life, and her recurrent hallucinations insist that which is excluded be given voice and presence.

Seeking to understand the hallucination-charged consciousness of Lisa, Thomas's Freud considers, "What she had in her consciousness was only a secret and not a foreign body."[60] Lisa can see her own imagery only as a malignant force that pushes its way into consciousness in order to torment her, but Freud sees the imagery as a clue to a puzzle. He suggests:

In a sense . . . her mind was attempting to tell us what was wrong; for the repressed idea creates its own apt symbol. The psyche of an hysteric is like a child who has a secret, which no one must know, but everyone must guess.[61]

As Freud helps Lisa to remember her past and understand her mental life, Lisa is drawn to produce two literary compositions, a poem and a surrealistic autobiographical narrative. These literary works express a flood of imagery. There are fires and storms in these works, but these images are not frightening in this context. The aesthetic context of Lisa's writing is in fact much like the context of psychoanalysis. It is a safe protected space, narcissistic and regressive, but it is also an experimental space where libidinal organizations that cause conflict can be safely expressed and considered. Lisa is able to imagine this space "inside" her because she has already experienced this space in her transference response to Freud, who listens to her as an interested ally in her experiences of conflict.

The literary works show that Lisa's imagery of fire and storm is related to a system of emotional relationships that need more careful attention. Later in therapy Lisa wants to destroy her writing because they are "devilish fragments thrown off by the 'storm inside her head.' "[62] Freud, however, encourages Lisa to pay attention to her imagery, and as the two of them begin to make sense of things, they piece together a narrative past that has not been told. In its totality, this new alternative past is "more true" to the past, and a better representation of Lisa's own identity.

In coming to see herself differently, to see herself in relation to this new version of the past, Lisa is required to modify many of her ideals, and this is very painful for her. Because she has so tenaciously invested in certain ideals, she has repressed certain events. The same forces that idealize Lisa's parents also regulate Lisa's libidinal attachments and repress her memories of the past. (Freud's "hydraulic" model of libidinal flow is not entirely convincing, but it is a good metaphor for drawing attention to dynamic interrelations within the self system.) Through Freud's therapy, Lisa learns to change her idealization of her mother, to change her impressions of her father and early lover, and to judge her own professional and sexual needs less critically.

Freud finds all these structures related: parental ideals (idealized libido regulating structures internalized in the superego), libidinal attachments (represented by Lisa's repressed relationship with her husband), and memory. To reduce Lisa's suffering, Freud first helps her to suffer. He investigates her parental ideals, her libidinal attachments, and her memory, seeking to recover the various conflicts compacted in each structure, as well as to have Lisa consciously structure these conflicts herself rather than merely to suffer as one who has received these structured conflicts from others.

Freud provides Lisa with narcissistic support in the transference relation of therapy, so that she is better able to visualize her own conflicts. As she comes to understand them better, she formulates different controls for them. She changes. As a result of these changes, Lisa derives three benefits. First, she no longer suffers from the hallucinatory imagery that tormented her earlier years; Lisa sometimes experiences these images, but they no longer produce such intense affect. They have been drained of an intensity of emotion attached to them. Second, Lisa recovers memories that she has lost, and these memories give her a more true representation of her own history. She can now remember the "bad" things that she and her parents have done. Third, as Lisa remembers more and judges less, she is able to derive more satisfaction from personal relationships. She learns to see people more realistically and to judge them less harshly. She is no longer tormented by her hallucinatory images. And because she both "sublimates" and expresses repressed desires, she is able to remarry and to enjoy both professional satisfaction and sexual intimacy.

Thomas's *White Hotel* shows Lisa able to gain "real" satisfactions when she learns to "read" primary process images. Lisa's health improves when she expresses hallucinatory primary process imagery and places it meaningfully within the context of a larger and more realistic vision of her own life. Lisa's engagement with imagery is a highly rhetorical event because it greatly changes her values, her self-image, and her "characteristic" experience of life.

A reader's response to the imagery produced by literary absorption is not usually as consequential as Lisa's therapeutic response to her hallucinations. But it can follow a similar path and also have powerfully rhetorical effects. In the structure of Lisa's change it is not hard to see a less intense but nonetheless similar process shaping the response of some readers to literary texts. As imagery recovers repressed desire, there is a restless but engaged movement to grasp these images and give them narrative form. Caught in the grip of conflicting fantasies and ideals, students feel a need to synthesize their feelings and thoughts, to idealize differently. This process often contributes to an experience of insight that is often pleasantly painful, exhibiting an almost hypnotic moment of recognition. This recognition usually takes time to process. But when it has been internalized students are prone to generalize about their value alterations, as when Holland's Sebastian says, "I can feel more sympathetic with other old ladies." Often, as teachers who have heard many generalizations from students, we are not fully attentive to those moments when students wrestle with troubling images (Holland describes Sebastian's attraction/repulsion for Emily), release repressed material, and integrate it within a larger, changed view of life. But perhaps if we are more attentive to this process we can be more helpful in facilitating it.

Imagery and Cognitive Processes

Traditional psychoanalytic theory has not fully appreciated how primary process signification contributes to progressive modes of cognition. Traditional theory assumes that unconscious signifiers refer only to a clearly knowable signified located in the subject's past. Thomas's Freud, for example, understands Lisa's imagery of fire and storm almost entirely in terms of her past. Because of this preoccupation with learning the past, traditional psychoanalytic accounts of reader response emphasize reading as a process libidinally invested exclusively in the memories and fantasies of a reader's past. This perspective fails to see how reading, and the imagery produced by reading, serve as experimental forms of libidinally charged cognition.

When Freud follows the logic of imagery to recover the lost past for a patient, the meaning of imagery becomes entirely equivalent to buried and forgotten memories, desires, and traumas. But to designate in general the psychoanalytic meaning of repression as forgotten memories, desires, and traumas muddles our understanding of how and why forgotten memories, desires, and traumas repeat themselves so passionately.

Do these unconscious signifiers recur merely to designate a signified of the past? Or is there more at stake? Contemporary analysts argue, first, that these signifiers indeed refer to signifieds of the past. But second, these signifiers, even after we exhaust their references to the past, continue working to represent the signifieds of the present and future. Patients use unconscious signifiers to "project" past signifieds upon present situations. (Peter Brooks points out that readers do the same thing in response to literature.)[63] The point of analysis is not to expunge unconscious signifiers by revealing their origin in the past, but to discover how our libidinally organized perceptions of the present and future *derive* from the past but differ from it in significant ways. Past signifiers, then, refer to the past, but also necessarily labor to signify the future. They do so precisely because such signifiers cannot be exhausted by the signifieds of the past.

The overdetermined networks of desire and reference condensed with unconscious signifiers allow them to compound meaning. These signifiers thus begin from a kind of capital of invested meaning. They are examples of especially strong bindings of libido to signification. In time these signifiers offer a return on such libidinal investment. They come to produce a surplus of meaning.

What does it mean to say that unconscious signifiers have a surplus of meaning? It means that unconscious signifiers are libidinal strategies for understanding experience. They are thus not "things" that can be designated or contained by linguistic names. They are characteristic libidinal patterns used in experiencing events.

What does the child first desire such that later signifiers designate that desire? What do sobbing children really want when they say, "I want my mother"? Children clearly want the mother, but they also want something more: Security, support, and recognition are part of a whole host of powerful but primitive affective and emotional experiences that are related to the mother, but are not in any strict sense of the term designated by "the mother." This host of powerful emotions, however, recurs as surplus in later life. The adult wants security, support, recognition, as well as power, wealth, and influence. In wanting these things we may say that the adult wants the mother. But the adult does not *really* want the mother, for no scenario of "having" the mother would satisfy this want. (Many neurotics prove this by exhausting, without satisfaction, various scenarios of "having" the mother.) What the adult really wants is something related to the situational context in which the term *mother* has assumed metaphorical (and metonymical) power. We might say that "the mother" is a metaphor for grandiose ambitions that cannot be satisfied in terms of "objects." The "mother" designates a biological signified linked to a host of narcissistic processes endowing the signifier "mother" with a surplus of diffuse but insistent aspirations. The signifier "mother" thus (when it works as a signifier of the unconscious) does refer to a past signified "mother," but it also necessarily works to imagine an otherwise unimaginable future where the surplus of the meaning of the mother can be enjoyed.

Freudian analysts are often very literal minded; the child wants *the mother*. Stephen Mitchell points out that Freud's theory of sexuality is composed of two curiously contradictory claims. On the one hand, for Freud sexuality was a kind of bestial drive without a proper aim. On the other hand, sexual libido becomes inexplicably "adhered" to early objects.[64] Thus although Freud saw sexuality as an open-ended drive, he insisted that patterns of sexuality in human beings become defined in terms of specific signifieds the unconscious repeatedly yearns for. For Lacan, however, unconscious desire is not determined by an incontrovertible unconscious paradigm named by the signifiers of the unconscious. There is no one thing, no single namable signified (i.e., the mother), that unconscious desire "wants." Unconscious signifiers of desire for Lacan (unlike Freud) maintain a great deal of fluidity and plasticity. The unconscious contains codings of desire, but the signifieds these codings make possible are dispersed both by the rails of metonymy that transfer desire from one signifier (and signified) to another and by metaphors that structure and re-restructure symptoms. Unconscious signifiers, thus, do not simply take the self backward in time to a lost signified, the mother. They also take unspecifiable aspirations of the self forward to a wide variety of fantasies and real situations of the future.

Unconscious signifiers refer to a past, but they also (and more importantly) serve as mechanisms for changes in the experience of desire. When libido invested in one signifier is shifted and invested in another related signifier, the self pursues a new ambition. Lacan argues that "need" (distinct from desire and demand) may find satisfaction. Hunger, for example, is a "need" satisfied by feeding. But desire is different from need. Desire, unlike need, has no real or necessary aim other than recognition and constancy from an ideal figure (mother) in the self's developmental environment.

All this means that we need to broaden our understanding of the relationships between imagery and repressed sexuality. Freud's *Civilization and Its Discontents* provides a powerful argument for seeing sexuality as constantly at war with culture. In this model, sexuality constantly seeks expression and culture constantly represses it. We have learned from Lacan and others, however, that culture does not just repress sexuality. It also provides countless unconscious models for the satisfaction of sexuality. Anthropologists and New Historicists provide powerful evidence of how sexuality is often happily shaped and configured by cultural images and ideals. Biology and anatomy, of course, provide general terms for erotic focus, but culture provides its own powerful images that specify the focus and circumstance of sexual arousal. For any culture, status, clothing, and physical beauty provide important cues for sexual satisfaction. This means, then, that as a site of sexual conflict, the unconscious is not simply a scene defined in terms of battle between libidinal expression and the "law" of culture. It is the site of conflicts between different codings of libidinal investment and between different desired formulations of libidinal control.

Culture, to the extent it defines characteristic sexual fantasies, ambitions, and self-images, provides generalized structures for libidinal investment. Individuals find their subjectivity positioned by these culturally idealized and normalized libidinal structures. But individuals also have their own unique way of defining themselves in relation to these structures. Each individual has a unique memory and imagination, and a unique relationship to imagery. There is seldom a perfect fit between an individual and the coding of libidinal investment offered by a culture. To the extent that individual subjects are the site of unique memories and uniquely configured ideological alliances, individual subjects participate in cultural norms in unique ways. Often such participation, or lack of it, causes conflict. When an individual, responding to personal conflict, can commodify through language or performance or image a more desirable libidinal script—a better fantasy or idealization—to resolve some of the tensions normally held in place by culturally prescribed repression, this structure has enormous rhetorical potential.

Imagery and Rhetoric

Rhetoric, to work and to change us, must persuade us that our customary values and desires are not as good as we imagine them. I have argued that a text can exacerbate conflicts between the orders of the Imaginary and the Symbolic, exacerbate conflicts between primary process thinking and secondary process thinking, and exacerbate conflicts among different libidinal structures. I have argued that these conflicts are structured by our involvement with plot and character. I now want to describe more carefully the role of imagery in textual conflict.

Our *response* to textual imagery and our *production* of textual imagery can contribute to our awareness of these conflictual systems. Imagery can play many roles in reading. It can make repressed desire visible. It can, as in Lisa's case, facilitate the translation of unconscious drives into conscious thought, thereby offering opportunities for control over what was formerly affect. Imagery can give form to desire, but it can also help us visualize the real more adequately. Most importantly, perhaps, imagery can serve as a marker for sites of emotional conflict, sites where one system of libidinal organization competes with another.

Clinical research suggests that imagery, as it is produced by men and women, often emerges from sites of conflictual perception. Mardi Jon Horowitz, summarizing the findings of numerous researchers, observes that

thoughts involved in an impulse-defense conflict often enter awareness first in the form of visual images. . . . [I]mages are the first vehicle for expression of repressed mental contents. They also emerge in resistance to expression of ideas in words. . . . [T]here may be an oscillation between image formation and lexical representation and . . . image formation tends to occur during transitions in the state of consciousness.

Why should some conflictual ideas gain representation first as visual images and not as lexical thoughts? To summarize, image formation is a more primitive system, and it tends to be under the influence of a primitive system of regulation, the primary process.[65]

If images express primary processes and often "emerge in resistance to expression of ideas in words," then images often emerge from sites of emotional conflict. At this scene of conflict, the representational implication of the image opposes the representational implication of the word and thus provides an entry way for awareness for conflictual experience.

Horowitz's observations suggest that, first, we can often image what we cannot think, and, second, the image may help to translate into thought aspects of life we resist thinking about.[66] W. J. T. Mitchell has shown, however, that the term *image*, especially the literary image, has been notoriously difficult to define.[67] And before we discuss imagery further, we need some clarification of the term. Although most theorists agree that a mental image can be both much more than and much less than simple visual information, there is experimental evidence indicating that images can often be strongly and distinctly visual. In his investigation of the nature of imagery, Ulric Neisser discovered:

An eidetic image is an imaginative production that seems to be external to the viewer and to have a location in perceived space; it has a clarity comparable to that of genuinely perceived objects; it can be examined by the *"Eidetiker,"* who may report details that he did not notice in the original presentation of the stimulus.[68]

On the other had, the word "image" can refer to something not at all visual, but something distinctly cognitive. Wolfgang Iser stresses this dimension of the image when he argues:

The image . . . is basic to ideation. It relates to the nongiven or to the absent, endowing it with presence. It also makes conceivable innovations arising from a rejection of given knowledge or from unusual combinations of signs.[69]

These descriptions suggest that images can be on one end of the scale distinctly perceptual phenomena, and on the other end of the scale, distinctly conceptual phenomena. Various readers, in fact, may experience images habitually more toward one end of the scale than the other. However, this very ambiguity may well indicate the role the literary image plays: If images are sometimes experienced as words and some-times as images, it may be that this experience occurs because the literary image effects a transfer of intelligibility. The image transfers affect (often across a field of resistance) into idea, or it plays on a conflictual boundary between two systems of representation, one highly affective, the other highly cognitive.

The image's translation of affect into concept might be an important aspect of "insight" experience. David Bleich, for example, observes:

In psychoanalysis, as anyone like myself who has gone through it will testify, the moment of insight, in which the patient "knows" for the first time how to identify certain thought, behavior, or dream patterns recurring in his or her personal history, is always a moment of finding the right language, the right name for something that has been previously experienced only as disturbance or suffering or frustration.[70]

If insight can be considered something like the translation of feeling into thought, then proper attention to imagery or proper manipulation of imagery can promote insight. Clinical experimentation, for example, indicates that imagery production can be an important technique of analysis because it contributes to the signification of ideas that cannot easily be thought.[71] When we produce imagery, or respond to the pro-duction of imagery, we can be brought closer to thinking thoughts that we otherwise would resist. If clinicians can manipulate imagery for insight, so might authors.

If imagery can translate feeling into thought, it can also work in reverse either to recover feeling latent in thought or to charge thought with added feeling. Rhetorical theorists promote the image as a device for infusing thought with emotion. Longinus's theory of the sublime in particular emphasizes the use of the image as a major rhetorical power. The image, brought by the artist into the domain of language, performs a "dramatistic" function: An event is staged before the reader's eye. Rhetoricians are advised to use strong images while speaking because such imagery will give strength to a speech. Emotive power can appar-ently be tapped by imagistic language because the imagistic experience draws heavily from its roots in the domain of primitive affective forces.

Clinical research indicates that images can be effective at releasing emotion because they are at the center of powerfully invested emotion, or conflictually invested emotion. Biographical considerations of an au-thor's use of imagery would seem to support this. If we probe an author's most consciously used images, we often find conflictual forces intersecting at the signifying locus of the image.

Gilbert Rose's analysis of the "inner splitting and reintegration" in *The French Lieutenant's Woman* begins by giving attention to an image that was for Fowles the "seed" of the novel. The image seems to originate at the center of a conflict "inner splitting and reintegration" that germinates the novel. Fowles writes about his first awareness of the image:

> It started four or five months ago as a visual image. A woman stands at the end of a deserted quay and stares out to sea. That was all. This image rose in my mind one morning when I was still in bed half asleep. I ignored this image; but it recurred. The woman obstinately refused to stare out of the window of an airport lounge; it had to be this ancient quay. An outcast. I didn't know her crime, but I wished to protect her. That is, I began to fall in love with her. This—not literally pregnant—female image came at a time when I was already halfway through another novel. It was an interference, but of such power that it soon came to make the previously planned work seem the intrusive element of my life. Once the seed germinates, reason and knowledge, culture and the rest have to start to grow it.[72]

Conrad's *Heart of Darkness* is another work that wrestles quite literally with an image. Conrad's Kurtz is an image collecting an assortment of both polymorphous-perverse sexual innuendoes and poorly repressed narcissistic ambitions (biographers of Conrad discuss his rising artistic ambitions in 1899).[73] As an image, however, Kurtz is also an icon for a text, that is, an image that drives a narrative. Marlow identifies with Kurtz's desires, but he also disdains them. As an icon, Kurtz gathers a collection of signifiers attempting to judge and understand Kurtz.

As an image, "Kurtz" is a network of strong affects, and from an experiential standpoint, these affects have a great deal of "presence" but very little meaning or intelligibility (exactly the adjectives critics of the novel habitually employ). But because the emotions associated with Conrad's Kurtz lack "meaning," they need narrative. Just as Sandra produces a narrative to make sense of her image of Homer Barron, Conrad produces a narrative to understand his attraction to Kurtz. Narrative provides a conflictual verbal contextualization that supports meaningful reflection. Kurtz is a network of strong affects packed (or condensed) into an image that gives purpose to the collecting of signification that is the drive to narrative. Geoffrey Harpham observes, "It is remarkable how many discussions, how many discoveries, how many narratives, begin with paradox, contradiction, apparent confusion." He proposes that as "a general rule . . . narratives begin with such knots, whose self-interfering energies demand to be released or dissipated."[74]

Lacanians might say that narrative labors to translate Imaginary representations into Symbolic representations. Through such Symbolic translations a relatively undifferentiated sensorium of affect gains particularity, differentiation, and hierarchical value. All this means, however, that Kurtz becomes, through narrative, more than an image. He becomes a signifier that presides over and finally even in its ambiguity anchors a collection of images, imaginary relations, and symbolic relations produced by Conrad, and produced after Conrad by his readers.

Readers easily detect the tension between imagery and language in *Heart of Darkness*. In the middle of his narrative, Marlow despairs that Kurtz cannot be seen by his audience. Yet for Marlow himself Kurtz's image is almost too tangible in its "presence." It is as if for both Marlow and Conrad, Kurtz's image is uncomfortably loaded with "presence." The image of Kurtz, which Conrad himself complained was "too symbolic," lies at the intersection of anxious and ambivalent visions of culture, ambition, and nature. Marlow's story does not resolve the conflicts that Conrad senses. But Marlow's narrative resists moral oversimplification and resists allocating authority to the domain of any one ideological network. The text insists that certain "primordial desires" must be faced, but at the same time advocates ideals to restrain such desires. The text continues to suffer and affirm this tension, even in the face of its apparent confusion.

I argue that readers respond strongly to images, and that authors create strong images. Many critics, however, might insist that literary images are *always* created by readers; they are never clearly delivered over to readers by authors who, in seeing them, force their readers to see them in a similar way. Authors, it might seem, can produce only signifiers, not images, for the reader's consumption. The reader necessarily supplies the text with its imagery.

Such claims fail to appreciate the complex interactions between writers and audiences. We have long assumed that rhetorically sensitive orators can move their audiences by endowing their language with imagistic effects—effects that they both intend and manipulate because they sense an audience's libidinal investment in signification. Good orators, most people agree, "have a feel" for the effects of various language strategies.

They know in advance what effect a particular image or rhetorical trope will have. The dominance of deconstruction has suggested that writers have no ability equivalent to speakers. Their signifiers cannot be aimed at readers, but only dispersed among varied contexts of appropriation. Such an assumption is a useful corrective for many critical assumptions about the authority of the text. But it oversimplifies the rhetorical complexity it seeks to analyze.

It is shortsighted to imagine that an orator can be rhetorically effective where a writer cannot. Writers, like orators, manipulate rhetorical effects through linguistic strategies. Writers are knowledgeable about how experience is shared and narrated by a culture. Writers understand the cultural signifiers that structure the libidinal investments of individuals. Writers, in their appreciation of words, sense the libidinal power of words. They understand that words are not empty structures for arbitrary signification; rather, words are structures for the cultural communication of libidinal investments.

When the U.S. military wants to increase its number of volunteers, it enlists the aid of professional film producers. When a required sum of money is paid, football games are interrupted by footage showing handsome, strong-looking, young men driving tanks and scouting out dense forests with machine gun in hand. The images in these films are carefully selected to trigger a desired response. Clearly there can be many different possible responses to these ads. Veterans may think about friends instantly transformed into stumps of human suffering. Sports enthusiasts may daydream about the importance of looking fit, confident, and winning. But many young men and women will consider talking to an army recruiter. The imagery of film, perhaps because it is close to the imagery of fantasy life, seems particularly able to trigger rhetorical effects. We know that certain ads can increase the number of products sold. Ad producers cannot predict for certain which advertisements will be successful, but they have an "artful" understanding of how to manipulate the libidinal investments of viewers. They understand the "language of imagery."

This understanding of the language of imagery is not as mysterious as all that. Good writers, like competent producers of television commercials, understand how to direct effective assaults on readers' emotions, and can skillfully construct and employ signifiers pregnant with imagistic and emotional effects.

Patrick Brantlinger describes Conrad's abiding interest in the adven-

ture stories of Capt. Frederick Marryat and others.[75] Conrad read enough
of these boy's adventure tales to understand the powerful libidinal structures defined by such stories, and he understood the spirit of adventure
that these stories communicated to early Victorian readers. It is no
accident that *Heart of Darkness* appeals to the imagery of such stories
even as it attempts to explode their libidinal organization. In chapter 1 I
quoted Conrad to illustrate how imagery can indicate when mere representation has been transformed into libidinally invested representation.
Marlow complains that, though he has heard much about Kurtz, he still
has no good image of him.

I had heard Mr. Kurtz was in there. I had heard enough about it, too—God
knows! Yet somehow it didn't bring any image with it—no more than if I had
been told an angel or a fiend was in there. I believed it the same way one of you
might believe there are inhabitants on the planet Mars.[76]

A few pages later, however, Marlow hears the manager and his nephew
talk about Kurtz. They are bewildered about Kurtz's motives, and in
this context of their lack of understanding, Marlow has an insight. He
suddenly gets a vivid image:

As to me, I seemed to see Kurtz for the first time. It was a distinct glimpse: the
dugout, the four paddling savages, and the lone white man turning his back
suddenly on the headquarters, on relief, on thoughts of home—perhaps; setting
his face towards the depths of the wilderness.[77]

This image, produced when Marlow considers Kurtz's motive, seems
ignited by the boy's adventure fantasy that Marlow, as Conrad, has
received from Marryat, and himself passionately lives. Conrad can use
the language of this imagery because he understands how he has been
used by it.

The image marks the moment when Kurtz becomes not simply an
abstract figure, but a figuration for Marlow's own narcissism. An abstract other, a remote human being, suddenly enters Marlow's inner life
as an image of the great explorer. Conrad is clearly manipulating this
image, inviting readers to savor it when he emphasizes the details of the
image—the dugout, four paddlers, lone white man. If we examine the
response of modern critics to the novel, however, we discover that this
image is not the one most often discussed.

Later in the novel, Conrad seems almost consciously concerned with
disciplining his early, painfully constructed and idealizing image of Kurtz

in the canoe with another, more closely inspected image. This is the image of Kurtz most often "seen" vividly by modern critics. It clearly imagines Kurtz in terms of a moral judgment of him, and it is an image that directly contributes to an easy moralizing interpretation of the text.

When Marlow first *really* sees Kurtz, through a spyglass (in order to bring something distant more close), he sees something much more like a hallucinatory image than a realistic picture. This is a curious moment in Marlow's narrative. Kurtz looks empty and skeletal, and this oddly constructed literary image combats the idealizing image of adventure (embodied by Kurtz) that Marlow had constructed earlier on. Clearly Conrad, at some level, is manipulating the imagery of his text, and critical response shows that many readers follow the patterns of imagery Conrad constructed, responding to the moral judgment Conrad seems to intend. This is not really so surprising; countless white males, like Conrad, are nurtured on similar fantasies of exploration and adventure. These fantasies (culturally defined libidinal structures) prompt such readers to "see" Kurtz much as Conrad "saw" him and to experience the libidinal attachments manipulated by such imagery.

It is difficult to generalize about literary images because literary authors make more complex rhetorical use of narcissistic conflict than orators. Literature seems to engage an aesthetics of self-division that tolerates an ambiguous rhetorical message; it commonly allows a reader relative freedom in formulating that message. The rhetoric of public address seems to require a more dependably stable "message," and it thus perhaps precludes the degree of self-division (a tragic vision of self-division, for example) permissible to literature. For this reason literary imagery frequently seems more restlessly overdetermined—easier to deconstruct—than oratorical imagery.

In both cases, however, imagery illuminates the domains of the Real and Symbolic with the magic of narcissistic promise. Entering into language and consciousness, the image alters the reader's sense of textual presence. The image can ignite ambition, but it can also discipline desire. Images can suggest to us that which we want to have, places we want to go, situations we want to master. This unveiling of desire is central to literary production. But we can do many things with this desire expressed in images; we can use images to discipline ambition, and even take pleasure in this act of judgment.

As the image channels narcissistic forces into signification, it exposes these forces to consciousness, and thus exposes them to the compromising demands of the ego's censorship. In normal thought, these forces might be repressed. But reading, like daydreaming, is less under the rule of the ego. Rather than undergoing repression in the face of the reality ego (as is commonly the case with narcissistic aspirations), sublimating or idealizing forces linked to narcissistic mechanisms find signifying possibilities in images wherein narcissistic energy can take up residence. The image helps readers enact a compromise to save narcissistic ambition from repression. Images can prompt us to formulate new fantasies acceptable to our ego, and they can prompt us to fantasize ideals that synthesize our libidinal investments.

As certain images (people, situations, ambitions) are "lit up" by investments of idealizing energy, they become, as Laplanche and Pontalis note, "exalted and aggrandized in the subject's mind."[78] Thus although the things themselves do not change, our perception of their qualities, or their value, can change. In the case of Conrad's skeletal image of Kurtz, what is admired is no longer Kurtz, but Marlow's improved understanding of him. Thus narcissistic libido initially prompts us to identify with Kurtz, to "see" him rather than just follow a flow of words. Later, however, narcissistic forces prompt us to judge Kurtz, and to experience the judgmental satisfactions accorded the superego. Experiences such as this, in which investments of narcissistic libido swing sharply from one pole to another, can occur in reading. They are also part of the normal process of psychological development. They often mark major changes and sometimes advances in adjusting to the difficult complexities of life. They can help us generate solutions to the problems that make us suffer.

Imagery gains particularity as it is carried forward by plot and manipulated by character interaction. Such imagery, precisely because it is imagery, draws emotional power from early repressed imagistic "visions" of desire. This manipulation of repressed desire attached to imagery can have important political effects. In her reading of *Little Women*, Jean Wyatt argues that a woman's participation in the kinetic imagery of the text can release aspirations for autonomy that are normally repressed by the patriarchal structures of society:

What messages does a girl reader take away from this novel's contradictions? If *Little Women* speaks to all levels of a girl reader—to her who tries to be a good girl in conformity with the wisdom of parental figures as well as to her who wants something different—surely the images speak louder than the words. The father's gender storyline may dominate the novel's structure. But scattered representations of autonomy and creativity as concrete action and concrete space speak directly to a reader's unconscious. The repeated images that express Jo's exuberant ambition and independence—running, climbing, writing a story and setting off into the world to get it published—engage the primary processes whose function is to assimilate new experience into the ongoing structures of the self. The vivid visual and kinetic imagery of the subtext should thus enable girl readers to take in and make their own Alcott's model of creative autonomy.[79]

The implications of Wyatt's claim are clear: Primary processes involved in reading help ignite images that take on narratable form. The "story" these images tell prods readers to construct and become consciously attached to fantasies and fantasized ideals that can resist cultural prescriptions.

Vivid "novel" fantasies thus can contribute to the transformation of libidinal bindings scripted by culture. In *Little Women* the conflict between patriarchy and autonomy is latent in the text, but not plotted by it. In *Heart of Darkness* the conflict between imperial exploration and moral restraint is emplotted and deeply suffered. In both cases the novels become vehicles for awareness and self-definition, forms for resisting the libidinal bindings of prevailing ideologies.

Notes

1. Victor Nell, *Lost in a Book* (New Haven, Conn.: Yale University Press, 1990).
2. Ibid., 214
3. See Josephine Hilgard, *Personality and Hypnosis: A Study of Imaginative Involvement* (Chicago: University of Chicago Press, 1979).
4. Skura, *The Literary Use of the Psychoanalytic Process*, 178–84.
5. A. Tellegen and G. Atkinson. "Openness to Absorbing Self-Altering Experiences ("Absorption"), a Trait Related to Hypnotic Susceptibility," *Journal of Abnormal Psychology* 83: 268–77.
6. Fredric Jameson, *The Political Unconscious: Narrative as a Socially Symbolic Act* (Ithaca, N.Y.: Cornell University Press, 1981), 59.
7. Geoffey Galt Harpham, "The Fertile Word: Augustine's Ascetics of Interpretation," *Criticism* 28 (1986): 237–53.
8. Kohut, *The Analysis of the Self*, 41.
9. See Heinz Kohut, "Clinical and Therapeutic Aspects of the Idealizing Transference," in *The Analysis of the Self*.
10. Ibid., 41; This description of the formation of the superego, a process

whereby libido is withdrawn from figures we are strongly attached to and then utilized in the formation of drive-controlling structure within the self, offers a parallel to how literary experience can exert rhetorical pressure on the self.

11. Susan R. Suleiman, "Introduction: Varieties of Audience-Oriented Criticism," in *The Reader in the Text*, ed. Susan R. Suleiman and Inge Crosman (Baltimore: Johns Hopkins University Press, 1980), 8.

12. Holland's description of the personal and idiosyncratic unconscious content of reading should not be ignored by poststructuralist critics who seek a more thorough understanding of intertextuality. It should prompt us to recognize that the idiosyncratic fantasies of a singular subject are libidinally charged structures that commonly become part of the material of intertextuality.

13. Kohut, *The Analysis of the Self*, 41.

14. If simple changes in perception can be imagined as primitive changes in value (in so far as they formulate different relations between elements), then these changes in value might be a constant and almost subliminal chatter circulating around the margins of all textual response. We often appreciate this chatter when we read, but we do not often acknowledge its importance for interpretation. This subliminal chatter of simple "idealizations" could have decisive results whenever particular interpretive gestures manage to give it precise and concrete form. In this case an interpretive gesture successful at accumulating and giving particular form to a network of simple idealizations would lead to a more complex idealization.

Textual interpretation, however, might also work in the opposite direction. Instead of recovering simple idealizations from within the text in order to provide a complex idealization, an interpretive response might appeal to a complex and shared idealization between readers outside the text. It might then seek to bring into recognition an awareness of a network of representations within the text that would support the shared complex idealization serving as an interpretation.

15. There is a need, I think, to explore those facets of literary experience hidden by Jameson's remark in *The Political Unconscious* that "the program for libidinal revolution is political only to the degree that it is itself the figure for social revolution" (74). Until we have a clear understanding of libidinal changes at the collective level, we must make use of those explanations psychoanalysis offers for understanding libidinal changes at the level of the individual subject. Jameson is shrewd in insisting on the importance of a collective vision when imagining libidinal revolution. But Jameson is shortsighted in downplaying the role of the singular subject in formulating psychological-political imaginative structures. Jameson seems unable to understand how difficult it is to overcome psychological resistances to political change. Changes in our images of authority and desire, as most political change requires, demand changes in ourselves, changes in our internal libidinal organizations. Not always, but sometimes, these changes require growth in ego strength and reality testing.

16. Kohut, *The Analysis of the Self*, 77.

17. Holland, *Five Readers Reading*, 183.

18. Wolfgang Iser, *The Act of Reading* (Baltimore: Johns Hopkins University Press, 1978), 187.

19. Hans Robert Jauss, *Aesthetic Experience and Literary Hermeneutics*, trans. Michael Shaw (Minneapolis: University of Minnesota Press, 1982), 153.

20. Identification need not promote empathy. Jeffrey Berman, *Joseph Conrad: Writing as Rescue* (New York: Astra Books, 1977), observes that Conrad's identification with one of his own characters, Martin Decound of *Nostromo*, does not allow for empathy.

21. Holland, *Five Readers Reading*, 194.

22. Jauss, *Aesthetic Experience*, 153.

23. Carl E. Bain, Jerome Beatty, and J. Paul Hunter, eds., *The Norton Introduction to Literature*, 4th ed. (New York: Norton, 1986), 91.

24. Maynard Mack, "The Jacobean Shakespeare: Some Observations on the Construction of the Tragedies," in *Essays in Shakespearean Criticism*, ed. James L. Calderwood and Harold E. Toliver (Englewood Cliffs, N.J.: Prentice-Hall, 1970), 43.

25. Quentin G. Kraft, "On Character in the Novel: William Beatty Warner versus Samuel Richardson and the Humanists," *College English* 50 (1988): 40.

26. Gilbert Rose, *Trauma and Mastery in Life and Art* (New Haven, Conn.: Yale University Press, 1987), 113–14.

27. Skura, *The Literary Use of the Psychoanalytic Process*, 181.

28. Kenneth Burke, "Literature as Equipment for Living," in *The Philosophy of Literary Form* (Berkeley and Los Angeles: University of California Press, 1967).

29. Hayden White, "The Value of Narrativity in the Representation of Reality," *Critical Inquiry* 7 (1980): 23.

30. Ibid., 16.

31. Peter Brooks, *Reading for the Plot* (New York: Random House, 1985), 37.

32. Ibid., 37.

33. Ibid., 38.

34. Ibid., 61.

35. Geoffrey Galt Harpham, "Language History, and Ethics" *Raritan* 7 (1987): 141.

36. It can also be a kind of empty self-assertiveness where value assertion compensates for an underlying hollowness or anger. Kohut, for example, speaks of "idealizations which (emanating from temporary ego attitudes or from chronic characterological positions) buttress secondarily repressions of, reaction formations against, or denials of a structurally deeper lying hostility," *The Analysis of the Self*, 75.

37. Holland, *Five Readers Reading*, 192.

38. Ibid., 192.

39. Ibid., 199.

40. Ibid., 199.
41. Ibid., 195.
42. This mode of shifting desire might well be more "fluid" than the other modes. Various objects of desire could successfully compete with each other, thus changing and redirecting desire, but such change would be cosmetic rather than essential.
43. Freud distinguished between *idealization* and *sublimation* as follows:

> Sublimation is a process that concerns object-libido and consists in the instinct's directing itself toward an aim other than, and remote from, that of sexual satisfaction; in this process the accent falls upon deflection from sexuality. Idealization is a process that concerns the *object;* by it that object, without any alteration in its nature, is aggrandized or exalted in the subject's mind. (Freud, "On Narcissism," 94)

44. Laplanche and Pontalis, *The Language of Psychoanalysis*, 431.
45. Ibid., 433.
46. Kohut, *The Analysis of the Self*, 325.
47. See Ernest S. Wolf's discussion of Kohut in "Psychoanalytic Psychology of the Self and Literature," *NLH* 12 (Autumn 1980): 41–61.
48. Rose, *Trauma and Mastery in Life and Art*, 10.
49. Skura, *The Use of the Psychoanalytic Process*, 12. Skura's position breaks with traditional views of art that emphasize its childish quality. Artistic imagery, considered in traditional terms, is pure fantasy, something that satisfies childish desires in opposition to realistic modes of perception. Although Freud emphasizes the "sketchy" nature of his ruminations about artistic power, his authoritative influence on theorists has led to largely reductive forms of interpretation. For Freud's followers, the symbol systems of a work "mean" the primitive narcissistic and defensive forces that produce them. The text, thus considered, merely represents repressed fantasy and "primary process" thinking—and nothing more.
50. Sigmund Freud, "Formulations Regarding the Two Principles in Mental Functioning" (1911), *The Standard Edition* 12: 224.
51. Rose, *Trauma and Mastery in Life and Art*, develops a very cogent argument about this.
52. Traditional literary discussions of artistic images, in seeing significant positive resemblances between imagery and primitive thought processes, lend a certain intuitive support to my theory. T. S. Eliot, for example, acknowledges that "the artist is more primitive as well as more civilized" (essay of 1918 quoted by René Welleck and Austin Warren *Theory of Literature* [New York: Harcourt, Brace & World, 1956], 84). Welleck and Warren, discussing the psychology of the creative writer, observe that "some novelists may . . . have the capacity, common among children, but rare thereafter, of eidetic imagery" (83). They point out that another "primitive" feature found in a writer's repertoire is "Synaesthesia, or the linking together of sensory perception out of two or more senses, most commonly hearing and sight. . . . As a physiological trait, it is apparently, like red-green colour blindness,

a survival from an earlier comparatively undifferentiated sensorium" (83). These "primitive" properties of imagery and synaesthesia have been admired ever since poets have been considered "visionaries." But, until recently, such admiration has been largely relegated to an unscholarly status. We have only recently developed psychoanalytic concepts sophisticated enough to probe the function of mental imagery in ego development.

53. Ragland-Sullivan, *Jacques Lacan and the Philosophy of Psychoanalysis*, 141.
54. Ibid., 140.
55. Ibid., 138.
56. Gabriele Schwab, "Genesis of the Subject, Imaginary Functions, and Poetic Language," *NLH* 15 (1984): 456.
57. Ibid.
58. Ibid., 458–59.
59. Ibid., 464.
60. D. M. Thomas, *The White Hotel* (New York: Pocket Books, 1981), 115.
61. Ibid.
62. Ibid., 136.
63. Peter Brooks, "The Idea of a Psychoanalytic Literary Criticism."
64. Stephen Mitchell, *Relational Concepts in Psychoanalysis*, 74–79.
65. Mardi Jon Horowitz, *Image Formation and Psychotherapy* (New York: Jason Aronson, 1983), 110–11.
66. This may suggest a relation between imagery and metaphor. The image, as Horowitz notes, is "the first vehicle for expression of repressed mental contents" (Ibid., 111). The image transfers "information" from the unconscious to the conscious, and thus has capability to broadly signify what the conscious mind may resist or deny.
67. W. J. T. Mitchell, "What is an Image?" *NLH* 15 (1984): 503–38.
68. Ulric Neisser, "The Processes of Vision," in *The Nature of Human Consciousness*, ed. Robert Ornstein (San Francisco: W. H. Freeman, 1973), 208.
69. Iser, *The Act of Reading*, 137.
70. David Bleich, "Intersubjective Reading," *NLH* 17 (1986): 412
71. See Horowitz, *Image Formation and Psychotherapy*, xii.
72. J. Fowles, "Notes on Writing a Novel," *Harpers*, July 1968, 88–97.
73. Frederick Crews, "The Power of Darkness," *Partisan Review* 34 (1967): 507–25, suggests that the "unspeakable rites" of *Heart of Darkness* are associated with incest and the "primal scene."
74. Geoffrey Galt Harpham, *On the Grotesque* (Princeton, N.J.: Princeton University Press, 1982), 147.
75. Brantlinger, *Rule of Darkness*, 49, 55, 69–70.
76. Joseph Conrad, *Heart of Darkness*, 81.
77. Ibid., 534.
78. Laplanche and Pontalis, *The Language of Psychoanalysis*, 202.
79. Wyatt, *Reconstructing Desire*, 63.

The Narcissism of Creation and Interpretation: Agon at the *Heart of Darkness*

The passions, when we know that they cannot find fulfillment, become vision.

W. B. Yeats

Every author strives to create a work of substance. We might modify this truism to suggest that authors strive to perfect and augment their own substance by means of the work they create.[1] In a letter of 1899, close to the time he was working on *Heart of Darkness,* Conrad complains of a fear that his work lacks substance. As he makes this complaint, he imagines himself face to face with a monster threatening to consume him, threatening to deprive him of his own substance:

The more I write the less substance do I see in my work. The scales are falling off my eyes. It is tolerably awful. And I face it. I face it, but the fright is growing on me. My fortitude is shaken by the view of the monster. It does not move; its eyes are baleful; it is still as death itself and it will devour me. Its stare has eaten into my soul already, deep, deep. I am alone with it in a chasm with perpendicular sides of black basalt.[2]

As the "scales" fall off his eyes, Conrad sees with increasing fear that his text lacks substance. But as he faces his failure of vision, he sees the meaning of that failure reflected back to him in the vision of a monster threatening to consume the substance of his body. The monster's message is clear: To fail to produce substance is to lack substance. Curiously, however, the monster Conrad's vision successfully embodies announces a failure of vision. The image of the monster thus contradicts, on one level, the very claim Conrad himself asserts. The monster is a substantive product of the very sort the author seeks. Despite this paradox, however, we have little trouble understanding the gist of Conrad's assertion. Conrad does not want the rhetorical "substance" of a merely private vision. He wants to coin the "substance" of a public vision. Conrad's letter, then, allows us to see his "vision" in action: Conrad's passionate complaint about his failure of vision *images* forth with remarkable force and clarity his own most ambitious demands and desires.

Jeffrey Berman, who argues that writing may have served to "rescue" Conrad from suicidal temptations, points out that Conrad's letters to his uncle Thaddeus during another depression in 1890–91 suggest another "serious battle against suicide."[3] During the time he was working on *Heart of Darkness*, Conrad was again experiencing depression, as he did recurrently throughout his life, but he was also pursuing rising ambitions as an author. His audience for writing—no longer only his uncle Thaddeus—was the reading public of Britain.

Conrad's monster expresses for him a certain ideal "vision" of textual creation. Textuality must have "substance," and something Conrad liked to call "truth." For an ambitious author like Conrad, a deficiency in vision—in truth—is tantamount to a deficiency in being. The "logic" of Conrad's passion seems rather simple: If the literary text does not create substance for others, it does not contribute to the substance of its author. And an author without substance is better off dead.

We should pause here at the image of an author disemboweled by his own creation, a monstrous being who reflects to the self its own deficiency, a fictive other whose imagined presence, unlike the successful artwork, depletes rather than augments or supplements the self's presence. This image marks the convergence of a number of restless forces at the origin of the work: the emptiness of the self, the substance of language, and somewhat hidden yet nevertheless insidious in its suggestion, the power of desire.

Conrad desires to create, through the visionary power of the text, the substance of his own being. But the monster of the chasm, whose power of vision is more powerful than Conrad's own, mimics in his "baleful eyes" and his location in "bottomless perdition" that "unconquerable Will," of Paradise Lost, Satan. Also, however, the monster of the chasm whose stare (an act of vision) acts like a mouth (an act of consuming), weds in one image two of Kurtz's most excessive traits: his vision, "piercing enough to penetrate all the hearts that beat in the darkness," and his desire, voraciously insatiable and intent to consume "the air, the earth, all men." Satan loses being and falls from the plenitude of Paradise because of his rebellion, his overweening desire, and his egotistical intensity of vision. Conrad's Kurtz also loses being and wastes his life because of the intensity of his vision and desire.

Although *Heart of Darkness* often serves many readers as an illustration of the deathly effects of "satanic" unbounded desire, a central puzzle about the work focuses on Marlow's ambiguous moral judgment of Kurtz. Kurtz's story clearly suggests that destructive consequences follow from heedless, self-serving, unrestrained, and pathologically narcissistic desire. But many readers also see a kind of heroism in Kurtz's unrestrained desires. Some even feel impelled to argue that the novel's major achievement is its emphatic illustration of Kurtz's heroism. Peter Glassman comments:

Against the indifference of the universe and all the insipidity of men, he has forced life to expand to the pressures of the self, to yield to human need energy and excitement, tangibility and form. Against the bleak nonurgency of ordinary life, Kurtz has discovered a locus for feeling—an uncommon achievement in the last days of the nineteenth century.[4]

It seems significant that this critic sees Kurtz as one who wrenches "tangibility and form" from the "insipidness" of existence. In order to make this assertion, critics must participate in its apparent truth. They must feel expansiveness in their own being as they read Kurtz's story. To one critic at least, then, Conrad's Kurtz offers the prized reward "substance."

Reading criticism published on *Heart of Darkness* demonstrates that a close reading of the text can support a response that admires the dark and problematic hero (or antihero) of the story. But it is also clear that a close reading of the text can support a much more critical response to Kurtz. Joseph Warren Beach, for example, argues: "Kurtz is a personal embodiment, a dramatization of all that Conrad felt of futility, degradation and horror in what the Europeans called 'progress,' which meant the exploitation of the natives by every variety of cruelty and treachery known to greedy man."[5]

Beach's reading of the text and its opposite are not misreadings of the text. Conrad's work allows both Glassman's vicarious exhilarating participation and Beach's sober moralization because the desires that form Conrad's text are as divided as the critical values that respond to the text.

Just as the imaginary monster of Conrad's letter is both a visionary reward and a visionary threat, the images of Conrad's Darkness are inherently conflictual.

The sharp contrast between the two different value judgments (the values of Glassman and Beach) is a major interpretive focus of Conrad's story. And the interpretive focus of the text is, in this case, the site of the text's rhetoric. Readers who respond to this challenge in interpretation easily embrace one value and suppress the other. This suppression of one of the text's values, however, is not so much directed by the text as demanded by readers. Readers embrace one value and suppress the other because the two systems of values expressed by the text are incompatible. Texts do not truly suffer from incompatible values, but readers do.

The conflict within the text creates a place for the reader in the text, a place where the reader, lead to suffer certain conflicts, seeks to resolve them. In short, the reader's place in the text is at the site of the text's rhetoric. The structured conflict and incompatibility within the values of *Heart of Darkness* define its rhetorical strength.

As suggested earlier, the rhetoric of a text is not most effective when it *silences* its opposition. Rather, rhetoric can be most effective when it *hears* the opposition and gives readers an increased power to consciously suppress (and not unconsciously repress) a value position they might in extratextual contexts, by acknowledging, be overwhelmed by. Seen in this light, interpretation becomes an emphatically rhetorical gesture.

I have argued that the text's rhetoric is that place in the text that most engages the reader. But I want to emphasize here that the scenes of the text's rhetoric that engage readers are also often those sites that most express an author's self-division. Rhetoric appeals to the conflicts of self-division, and it does so because it stems from conflicts of self-division. Conrad, for example, feels both positively and negatively about Kurtz. Both attitudes are present at the conflictual germinating core of the story, and in writing it, Conrad's identity is at risk in the text's confused rhetorical insistence.

If identity is, in part, a structure of desire, then Conrad's story both makes and unmakes this structure as it seeks to speak "substance" and formulate a rhetoric of identity. We witness in the story a moral dilemma embodied in Conrad's self-divisive identification with Kurtz. Conrad's predicament is mirrored in Marlow. Although he wants Kurtz's power, he fears the corrosive effects of the desire that enables Kurtz's power. A similar predicament surfaces in Conrad's *Personal Record*, where he argues on the one hand that "all intellectual and artistic ambitions are permissible, up to and even beyond the limit of prudent sanity."[6] Yet, on the other hand, he complains that real artistic power is suspect, achieved when one "surrender[s] oneself to occult powers," a surrender equivalent to selling one's soul "for love or power to some grotesque devil."[7] Marlow's narration embodies the same duality. Marlow, in wanting Kurtz's artistic power, admires Kurtz's intensity of desire. But he also does not admire it; he wants somehow to purify it. Marlow's narration, for example, is the act that most closely imitates Kurtz. But this act of imitation imitates his speech—and it emerges from Marlow's body only as he assumes the desire-denying posture of Buddha.

A key question I and other critics ask about the text is: How does Conrad identify with Kurtz? In asking this question, we are asking about the text's origin, the text's rhetoric, and the text's mechanisms for signi-fication.

To understand the text's origin, I need to understand Conrad's own interaction with his text. I want to know, not how Conrad judged his text, but how he responded to his own text.

It is quite probable that Conrad's identification with Kurtz is reflected in Marlow's identification with Kurtz. Marlow is not simply a character. He is a point of view. Marlow is an embodiment of Conrad's response to his own narrative. Marlow offers us a glimpse into Conrad's sense of the story, his feelings about the moral dilemmas of his narrative. Daniel Schwarz argues that for Conrad

fiction writing is a self-conscious process in which he tests and explores his intellectual and moral identity. He created Marlow to explore himself. Marlow is a surrogate figure coping with a version of Conrad's own psychic turmoil and moral confusion.[8]

I argue that in *Heart of Darkness* Marlow acts out Conrad's own identi-fication with Kurtz as Conrad experienced that identification in the process of discovering his narrative. Critics have long argued that this identification between Marlow and Kurtz is a very complex if not con-fused matter. This confusion and complexity is precisely what I wish to examine in my analysis of the text's rhetoric.

There are three distinct stages in Marlow's identification with Kurtz, and the pivotal points in each stage are formulated through changes in identification that can be understood as "redistributions" of narcissistic investments.

The act of identification seems most critical to the libidinal economy of Conrad's text. This crucial act of identification clearly divides the responses of readers who write about the text. Each reader makes sense of the text in terms of a different libidinal organization of response. This struggle with identification also clearly divided Conrad himself as he produced the text. Conrad's story reflects the agonies of an author caught within bewildering and shifting configurations for investments and disinvestments of narcissistic energy. The text and the story it tells are confusing because we do not find a clear resolution to its conflict of identification. But this irresolution only means that in order to explain the story of the responsive dynamics of the text's rhetoric, we must tell a different story. We must tell a story about conflicts in identity. We must tell a story about narcissism—describe its drama and logic of conflict.

Conrad and Narcissism

Critics largely agree that from The Nigger of the "Narcissus" to The Arrow of Gold, Conrad's prose abounds in mirrors, reflections, doubled selves, and generally narcissistic themes. Conrad's psychoanalytic biographer, Bernard Meyer, asserts the importance of "self-love" in many of the novels and argues further that the "fluid and amorphous sense of personal identity" plaguing many of Conrad's characters bespeaks the presence of similar problems in the author himself.[9] A more recent biographer, Frederick Karl, emphasizes creative features in Conrad's narcissism: "Conrad identified himself with the conjurers, with the narcissists, with the Don-Quixote-like bag of conjuring tricks."[10] Critical interest in Conrad's narcissism is not, however, limited to the author's personality and his cast of characters—it extends also to Conrad's relation to language. William Bonney, for example, discusses The Nigger of the "Narcissus" as a brooding meditation on the "narcissistic seductions of language," arguing that the self's desire for meaning in language betrays a potentially lethal narcissistic sentiment that Conrad manages to circumvent.[11] Given the wide range of contexts in which the adjective "narcissistic" is used, however, one wonders what the word means.

Does the adjective imply that Conrad had a narcissistic personality disorder? Or does the adjective merely suggest that Conrad's imagination betrays an uneasy "self-absorbed" style?

As I pointed out in chapter 1, *narcissism* can refer either to the broadest array of narcissistic cathexes present in the repertoire of human individuation, or the limited set of narcissistic cathexes common to narcissistic personality disorders.[12] Except where otherwise specified, I use the term in the broader clinical sense to refer to the interior relations of the self with itself. The phenomena that repeatedly characterize Conrad's fiction—identification, empathy, idealization—are not necessarily narcissistic in the pathological sense of the term. They are, however, processes central to ego growth, and they are best understood as narcissistic "variables," which an idealizing and reflective endeavor of fiction explores and makes use of.

Consideration of Conrad's work indicates that through time he became more comfortable with narcissistic processes and more skillful at employing them in his fiction. Much of his work wrestles with narcissistic ambiguities as it attempts to evaluate or work through various puzzling or disorienting narcissistic forces. The *Nigger of the "Narcissus,"* for example, explicitly thematizes narcissistic concerns, but carefully distinguishes the seductive (and narcissistic) attractions of empathy and identification from the self-sacrificing demands of duty. It is as if for the early Conrad identification and empathy were necessarily linked with pathological content—that is, were contagious pathogens that could swiftly infect and disable a healthy ego. After The Nigger of the "Narcissus," however, Conrad explores more minutely the narcissistic affiliations of empathy and identification; *Lord Jim* (written after "Youth" and *Heart of Darkness*), suggests that empathy, idealization, and identification are not evidence of psychopathology, but an arena wherein the various conflicts of identity are fought. Just as psychoanalytic understanding of narcissism evolved from an initial simple and negative view to a more complex and integrated understanding, so also Conrad's understanding of narcissism seems to evolve from an initial simple and negative view (seen, for example, in *The Nigger of the "Narcissus"*) to a more complex and positive vision (as in "The Secret Sharer" and *The Arrow of Gold*.)

In the progress of his work, Conrad seems to grasp more and more expansively the role narcissistic energy plays in the process of human individuation. This role is succinctly described by a recent psychoanalytic theorist:

As our knowledge of the ego, of the processes of introjection and identification upon which much of it is built, and of its various substructures has grown, so our understanding of the role of the investment of narcissistic energy has deepened. It is with this energy that the ego nourishes itself and those of its component parts whose successful and integrated functioning maintain that inner psychic balance. The distribution of narcissistic energy—whether it is vested in intrapsychic structures, in internalized representations of self and others or projected onto others in the world—is often an important indicator of the nature and extent of the psychic balance or imbalance of the individual. The ego-ideal, of all the substructures of the ego, is perhaps the most heavily invested with narcissistic energy.[13]

Numerous critics emphasize Conrad's moral commitments and his Victorian fidelity to ideals. But most critics find this simpleminded fidelity strangely at odds with Conrad's cynicism and tough-minded "realism." Conrad wanted to believe in morality, but visibly suffered constraints in this ambition because he believed in nothing that would metaphysically sustain his desire. Conrad's ideals, thus, are sustained by little more than a unique intensity of imagination. In reflecting on *Heart of Darkness*, Conrad's most puzzling work, I probe how the narrative both reflects and attempts to ameliorate the agonies of this problem. My analysis explores the relationship between Conrad's narcissism and those ego-ideals his fiction repeatedly explores, deflates, and supports.[14] But as I focus on the smaller psychoanalytic details of Conrad's text, I urge my reader to keep in mind the larger arc of my argument. Conrad's darkness tells a story about vision. According to this story, the substance of vision is narcissistic. The narcissism of vision can eviscerate a writer, but it need not. Narcissism can also contribute to the formation of the self and to a public and materially productive rhetoric. When narcissism "works" it gives substance to an image of value. But Conrad's imaginative discovery also seems to embrace the recognition that narcissism is relentlessly dialectical. Narcissism is both productive and destructive. When narcissism does not work, it empties substance from images of value. This threat of absolute metaphysical emptiness always stands just behind the machinery of narcissistic production.

Narcissism and Morality

The Nigger of the "Narcissus," Conrad's first major work, idealizes the seaman's honorable code of conduct and combats other seductive possibilities: the values that would result from identification with James Wait. The novel pointedly emphasizes that the seaman's code must withstand enfeebling temptations toward empathy with Wait. In idealizing the seaman's code, however, Conrad promotes identification with the ship's crew in order to combat identification with one highly individualistic member of the crew: Wait. On the surface, the novel seems to use imaginative forces to combat narcissistic forces. But in actuality Conrad only uses a disguised form of narcissism to combat another more self-indulgent style of narcissism. The novel seems to be denouncing narcissistic identification, but actually uses morally condoned identifications to counter morally suspect identifications. Conrad, then, actuates certain preferred narcissistic mechanisms in his reader in order to combat other nonpreferred narcissistic mechanisms. Some critics find this effort curiously self-divided.[15] But this self-division does not seem to trouble Conrad until his next major work, Heart of Darkness.

In Kurtz, Conrad intuits the narcissistic underpinnings of all idealizations and struggles to grasp the narcissistic ambiguities implicit in his own artistic ideal. David Thornburn argues that "it seems impossible not to recognize in Marlow's mingled admiration and disdain for Kurtz something of Conrad's deep ambivalence toward the profession of the artist."[16] Kurtz demonstrates an array of artistic talents, but more properly he suggests an artistic potential he does not fully embody. If, as Freud suggests, "artistic talent and productive ability are intimately connected with sublimation," then Kurtz's ambition is deflected from art to colonial imperialism because his African experience desublimates and activates the pathologically narcissistic elements of his personality. Through such desublimation, Kurtz's pre-Congo ideals are transformed into desperate and destructive compulsions.[17] Conrad confronts the unsettling truth that both sublimation and desublimations are empowered by the protean, Faustian, narcissistic energy embodied in Kurtz. Conrad must identify with and claim this energy as his own without at the same time identifying with the specific personality in which he sees this energy embodied—Kurtz. Kurtz evokes from Conrad essentially irreconcilable desires: admiration and disdain, identification and the rejection of identification.

Faced with this double-bind, Conrad turns to Marlow as a stable fictional identity, and a Virgilian guide for the descent into "darkness," the imaginative space the narrative explores. As an emotionally invested ego-ideal, Marlow helps Conrad to maintain his narcissistic balance, but more importantly, helps Conrad limit, direct, and specify his identification with Kurtz. The story of Marlow's uneasy relation to Kurtz (which enacts as it buffers Conrad's relation) follows a seesaw course of narcissistic attraction and repulsion very similar to the course of "transference" that operates in psychoanalysis. Like an analyst in relation to his patient, Kurtz elicits from Marlow a series of identificatory responses that work to "bind" narcissistic energy and reduce the conflictual aspirations and self-divisions manifested by the responses themselves. Kurtz himself, of course, has none of the properties of an analyst. He is merely a figure of the imagination. But precisely as an imaginative projection of a special sort, Kurtz evokes from Conrad a deeper insight into the forces with which the imagination works.

The series of identifications that Kurtz evokes from Marlow begins in an image of the child's earliest aspirations and ends with a vision of death. Each identification brings Conrad closer and closer to a grasp of Kurtz's central mystery. Before gaining firsthand experience with Kurtz, Marlow imagines him as a kind of super explorer, a "universal genius," a man of tremendous talent, ability, and stamina. The imaginatively elicited ego-ideal bathes in all the narcissistic grandiosity of Marlow's childlike infatuation with the "glories of exploration."[18] Later, however, as Marlow discovers the real Africa and encounters through his looking-glass a surreal image of the "real" Kurtz, he beholds the shell of a man wasted and consumed by the power of his own desires. Here, Marlow's original narcissistic cathexis of Kurtz dwindles as he faces the skeletal body behind the "magnificent eloquence." Still later, however, when Kurtz apparently judges and renounces his own personality, Marlow reinvests an intense identification with him, but it is an identification precisely with Kurtz's act of renouncing identity. Kurtz's final achievement reinstates his heroic stature and embodies an ideal of vision, "truth," and courage very close to Conrad's highest aspirations for art.

To trace the progress of Marlow's fluctuating identification with Kurtz, it is necessary to examine the stages of Marlow's identifications and the various layers of Kurtz's narcissism as Marlow perceives them in each stage.

The origin of Marlow's African adventure begins with a child's wondrous self-loss in the innocent and unbounded desire of daydreams. "Now when I was a little chap," Marlow relates, "I had a passion for maps. I would . . . lose myself in all the glories of exploration."[19] For the child the "blanks spaces" of the earth are a magic lantern wherein the dreamlike obscurity of imaginative indulgence mirrors the self's deepest aspirations. In the child's fantasy world, exploration offers to extend the self's ontology effortlessly outward. The explorer's map indulges a fantasy of narcissistic omnipotence in which all things beyond the self can be inhabited and appropriated without pain and resistance. The first stories Marlow hears about Kurtz partly reactivate this youthful fantasy, and Marlow imagines him to be a superhuman explorer carrying light to the dark places of the earth. Kurtz thus radiantly embodies the child's omnipotent fantasies.

But Marlow indulges himself and his audience with an image of his youthful hopes and memories only to shatter the child's fragile dream. The real story of unbounded desire, he subsequently suggests, is not the child's dream, but the history of Kurtz. Marlow's first real images of Kurtz are nightmarish images of death and the dispensing of death. The imagery of Conrad's narrative thus reflects ironically on Marlow's youthful admiration, arguing that Kurtz's unbounded desire is not heroic but demeaning.

Marlow twice pictures Kurtz as a huge, voracious, and indiscriminately consuming mouth: "I saw him open his mouth wide—it gave him a weirdly voracious aspect, as though he wanted to swallow all the air, all the earth, all the men before him" (134). During the discussion with the Intended this image recurs as if it were Kurtz's most indelible signature: "I had a vision," Marlow confides, "of him on the stretcher, opening his mouth voraciously, as if to devour all the earth with all its mankind" (155). It may be an understatement to suggest that Kurtz's huge and clearly hostile mouth indicates flaws in his moral character. These flaws, however, are associated with the disturbances of pathological narcissism. Heinz Kohut, describing the narcissistic patient, emphasizes the feeling of inner emptiness from which patients often defend themselves by delusions of personal grandiosity.[20] Otto Kernberg observes that the narcissistic personality exhibits unusual degrees of self-reference in interactions with others, a great need for esteem, and oral rage when confronted with disappointment.[21] Kurtz's huge mouth combines in one image both qualities of inner emptiness and oral rage. This desperate attempt to "devour all things" suggests that Kurtz (as Marlow envisions him) is obsessed by a need to internalize and possess all things of value so that his own self can have value.[22]

Like a child—"sometimes he was contemptibly childish," Marlow reports (148)—Kurtz responds to the awesome potentiality of the jungle as if it were a huge reservoir for narcissistic gratification. Kurtz takes advantage of his unique role in the colonization process to indulge his infinite ambitions and "feed" his intense and childish need for esteem. In Marlow's eyes, however, Kurtz's childlike attachment to the jungle impoverishes rather than nourishes: "The wilderness had patted him on the head, and, behold, it was like a ball—an ivory ball; it had caressed him, and lo—he had withered; it had taken him, loved him, embraced him, got into his veins, consumed his flesh. He was its spoiled and pampered favorite" (115). The jungle stimulates Kurtz to fantasies of "inner plenitude," but it does not nourish him. Kurtz's esteem feeds on and is inflated by the quantity of ivory he is able to collect. But while Kurtz's esteem feeds on images of wealth, his body starves. When near death, Kurtz takes on an aged ivory pallor reminiscent of bone, and symbolic of the inner deadness and emptiness of his being.

Marlow recognizes that Kurtz, despite his energy and brilliance, cannot fill the emptiness at the core of his being, cannot nourish his inner self. Approaching death, Kurtz fantasizes that the ivory can be traded for wealth and fame, and that at last his inner hunger can be satisfied. But Marlow's recurring image of Kurtz's huge mouth suggests that he perceives a flaw in Kurtz's imagined program of self-nourishment. Kurtz's passion to consume, by its very nature, destroys the possibility of satisfaction through consumption. The obsessional torque in Kurtz's urge to consume dictates that he cannot internalize nourishment; he can only reduce to nothing all things that can nourish. In attempting to claim, possess, and control all things, Kurtz denies their intrinsic value, makes them dead "substance," and thereby denies himself the possibility of gaining "substance" (satisfactory self-confirmation) from them. Like the pathological narcissist, Kurtz makes exploitative demands on the external world, but because these demands inherently deny the value of external things, they ultimately impoverish the self, which attempts to appropriate such objects. Furthermore, Kurtz's internal emptiness exponentially generates an increasing frustration and anger by virtue of the distance between his ability to imagine satisfaction, and his inability to obtain it.

If the desperate attempt to devour all things were the only component of Kurtz's restless narcissism, Marlow's judgment of Kurtz would be clearly and unambiguously negative. But Marlow spares Kurtz total condemnation because he admires his linguistic accomplishments. The relation between Kurtz's narcissistic emptiness and his linguistic competency is unclear. But it is exactly this obscurity that both haunts and disrupts Marlow's story. Until the last impoverished words near death, Kurtz's verbal plenitude contrasts ironically with his inner emptiness; his linguistic eloquence compensates for his inner emptiness as it serves to woo or coerce admiration from others. Marlow perceives the deceptive features of Kurtz's speech, but he also admires its power. Near the end of the journey to the "Inner Station" when Marlow despairs of his hope to meet Kurtz, he dismisses the charges of moral misconduct brought against Kurtz:

That was not the point. The point was in his being a gifted creature, and that of all his gifts, the one that stood out preeminently, that carried with it a sense of real presence, was his ability to talk, his words—his gift of expression, the bewildering, the illuminating, the most exalted and the most contemptible, the pulsating stream of light, or the deceitful flow from the heart of an impenetrable darkness. (113–14)

Kurtz's speech has the magical power of "real presence." In its most urgent moment it achieves more than "presence"; it achieves a "glimpse of truth." Kurtz's final moment of vision, "piercing enough to penetrate all the hearts that live in darkness" (151), and his "magnificent eloquence," which carries with it a sense of "real presence," nominate him as a personification of all those grandiose claims that Conrad himself wants to make for fiction. Kurtz becomes the projected image of Conrad's fictional ambitions, and a tutelary spirit of what Conrad in a letter called the "creative darkness."

Kurtz's speech emerges from the darkness, as it emerges also from the ambitious inner emptiness of his narcissism.[23] Issuing from the dark invisible spaces of his own being like a "pulsating stream of light," Kurtz's speech illuminates "things" and confers on them a sense of "real presence." Kurtz's uncannily effective "terms of appeal" and his apparently hypnotic control of "real presence" assuage his inner emptiness by seeming to give him control of "being" itself. Kurtz's power of speech brings things into being for others: "He made me see things—things," the Russian says (127), and in this manner Kurtz's speech seems to embody a very potent idealization—the greatest power to which any writer could aspire.

Spoken by a "universal genius" who was "essentially a great musician" but whose talents also included painting and journalism, Kurtz's words characteristically combine the power of vision with the immediacy of sound, synaesthetically, to overburden subjectivity with a sense of "presence." We are asked, for example, to "see" Kurtz's speech as a "stream of light," and to "hear" in Marlow's last "image" of Kurtz the "faint ring of incomprehensible words" (159). Conjuring the wonders of vision through the ringing tonality of verbal eloquence, Kurtz articulates the illusion of "real presence," and commands a rhetorical energy essential to both the artist and the politician. This power to unveil the "seen" through language echoes Conrad's own desires, as stated in the preface to *The Nigger of the "Narcissus"*:

All art . . . appeals primarily to the senses . . . to the plasticity of sculpture, to the colour of painting, and to the magic suggestiveness of music. My task which I am trying to achieve is, by the power of the written word, to make you hear, to make you feel—it is, before all, to make you see.[24]

Kurtz clearly epitomizes a power to which Conrad himself aspires. But this power to unveil the "seen" frequently eludes Marlow. One can detect a hint of Conrad's own anxiety in Marlow's exclamation: "Do you see him [Kurtz]? Do you see the story?" (82). Marlow's restless self-doubt ends on a pessimistic note: "It is impossible to convey the life-sensation of any given epoch of one's existence. We live as we dream—alone" (80).

At a later stage of the narration, however (exactly where Marlow begins to gain power over Kurtz by speech), the solipsistic analogy of the dream is abandoned. Through the "terrific suggestiveness of words heard in dreams, of phrases spoken in nightmares" (144), Marlow "talks" Kurtz into "seeing" things his way and persuades him to return to the boat. Marlow's control of dreamlike words suggests that the "dream" speech is not as powerless as he had thought, and further, that the "dream images" of speech are not as solipsistic as they seem. Indeed, the magical, rhetorical "real presence" of Kurtz's speech seems inextricably bound to the seductive and narcissistic power of the dream.

Kurtz's Rhetorical Power

Dream imagery bespeaks desire as it also betrays an inner poverty of need. "The elaboration of the dream," Lacan comments, "is nourished by desire." The dream is a "narcissistic folding back of the libido and disinvestment of reality."[25] Like childhood fantasies of primary narcissism, the dream erases the tyranny of subject–object distinction and refutes the essential otherness of the objective world in order to picture desire's satisfaction. The dream, Lacan suggests, pictures the desired object, not in terms of a "reality principle," but as the self would wish it to be. The dream expresses a narcissistic fantasy about desire's immediate satisfaction as it strives to signify desire. Similarly, Kurtz's "rhetoric," his power of "real presence," seduces the vision as it pictures desire with the immediacy of dream images.

Kurtz's power of real presence, then, lies not in his use of language to represent the "real," but in his ability to unveil desire, and to announce, advertise, and "market" it in language. Real presence addresses narcissistic aspiration through revelatory imagination, the metaphor, the newly created image. Kurtz's power of real presence lies in his power to direct and accelerate (in Lacan's terms) the metonymic sliding of the signifiers of desire. Kurtz's control of real presence reflects his ability to reveal objects of desire in more immediate and seductive terms, that is, in more "desirable" metaphors.

Ultimately, the discrepancy between the desire that can be pictured in dreams and the desire that can be satisfied by reality presents grave problems for the narcissist attempting to satisfy grandiose imaginative needs. But in the realm of politics, as well as in the realm of art, the discrepancy between the real and the imaginary empowers language with vital and dynamic potency. Because language can fill in the gaps of the unsatisfactory real with the imagined, it offers a new horizon for action and self-definition. Kurtz has the potential to be a "splendid leader" because he excels in manipulating through language the narcissistic cathexes that bind people to ideals and to ideas of action.

Kurtz's dazzling linguistic power gives him social power, but it fails to nourish his own inner hunger. Kurtz can win adulation from others, but such adulation offers no secure comfort. Kurtz can control and direct the enthusiasm of others, but he cannot satisfy his own inner emptiness. He is unable to establish any psychologically sustaining bonds with other people. Indeed, other people have no real value for Kurtz. He evokes empathy from the Russian, for example, but returns no empathy to him. He is ready to kill him for the sake of ivory. So also, Kurtz leads the natives, earns godlike respect from them, but fails to reciprocate the

admiration he is given. His feelings for them express more than con-
tempt. They express overt and intense hatred: "Exterminate all the brutes"
(118). Kurtz's hatred defends him from fears of dependency (a dependency he clearly has in relation to the jungle), but it does not give him
independence.

These pathological and self-protecting patterns of socialization seem
characteristic of Kurtz. He forgets his "Intended" though he "values"
her highly. Because he cannot "internalize" the value of other people,
Kurtz's loyalty cannot remain attached to other people. But Kurtz's
inconstancy to people also extends to his relation to ideals. Paradoxically, Kurtz is a powerhouse for the generation of ideals. But he has a
special "hollowness" in relation to them. He can manipulate ideals as
projections of his own grandiosity, but he is unable to internalize and
gain satisfaction from them.[26]

Kurtz's desires are heavily funded by primitive primary process thinking (thinking not conditioned by the "reality principle"), so his desires
animate his language with a dazzling imaginative power and freedom.
But because Kurtz's imagination is compelled to serve his grandiosity,
he becomes the victim of his own talents. Any image or idealization that
might psychologically sustain Kurtz decomposes into the more remote
and imaginary primary processes that are its structural foundation. Paradoxically, then, Kurtz becomes the delivery system for a load of wealth
from which he himself cannot benefit.

The narcissistic delusions that empower Kurtz's language, however,
are difficult to distinguish from the narcissistic illusions sought by Conrad and Marlow. Both the delusions and the illusions gain their strength
from the lyric and dreamlike immediacy with which language unveils
desire. Illusions differ from delusions, however, in that they are devel-
opmentally enabling. Esther Menaker emphasizes the role that narcissistic energy takes in developing "illusory" but "beneficial" ego-ideals.

When a child idealizes a parent he [she] is in the grip of a creative ego process,
for he [she] is taking the reality of his experience—as it exists in his [her] memory
imagery, both conscious and unconscious—and embroidering, embellishing,
altering it to create illusion. But because the child believes his [her] idealization
to be real . . . in the course of the growth of his [her] ego he [she] has the
potentiality for exceeding his [her] predecessors. Thus the capacity for idealization through the use of the creative imagination is a major factor in man's socio-
cultural evolution as well as in the psychological evolution of the ego. Obviously
not all idealizations are used constructively, in individual development, nor is

the course of cultural history a consistently progressive one. Nevertheless, it is the ability to idealize that makes for change in the direction of higher levels of organization, both in the individual and in social history.[27]

We know from the preface to *The Nigger of the "Narcissus"* that Conrad actively sought to "embroider" and "embellish" memory in order to develop illusion. And we also know from the Preface that Conrad sought to use art to foster worthy ideals. Ian Watt, responding to Conrad's use of illusion in *The Nigger,* argues, however, that there is an ethical paradox in this employment of illusions: "We are indeed made to wonder whether the most powerful form of solidarity manifested in the novel is not the 'solidarity in illusions' which Conrad mentions in the preface."[28]

But the paradox Watt observes did not go unnoticed by Conrad. Conrad clearly had conflicting feelings about his highly idealistic artistic ambitions. He was aware of both the illusions of art and the solidarity such illusions could promote. David Thornburn comments that "in his letters Conrad may be said to vacillate between moments of almost religious commitment to the act of writing and other moments of deep disdain for the passive, inactive life of the artist."[29] Clearly, Conrad indulged in grandiose aspirations. He sought, through the written word, to create literary "illusions" that would foster greater morality and "solidarity" in men's ego-ideals. In one of his grandiose moments, Conrad commented that the "imagination should be used to create human souls: to disclose human hearts."[30] But Conrad also feared, as Thornburn notes, "that the enterprise of literature is an impossible delusion."[31]

To "create human souls" (to foster illusions that promote ego-ideals) requires the manipulation of narcissistic energy—that "energy" as Esther Menaker comments "with which the ego nourishes itself." But there is a danger in manipulating narcissistic energy because it is a notoriously unstable quantum: Ideals and morals maintained by narcissistic energy can also be dissolved by narcissistic energy. The power of an illusion may be exceedingly great, but it rests, finally, on a purely imaginary "ground," especially susceptible to transmutation.

For Conrad, Kurtz is a case study for the problems of a morality sustained entirely by art and artifice. Kurtz came to Africa intending to be an example of the highest of Western ideals, "an emissary of pity, and science, and progress" (79). But the strains that Kurtz undergoes transform his excessively moral pre-Congo idealistic illusions into excessively

narcissistic self-aggrandizing delusions. "He desired," Marlow comments, "to have kings meet him at railway stations on his return from
some ghastly Nowhere, where he intended to accomplish great things"
(148). It is as if the easy narcissistic sublimations that Kurtz was able to
achieve before going to the Congo could not finally withstand the rigors
of isolation and the temptations of radical freedom conjured by the
jungle. The paradox, however, is that though Kurtz is victimized by his
own imagination, he is also the agent or agency of those same forces that
Conrad wants to master.

Kurtz and Conrad's Artistic Ideals

It would be difficult to determine those forces that caused Conrad to
imagine Kurtz. Clearly some of these forces were a function of memory
— Kurtz is in part modeled on Klein, the subordinate agent who died of
dysentery aboard the *Roi des Belges* at Stanley Falls.[32] But other causal
forces undoubtedly reflect Conrad's emerging and ambivalent awareness
of the role of the artist and the tools of his trade. On one side of this
ambivalence, Kurtz serves Conrad as an image of a more powerful mode
of being, an alter ego or double. Kurtz offers a vision of an alternate and
more powerful mode of existence: a grandiose vision of the artist's life.
Kurtz then expresses an image of Conrad's most idealistic ambitions —
to be an artist. But he also simultaneously awakens and expresses primitive narcissistic desires associated with that ambition. Freud's comments
on the "double" are illuminating here:

It is not only this latter material [narcissism], offensive to the ego-criticizing
faculty, which may be incorporated in the idea of a double. There are also all the
unfulfilled but possible futures to which we still like to cling in phantasy, all the
strivings of the ego which adverse external circumstances have crushed, and all
our suppressed acts of volition which nourish in us the illusion of Free Will.[33]

Freud comments that the image of the double dates "back to a very early
mental stage," a stage closely allied to "primary narcissism" and to
primitive, magical, and infinitely grand ambitions. Clearly Kurtz suggests these ambitions to Marlow, as he himself seems to live in a world
animated by primitive, magical, and infinitely grand forces. Kurtz's
residence at the "Inner Station" of the "heart" of "darkness," for example, may suggest his colonization of the "primitive" areas of the
unconscious.[34]

Clearly, the metaphor of darkness has imaginative appeal for a Romantic like Conrad. Marlow, for example, sees Kurtz as living uncontaminated by the conventional, very close to the well-springs of human imagination. He would himself like to "have" access to Kurtz's imaginative power. But Marlow's conflicted image of Kurtz indicates that Kurtz does not merely express an imaginative power; he is victimized by this power. He is emotionally isolated and impoverished by the imaginative power that is his chief glory.

It would have been easy for Conrad to sever his own identification with Kurtz, to curb his admiration on moral grounds. But he does not. A younger Conrad might have done so, and a writer of lesser stature might have done so. Instead Conrad, driven by a desire he can neither fully affirm nor fully abandon, continues to pursue and unfold an uncomfortable narrative.

The defenses Conrad employs to isolate himself from Kurtz's moral contamination, even as he admires his power, seem clear. Marlow's preoccupation with the "steam" within his boiler, his concern to keep it within "safe" levels of pressure, seems to express his need to control the powerful forces the narrative ventilates. This control of steam may seem merely a self-deceptive defense: a refusal to acknowledge those huge and powerful forces of the jungle. But Marlow's attention to work and his concern for "duty" are not as simple as this. Marlow is able to continue in his journey precisely because he is able to keep his engine running. Attention to the boiler does not elide Marlow's perception of the real nature of the jungle; it allows Marlow to journey into the jungle so that his story can be told. Attention to the boiler, then, is a kind of defense, but it also expresses a need to bind and discipline various narcissistic energies associated with identity.

If the appeal of the jungle symbolizes in part the appeal of the "archaic grandiose self"—the self that Kohut postulates as historically primary in our journey to self-autonomy and typically the center of the pathological narcissist's defense against a world that offers insufficient adulation— Marlow himself realizes that he must "explore," "pass through" (in a psychological sense), and even recover the potency of this narcissistic energy.[35] He must use its steam. But he must do so without becoming, as Kurtz, captivated or totally identified with it. He must, essentially, "meet that truth with [his] own true stuff," his "inner strength" (37).

Another apparent defense that Marlow uses to curb his admiration of Kurtz is, quite simply, his insistent and repeated criticism of him. Seeking to fathom Kurtz's mystery, Marlow fixes on Kurtz's "inner emptiness." Marlow suspects that Kurtz cannot withstand the temptations of the jungle (withstand the temptations to desublimate narcissistic needs) because he is "hollow at the core" (131). He lacks an inner power to remain loyal to ideals sublimating deeper and more primitive desires. There is "something wanting in him . . . which . . . [can]not be found under his magnificent eloquence" (131).

Marlow's criticism of Kurtz, of course, alternates with admiration, and this is confusing. But it is not as futile and irrational as many critics think. By means of this painful and protracted alternation in value, Marlow slowly comes to formulate a moral and artistic ideal that taps Kurtz's energy without becoming enervated by it. This formulation of a moral ideal charged with some of Kurtz's own nature is not fully imagined in the text, but we can see the traces of it in various puzzling scenes: It explains, for example, the curious nature of Marlow's final identification with Kurtz's death. It also explains a major change in Conrad's vision of fiction as he ceases to write narratives of complacent moral assertion and takes on tasks of far more complex moral vision.

In opposition to Kurtz's inner emptiness, Marlow attempts to idealize a moral value of "inner strength." He hopes that if, unlike Kurtz, he can manipulate the narcissistic forces of the imagination from an idealized position of inner strength, he can constructively invest the power that formulates ideals and "nourishes" the ego. By means of the narrative, Conrad finally formulates (although in a primitive symbolic form) an ideal of inner strength that allows him both to identify with Kurtz and to have access to his imaginative energy. It seems to me that this formulation is a major achievement of the work, and an important one for Conrad's later work. But this formulation occurs only because Conrad allows himself to respond to what he initially senses to be dangerous and primitive instinctual attractions. By allowing himself to suffer through his conflicted response to Kurtz, some quantity of primitive narcissistic desire seems to undergo sublimation and becomes carried forward and invested in ideals not in conflict with the ego. In becoming bound to nonconflictual ideals, these desires allow Conrad less defensive and more profitable, productive, and complex imaginative strategies.

What is Conrad's new moral ideal? It can be best explained by comparing it to his older moral ideal. Prior to *Heart of Darkness* Conrad endorsed in his fiction a rather simple moral code: the code of the seaman. We can see this code operating in *The Nigger of the "Narcissus"* where Conrad formulated an ideal of "inner strength" as a protection from seductive imaginative and narcissistic forces. "Inner strength" marks a mariner's disciplined willingness to perform the "sacrifices" required of sea duty. The ideal sailor ignores the call of his own inner imaginative world in order to meet the real challenges of the present: challenges of wind and wave. The best seamen of the *Narcissus*, for example, defend themselves from imaginative usurpations through a "self-sacrificing" "devotion" to duty. They abandon personal thoughts and grievances in order to work together to save the ship. They "sacrifice" their narcissistic concerns (their concerns for their own unique individuality) in order to effectively manage a threatening sea.

In *Heart of Darkness*, Conrad confronts a situation very similar to the one he had imagined in *The Nigger*. Both James Wait and Kurtz are men indifferent to wider social concerns beyond their own self-interests. In addition, the two works show a similar concern for language. Donkin's "writerly loquacity" and Kurtz's suspicious eloquence, as David Thorn-burn notes, clearly engage Conrad's interest:

The remarkable directness of Conrad's disapproval of Donkin's writerly loquac-ity and still more, his open and fully acknowledged ambivalence concerning Kurtz's dark eloquence . . . help to distinguish him from writers like Kipling, Marryat, the early Stevenson. The books of these men implicitly attack artifice, intellection, language, without ever accepting full responsibility for such an attack; while in Conrad . . . the man's suspicion of art and language, of the hesitations and limits of intellect, is translated into the artist's conscious subject matter.[36]

Clearly the similarities between *The Nigger of the "Narcissus"* and *Heart of Darkness* are remarkable. But the differences between the two works are perhaps more noteworthy. Conrad could have criticized Kurtz with the same smug moral assurance he used to criticize Donkin and Wait. He could have used the short novel as a sounding board for resounding and traditional moral rhetoric. But he does not. Conrad decides instead to suffer internal conflict, and this conflict funds a more complex textual rhetoric.

Like Wait, Kurtz is a moral outlaw. But Conrad has imagined him in a context that, in itself, links him to a variety of forces that encourage admiration and identification. One of these forces is Conrad's old and rather simple ideal of exploration. Much like the dark continent of Africa, Kurtz's personality is an unmarked space that tests a man's inner strength as it invites exploration. Conrad, thus, explores the internal psychology of Kurtz in order to know what is "in there," much as he would explore the internal geography of Africa in order to know what was "in there." In this sense, *Heart of Darkness* can be seen as an expression of the artistic geography Conrad formulated in the preface to *The Nigger.*

In this preface, Conrad suggests that the imagination arises from some source deep within us. The artist, he says, "descends within himself"; it is only through this descent within that the artist gains access to the imagination. Through this descent *within,* however, the artist, paradoxically, finds terms for rendering "justly" an image of what is *without*— reality. The artist, through the descent within, comes to "render the highest kind of justice to the visible universe." He "bring[s] . . . to light the truth manifold and one, underlying its every aspect."[37] *Heart of Darkness* clearly portrays a "journey within," a journey to the "inner stations" of the heart. But this journey, an imitation in some respects of Kurtz's own descent within himself, does not promise any easy access to truth. Instead the journey seems to question the very possibility of bringing truth to light.

This questioning clearly cuts against the grain of Conrad's most grandiose ambitions, for he believed that an artist's inner struggle to grasp imaginatively the breadth and complexity of the real world would be rewarded. Like Freud, Conrad felt that the self should "grow" by virtue of the pressures and conflicts imposed on it by external reality.[38] Its functions of self-regulation and reality perception should become more complex and coordinated through increased exposure to the "reality principle." Like Freud, Conrad believed that exposure to reality should stretch the ego's capacity to understand reality. For example, when Marlow, in *Lord Jim,* hears Jim's story, he struggles to grasp imaginatively the truth that is deeper than the "convention" that habitually "imagines" truth. "It seems to me," he says, "I was being made to comprehend the Inconceivable. I was made to look at the convention that lurks in all truth and on the essential sincerity of falsehood."[39] Here, the imagination that seeks truth is tested both by the "convention that lurks in all truth," and by the "essential sincerity" of falsehood. But this test is precisely the test imposed on the artist. And Conrad's response to this test here is characteristic of his response to the test elsewhere. He seeks to grasp what has not yet been conceived. He is led through the enigmas of Jim's story "to comprehend the Inconceivable." Achieving an imaginative and visionary breadth of this sort is, for Conrad, heroic, and the most idealized of Conrad's characters struggle within themselves to attain a similar breadth of perception.

Kurtz is an imaginary character who lies between the relatively easy imaginative tests of Conrad's earliest novels and the more difficult tests of the later novels. Kurtz both encourages and tests the artist's idealized inner struggle. He tests Conrad's courage in journeying inward because he illustrates a case in which the self's inward journey encounters a corrosive and contaminating alien reality. The journey within, the text intimates, need never encounter truth; it can instead engender a pathological fantasy that arrests the ego's growth and distorts its perception of reality. *Heart of Darkness* thus portrays an unusually sobering exposure to reality at the same time as it portrays disquieting truths about the plasticity of imaginative perception. Kurtz's experience engenders an imagination able to change the perceptions of others and a power able to endow words with "real presence," a power able to explode the conventions that disguise reality. But Kurtz's transformative imagination imprisons him within the delusions of an empty and distorted inner world. In *Heart of Darkness*, then, the imagination does not in any simple way provide the self with access to the truth; it seals the self within the various and captivating fantastic repetitions of an imprisoning inner fantasy.

Kurtz's story, then, presents Conrad with a powerful critique of the simple values embodied in the preface. Any simple description of Conrad's response to this critique will founder in the complexly overdetermined density of Conrad's prose. But let me sketch out a possible account for what happens. In response to the critique of the journey within, Conrad returns to his old values. But this return is also a transformation, because it occurs at the end of Marlow's narrative about Kurtz, and it occurs as a response to the complex forces brought into play by the narrative. Marlow's final stage of identification with Kurtz, then, is his response to the critique Kurtz embodies. This final stage of identification is both deceptively represented and idealized with tortuous misgivings. But this final act of identification also reasserts Conrad's commitment to imaginative exploration and redeems, rather than sacrifices, the imagination's alliance with narcissistic forces.

The final stage of identification helps Conrad formulate an artistic ideal to support inner exploration. It also redeems the imagination from its pathologically narcissistic affiliations. But this final stage of identification works precisely by rejecting the idealization of identity.

We can imagine Kurtz's death as a kind of fictional sacrifice. Sacrifice, however, is a complex gesture. It requires a giving up of one thing of value in order to obtain something of greater value. In primitive communities this giving up requires the killing of an animal or person. Yet this killing is not a murder; it is a mode of appropriation, transvaluation, a way of making something sacred. Sacrifice mysteriously transforms the value of objects: Something of concrete value is given up in order to assert the value of something else that becomes spiritually bestowed when the physical object disappears. Marlow's identification with Kurtz has all the markings of a ritual sacrifice. One could argue that Kurtz becomes a scapegoat for Marlow's own archaic grandiose narcissism. Marlow can identify with him, identify with his extravagant narcissistic faults, and then relinquish him to the death that is his due. "It is not my own extremity I remember best," Marlow confesses, "it is his extremity I seem to have lived through" (151). In identifying with Kurtz's death, Marlow purges himself of some of Kurtz's characteristics. But this mode of analysis, of course, is far too simple.

Marlow's final identification with Kurtz's "death" is not really an identification with a literal death; it is an identification with an imaginative act strongly analogous to death. The death that fascinates Marlow most strongly is not Kurtz's literal death (which occurs somewhere beyond and outside the text), but an imaginative self-annihilating recognition that Kurtz achieves before he dies. Kurtz's self-recognition resonates metaphorically with all the qualities associated with death, but his final vision occurs before he literally dies. "Perhaps," Marlow opines, "all the wisdom, and all truth, and all sincerity, are just compressed into that inappreciable moment of time in which we step over the threshold of the invisible" (151). Stepping "over the threshold of the invisible" has all the metaphorical associations linked to death, but this movement between the visible and the invisible does not literally refer to death; it refers to a transition between two models of perception. When Kurtz enters most deeply into himself, when he "crosses the threshold of the invisible" to utter his famous cry, he does not in "crossing" the "threshold" die. Rather in "crossing" the "threshold" he sees what before had been invisible to him. Crossing the threshold is a metaphor for access, and what Kurtz gains access to is a new exercise in imagination: a new conception of himself funded by a mode of imaginative "vision" significantly different from that associated with his "magnificent eloquence."

Near death, Kurtz becomes Marlow's hero because he achieves a new verbal power to complement the power of his deceptive eloquence. This new power is much less a power over images of desire than an access to images that produce insight. When near death, Kurtz has an image of himself that enables him to reinterpret the meaning of his life. Until this "vision," Kurtz's imagination communicates powerfully to others and allows them to see "things" differently, but it offers no power of self-insight. Kurtz's vision consumes things, but it does not reveal Kurtz to himself. Kurtz's unique being gives him a unique vision of "things." However, in seeing "things" as a function of his own narcissistic needs, Kurtz is blind to the limitations and distortions of his own vision. To free himself from his narcissistic perspective, Kurtz must see into the nature of his own seeing, must direct the powerful imagination that sustains his narcissism back on its origin to encounter not the "being" of "things," but the "being" of the observer—himself.

Kurtz's access to the origin of his own perspective—his vision of the "invisible" homunculus behind his own vision—occurs, however, only by virtue of a sacrifice of the sort Conrad is quite eager to idealize. To cross the "threshold of the invisible" Kurtz must abandon his claims to the "visible" (those self-sustaining illusions that have nourished his narcissistic drive), and give himself over to a metaphorical death. To see himself, he must finally see the darkness of his own heart. He must judge and acknowledge the "empty" cavity of his being that his imagination had attempted to deny. The cry that accompanies Kurtz's final vision— "the horror, the horror"—is necessarily problematic, a vortex for critical indeterminacy. We cannot know Kurtz's true attitude at death. But in so far as Kurtz serves to elicit and objectify Marlow's own feelings and values, those last words redeem for Marlow the imagination from its pathologically narcissistic affiliation. Moreover, for Conrad, these last words seem to mark something like the very bottom of the self's inner exploration of itself.

On the threshold of the "invisible" Kurtz seems to "live his life again in every detail of desire" and achieve (notice the idealizing insistence of these words) in a "supreme moment of complete knowledge" (149) an understanding of his moral "deficiency." Kurtz's near death "piercing vision" discovers a gap between his own deepest desires and the pattern of his aspiration. In an act of "self-sacrifice," he enters into a space hitherto "invisible" to him. Crossing the "threshold," Kurtz confronts the "appalling face of a glimpsed truth" marked by a "strange commingling of desire and hate" (151). As "desire and hate" commingle to reveal the apparent horror of his desire, Kurtz seems to undergo an imaginative but enabling self-alienation that puts his narcissistic perspective into a different perspective.

The proximity to death unveils to Kurtz the limitations of narcissistic desire. Recognizing at last the reality of his own finitude, Kurtz grasps the fraudulence of his imaginative attempt to defeat it. And in this recognition, Kurtz achieves his most heroic imaginative act. Or at least Marlow thinks so. Marlow idealizes this vision near death as Kurtz's most brilliant accomplishment. As his desperately self-sustained code of desire is unmasked by his intuition of death, Kurtz's imagination discovers and explores a cognitive space relatively free from desperate defenses and psychic bondage. In this space, vision can occur in a "new light," and "things" masked and distorted by strong ego defenses can be seen anew. This revelation, however, can only be achieved by self-sacrifice: To "cross" the threshold, Kurtz must sacrifice his allegiances to those pathologically narcissistic forms of perception that have defined and defended him. Kurtz's final vision has the form of a self-sacrifice, because to achieve his final vision his self-sustaining ego defenses must be abandoned. This loss is more than a loss of values; it is a loss of self because these defenses define and quite literally "authorize" Kurtz's identity.

Kurtz's final ability to sacrifice his ego defenses and confront his deeper emptiness illustrates a significant reformulation of the seaman's ideal of self-sacrifice. The self is, in a certain sense, sacrificed, but the journey within the self is not. Kurtz's final vision, then, reveals, for Conrad, the imaginative achievement of a great artist—and gives cogency to his aspiration to "use" the "imagination" to "create human souls: to disclose human hearts." Kurtz's final self-recognition, a "moral victory paid for by innumerable defeats, by abominable terrors, by abominable satisfactions," does not redeem Kurtz's life, but it does illuminate both Marlow's life and Conrad's ambitions. Marlow learns to chart his own course in relation to the narcissistic vortex by identifying with (a) the Faustian energy of Kurtz's narcissism, (b) Kurtz's "inner emptiness," and (c) Kurtz's insight into the "heart of darkness"—that is, Kurtz's recognition of the "deficiency" behind his energy and brilliance.

Through the figure of Kurtz, both Marlow and Conrad are able to achieve a certain stability and maturity in relation to the grandiose components of their own narcissism. They are able to recognize the ambiguities within the narcissistic attraction to the "glories of exploration," and through this imaginative vision they are able to retain, despite the ambiguities, an allegiance to that "energy with which the ego nourishes itself." It is this energy that finally (again embodied in the figure of Kurtz) allows an insight into the self. Kurtz's spiritually enabling self-insight reveals at last, for Conrad, a truth—truth not as any stable ontological ground, nor as anything that can be easily verified, but truth as an experience of a step forward in the ego's greater mastery of reality through the imagination, a step forward in the ego's ability to formulate ideals more consistent with the larger ideal to explore reality.[40]

In a 1905 essay on Henry James, Conrad speaks of "art" as a "temple" in which a "sacrifice" has to be made. He then applies this ideal of "sacrifice" to all significant human endeavor:

All adventure, all love, every success is resumed in the supreme energy of an act of renunciation. It is the uttermost limit of our power; it is the most potent and effective force at our disposal. No man or woman worthy of the name can pretend to anything more, to anything greater.[41]

As an author, Conrad perhaps sensed archaic grandiose aspirations reviving in himself as he discovered that art required an essentially narcissistic endeavor, a turning inward of the self on itself. Perhaps also, in his descent "within himself" to find "terms of appeal," Conrad encountered forces that threatened his narcissistic balance as he explored uncharted currents of aspiration and identification. Troubled by the vicissitudes of inner exploration, Conrad seems to have refined his ideal of self-sacrifice as a kind of ballast, a principle of internalized otherness to protect his ego from inflationary and pathological forces.

When "adventure" and "love" are "resumed" in an act of "renunciation," they are begun again after they have been purged of self-interest, purged of the self-aggrandizing quality often associated with aspiration. The narration of *Heart of Darkness* begins as Marlow assumes the posture of Buddha, and ends, strangely, with an image of the "Intended's" grief, her despair before the loss of Kurtz.[42] In gesture and theme the narrative bespeaks a loss, a renunciation of some sort. How we judge what has been lost depends on how we ourselves identify with Kurtz and judge the heroics of his aspirations. Clearly, however, the writing of *Heart of Darkness* gave Conrad an increased control of the narcissistic forces of the imagination. In "Youth," written just before *Heart of Darkness*, Marlow appears as a slightly romantic and ironic narrator commemorating the idealizations and lost illusions of youth. "Youth" records a nostalgic celebration of the delusional and narcissistic promise of youthfulness: "I remember my youth," Marlow says,

the feeling that I could last forever, outlast the sea, the earth, and all men; the deceitful feeling that lures us on to joys, to perils, to love, to vain effort — to death; the triumphant conviction of strength, the heat of life in the handful of dust, the glow of the heart that with every year grows dim, grows cold, grows small and expires — and expires too soon, too soon — before life itself.[43]

In *Heart of Darkness*, Kurtz's attempt to surpass, through consumption, the existential weight of "the earth, the sky, all men," betrays a naked emotional intensity not qualified by irony. Through the figure of Kurtz, however, Conrad's own narcissistic aspirations are, if not worked through, at least worked on. Given the work's preoccupation with mourning it may be that some of the more ambitious aspirations are abandoned.[44] In Conrad's next major work, *Lord Jim*, the theme of narcissistic aspiration, and Marlow's identification with it, explores new material as it achieves a new clarity and poignancy. Many of the same themes are present in both *Heart of Darkness* and *Lord Jim*: identification with a moral outlaw, illusional and delusional imaginative aspirations, and the reparational gesture of self-sacrifice. In *Lord Jim*, however, Conrad examines new complexities as he insists on a brooding respect for the narcissistic "dream" that underlies our ideals, and finally questions, rather than glorifies, the uncertain heroics of narcissistic self-sacrifice.[45]

Notes

1. The following are some of the better discussions of relations between writing and identity in Conrad: Jeffrey Berman, *Joseph Conrad;* Jeremy Hawthorn,

Conrad: Language and Fictional Self-Consciousness (Lincoln: University of Nebraska Press, 1979); and Edward Said, *Joseph Conrad and the Fiction of Autobiography* (Cambridge: Harvard University Press, 1966).

2. "To Edward Garnett," "Good Friday," 16 September 1899, *Letters from Joseph Conrad, 1895–1924,* ed. Edward Garnett (Indianapolis: Charter Books, 1962), 153.

3. Jeffrey Berman, "Writing as Rescue: Conrad's Escape from the Heart of Darkness," *Literature and Psychology* 25 (1975): 65–78.

4. Peter Glassman, *Joseph Conrad and the Literature of Personality* (New York: Columbia University Press, 1976), 234.

5. Joseph Warren Beach, "Impressionism: Conrad," in *The Twentieth Century Novelists: Studies in Techniques,* 337–65 (New York: Appleton-Century, 1932).

6. Joseph Conrad, *A Personal Record* (London: J. M. Dent, 1919), 17–18.

7. Ibid., 15.

8. Daniel R. Schwarz, *Conrad: Almayer's Folly to Under Western Eyes* (Ithaca, N.Y.: Cornell University Press, 1980), 52.

9. Bernard Meyer, *Joseph Conrad: A Psychoanalytic Biography* (Princeton, N.J.: Princeton University Press, 1970), 305, 319.

10. Frederick Karl, *Joseph Conrad: The Three Lives* (New York: Farrar, Straus & Giroux, 1979), 219, 425.

11. William Bonney, *Thorns and Arabesques: Contexts for Conrad's Fiction* (Baltimore: Johns Hopkins University Press, 1980), 217.

12. In his earliest work Kohut uses the word in its broadest sense. His preface to *The Analysis of the Self* begins: "The subject matter of narcissism, that is, of the cathexis of the self (Hartmann), is a very broad one since it can be said with justification that it refers to half of the contents of the human mind— the other half being, of course, the objects" (xiii). Kernberg, *Borderline Conditions and Pathological Narcissism,* prefers a more restrictive use of the term: " 'Narcissistic' as a descriptive term has been both abused and over-used. There does exist, however, a group of patients in whom the main problem appears to be the disturbance of their self-regard in connection with specific disturbances in their object relationships, and whom we might con-sider almost a 'pure culture' of pathological development of narcissism. It is for these patients that I would reserve the term 'narcissistic personalities' " (17).

13. Esther Menaker, "The Ego-Ideal: An Aspect of Narcissism," in *The Narcis-sistic Condition,* ed. Marie Coleman Nelson (New York: Human Sciences Press, 1977), 248.

14. Andre Green, "Moral Narcissism," *International Journal of Psychoanalytic Psychotherapy,* 8 (1980–81): 244–62, makes an interesting but discomforting argument about the relationships between morality and narcissism.

15. Ian Watt, *Conrad in the Nineteenth Century,* 115. Schwarz, in *Conrad,* observes: "As we have seen *The Nigger of the "Narcissus"* concludes with a reaching towards celebration which is belied by what precedes. While the

narrator desperately tries to impose a significance upon the disintegrating crew by means of his final reductive fantasy, the tale refutes the narrator's recollection as a narcissistic wish-fulfillment and makes us understand that the narrator, as much as Wait, belongs to the Narcissus" (62).

16. David Thornburn, *Conrad's Romanticism* (New Haven, Conn.: Yale University Press, 1974), 123.

17. Freud, in *Leonardo da Vinci and a Memory of His Childhood* (1910), *The Standard Edition* 11: 136, speculates that "artistic talent and capacity are intimately connected with sublimation." Art is concerned, he suggests with "instincts and their transformations," but with this observation he feels at the "limit of what is discernible by psychoanalysis."

18. In arguing that *Heart of Darkness* is about narcissistic energy, I do not mean to imply that the story is not about the colonization of Africa. Psychoanalysis itself argues that human signification is "overdetermined": More than one thing can be "meant" in any one signifier. *Heart of Darkness* is indeed about the colonization of Africa. But I believe it is also about the strange "states of mind" that too often accompany imperialistic ventures.

19. Conrad, *Heart of Darkness*, 52. Further citations of this work appear in the text.

20. Kohut, *The Analysis of the Self*, 16–17.

21. Kernberg, *Borderline Conditions and Pathological Narcissism*, 227–29.

22. Ben Bursten ["The Narcissistic Course," in *The Narcissistic Condition*, ed. Marie Cole (New York: Human Sciences Press, 1977)] suggests a fundamental affinity between narcissism and orality: "Because the earliest attempts to sense the self take place when oral sensuality is at its height, orality becomes a stage on which later struggles to preserve the sense of self are enacted. . . . The fantasies of taking in support the sense of self as within the body, and fantasies of the effects of eating help confirm the sense of self by the illusion of partaking of the mother's bigness and power" (115).

23. "To Edward Garnett," 8 November 1920, in *Letters from Joseph Conrad*, ed. Garnett, 273. See also, Elsie Nettles, "Heart of Darkness and the Creative Process," *Conradiana* 5 (1973): 66–73.

24. Joseph Conrad, "Preface," in *The Nigger of the "Narcissus"* (Garden City, N.Y.: Doubleday, Page & Co., 1921), ix–x.

25. Lacan, *Ecrits*, 260.

26. Kernberg, *Borderline Conditions and Pathological Narcissism*, observes that "the degree to which a patient is able to invest himself in a certain activity or profession beyond strictly narcissistic needs, the degree of gratification from such activity or profession, and the extent to which the patient is concerned about the intrinsic values of that activity or profession represent his sublimatory potential" (133). Narcissists have trouble in deriving gratification from sublimated activities; their "ideals" are generally unstable and reflect a "projection" of the "grandiose self."

27. Menaker, "The Ego-Ideal," 252–54.

28. Watt, *Conrad in the Nineteenth Century*, 115.

29. Thornburn, *Conrad's Romanticism*, 109.
30. "To Edward Noble," 28 October 1895, in *Joseph Conrad: Life and Letters*, vol. 1, ed. G. Jean-Aubrey (Garden City, N.Y.: Doubleday, Page & Co., 1927), 183.
31. Thornburn, *Conrad's Romanticism*, 111.
32. Norman Sherry provides photographs of the grave in *Conrad's Western World* (Cambridge: Cambridge University Press, 1971).
33. Sigmund Freud, "The Uncanny" (1919), *The Standard Edition* 17: 236.
34. Crews, "The Power of Darkness," suggests that the "unspeakable rites" of *Heart of Darkness* are associated with incest and the "primal scene." Like Crews, I believe that the text is charged with such "primary process" thinking. But unlike Crews, I believe that the central struggle of the text involves purposeful (although perhaps not self-conscious) "secondary process" thinking, attempting to responsibly "invest" the raw energy of "primary process" and narcissistic material.
35. Kohut, *The Analysis of the Self*, 17; 25–29.
36. Thornburn, *Conrad's Romanticism*, 115.
37. Conrad, "Preface," viii.
38. Freud, in "Formulations Regarding the Two Principles," argues that the ego "goes through its transformation from a pleasure-ego into a reality-ego" (224).
39. Joseph Conrad, *Lord Jim* (Garden City, N.Y.: Doubleday, Page & Co., 1921), 43.
40. I write about Conrad, in part, because I myself have come to idealize the imagination in a manner similar to Conrad. But I also write about Conrad because I want to illustrate the pattern of fantasy and idealization that many texts reveal. We choose to teach these texts because we too have participated in certain facets of their conflict and we too have ideals we want to promote. Just as Conrad's text struggles with expressing and regulating desire, readers of Conrad engage in a similar struggle. They may formulate very different ideals. But the ideals they formulate will organize and make sense of their own libidinal investments in life and in the text. A George Washington student, Andrew Barret, formulates his own ideals about *Heart of Darkness* when he argues:

    Marlow would rather be unsound, or numbered with the dead, a partner of sorts with the unfavorable Mr. Kurtz, than be associated with the other men from the company whom he calls "mean and greedy phantoms." Marlow cherishes his "choice" as a freedom in terms of his own existence, and he wouldn't trade it to be an average person unaware of the insincerity of their existence, "so full of stupid importance." (Unpublished paper, George Washington University)

    I do not fully understand Barret's description of the "unpleasant" truth Marlow learns from Kurtz, something regarding the average person's "insincerity of . . . existence," but I grasp the general form of this claim. I see myself valuing similar perceptions of the text in my own readings of it.

When a text engages the "fantasy" of an identification that finally triggers the disclosure of a perception initially resisted (linked to a "partner"ship with an "unfavorable" person), but finally acknowledged as true, such a process marks readjustments in the values that define and idealize subjectivity. Such a process engages the deepest powers of self-recognition and, in this manner, is a profoundly rhetorical event because such discovered values are experienced in the vital relation to the self, and not perceived as external claims advocated by a distant authority figure.

41. Joseph Conrad, "Henry James," in *Notes on Life and Letters* (Garden City, N.Y.: Doubleday, Page & Co., 1926), 16.

42. Henry Staten, "Conrad's Mortal Word," *Critical Inquiry* 12 (1986): 720–40, offers a very compelling account of the text's preoccupation with mourning.

43. Conrad, *Youth and Two Other Stories* (Garden City, N.Y.: Doubleday, Page & Co., 1921), 36–37.

44. Kernberg, *Borderline Conditions and Pathological Narcissism*, observes that "the prognosis improves for patients who preserve some capacity for depression or mourning." Narcissists are often "extremely resistant to any effort to mobilize their rigid pathological character defenses" and admissions of grief or sorrow are impossible for them. Melanie Klein, "Mourning and Its Relation to Manic-Depressive States," in *Love, Guilt, and Reparation and Other Works, 1921–1945* (New York: Dell, 1975), 344, finds a close relation between mourning and the testing of reality. Mourning allows us to accept the painful "truths" of the "real world."

45. Crews, "The Power of Darkness," suggests that "death is at once a symbol of castration and the surest escape from it, a flight from incest and a return to it" (512). I feel that a "literary" death may be even more overdetermined; it offers an opportunity to mourn narcissistic loss. This imaginary death, which occurs after the double revives repressed narcissistic aspiration, may, as Melanie Klein says of "painful experiences" ("Mourning and Its Relation to Manic-Depressive States", 360), "stimulate sublimation," that is, stimulate a deeper and more productive appreciation of "the visible universe." Fascination with a "literary" death of this sort is at the "heart" of our most profound respect for literature.

Language and the Substance of the Self: A Lacanian Perspective

And sometimes even music / Cannot substitute for tears.

Paul Simon, "The Cool Cool River"

This book has offered an extended discussion of relations between language and the subject. I have suggested that language can have a powerful effect on self-functions because the subject is, in part, a linguistic entity. For the most part, the theoretical underpinnings of my discussion have been eclectic. In emphasizing the self-divisive structure of the subject, I have used Freudian, post-Freudian, and even poststructuralist ideas to develop my argument. Because relations between language and the subject are central to my argument, and central also to many other influential theoretical positions, I want to devote this chapter to an extended discussion of Lacan's description of these relationships. Lacan is often misunderstood by his poststructuralist readers, and although I do not consistently utilize Lacanian theory in this book, a more sustained attention to this theoretical system will help clarify many of the abstract theoretical claims I have made. Readers who are uncomfortable with my claims about the libidinal organizations of subjectivity may be more comfortable with Lacan's analysis of the subject functions that negotiate relationships between discourse and subjectivity.

Increasingly, Lacan emerges as the preeminent theorist of relationships between discourse and the subject. Lacan is unique as a discourse theorist because his thinking synthesizes ideas at the interface of two very different conceptions of the subject, the psychoanalytic and the poststructuralist. As a practicing analyst, Lacan sought to understand the human subject. As a poststructuralist, he sought to understand the sub-

ject's constitution through and by discourse. But precisely because Lacan's theoretical work derives from and ultimately moves beyond the
theoretical limitations of two rather different perspectives on the subject,
his ideas about the subject require more careful attention.

Poststructuralists and Freudians hold very different assumptions about
the "subject of discourse." To understand Lacan's uniqueness as a theo-
retician, we must see where he stands in relation to Freudian and poststructuralist ideas. A central issue dividing psychoanalytic and poststructuralist theories focuses on the meaning of the prepositional phrase
following the noun "subject" in the phrase "subject of discourse." How
exactly is the subject related to discourse? Structuralists and poststructuralists assert that the subject is created by, derived from, and essentially
equivalent to discourse. Such an assumption emphasizes the primacy of
the prepositional phrase "of discourse." The subject is a secondary deri-
vation of discourse interaction, an illusory effect of discourse systems.
Discourse contains, causes, manipulates, and composes the subject, as in
the phrase "the puppet of wood," where "wood" describes the essential
nature of the puppet. If this description is correct, the relation between
discourse and the subject is one-sided. Discourse operates the subject as
it operates on the subject. To study relations between discourse and the
subject from this perspective, one must study those discourse systems
and mechanisms that (outside the psychoanalytically circumscribed sphere
of the subject) situate, position, constitute—*contain*—the subject.

Psychoanalysts, however, assert that it is not discourse that contains
the subject, but the subject that, in some sense, contains discourse. In
this case primacy is given to the noun "subject," and the prepositional
phrase "of discourse" describes something secondary and quite different
from the subject. Discourse here is something belonging to, worked on,
or contained by the subject, as in the phrase "basket of eggs," or perhaps
the more problematic phrase "pool of water." Here the emphasis of the
prepositional phrase directs attention to the subject's containment and
manipulation of discourse. Discourse does not animate and operate the
subject; instead, the subject operates discourse. A contemporary formulation of this perspective would suggest that the term *subject* defines
certain subject-specific discourse functions that, because they are characteristic of what subjects are, work distinctive (we might call them
"subject-driven") processes on the field of discourse. Just as the pool of
water, because it is a pool, affects what happens to the water within, the

subject, because it is a subject, has certain subject-specific effects on discourse. These subject-specific discourse functions derive from the nature of subjectivity and—rather than being mere reflections or internalized components of discourse systems external to the subject—alter, manipulate, resist, and transform those systems.

A central problem in the study of Lacan arises because the major theoretical schools that make use of Lacan tend to appropriate Lacanian thought from one pole of the subject-discourse relation and ignore the other pole. Structuralists and poststructuralists tend to ignore the specific discourse functions (described by psychoanalysts) that, lying within the subject-system, operate on language. Psychoanalysts tend to ignore the discourse systems (described by structuralists) that, lying outside the domain of the subject, compose and situate the subject. Both Freudian and poststructuralist appropriations of Lacan are one-sided in their perspective and vastly oversimplify an intellectual system promising to resolve many of the unproductive theoretical disputes attending poststructuralist and Freudian accounts of language. Lacan's position contains—and transforms—both polar formulations of the subject-discourse relationship. The phrase "subject of discourse" can easily be read in terms of only one meaning. Similarly, Lacan is frequently interpreted in terms of only one figuration of the subject-discourse relation—and not the other.

Poststructuralist appropriations of Lacan frequently follow a formula described by Frederic Jameson. In *The Political Unconscious*, Jameson continues his earlier support of Lacan's ideas and emphasizes the importance of Lacan's radical decentering of the ego:

Lacan's work, with its emphasis on the "constitution of the subject," displaces the problematic of orthodox Freudianism from models of unconscious processes or blockages toward an account of the formation of the subject and its constitutive illusions which, though still genetic in Lacan himself and couched in terms of the individual biological subject, is not incompatible with a broader historical framework. Furthermore, the polemic thrust of Lacanian theory, with its decentering of the ego, the conscious subject of activity, the personality, or the "subject" of the Cartesian cogito—all grasped as something like an "effect" of subjectivity—and its repudiation of the various ideals of the unification of the personality or the mythic conquest of personal identity, poses useful new problems for any narrative analysis which still works with naive, common-sense categories of "character," "protagonist," or "hero," and with psychological "concepts" like those of identification, sympathy, or empathy.[1]

Jameson applauds Lacan's "displacement of orthodox Freudianism" because he sees Freud's displacement leading to a suitable replacement. Instead of considering individuals, Jameson wants us to think about effects of subjectivity. Jameson's description of Lacan's subject—his attempt to characterize it as an entity "of discourse"—is an attempt to push Lacan's subject back into its proper poststructuralist place in the discourse systems that compose it. But we should note that Jameson is not simply describing Lacan's thought; he is appropriating it. Jameson argues that Lacan's displacement of "orthodox" Freudianism is promising; but at the same time, he admits that Lacan does not *really* displace Freud, does not really overcome an archaic belief in the "individual biological subject." Lacan's rejection and displacement of Freudian ideas is, to a large extent, something Jameson imagines. According to Jameson, it is something that is, in Lacan himself, "still genetic."

Jameson clearly wants to make use of Lacan and to appropriate his ideas for his own purposes. For many scholars, however, Jameson's highly persuasive appropriation of Lacan is less an appropriation and more a standardization of Lacan. Lacan, through the commentary of Jameson and others, becomes the kind of thinker Jameson imagines. Lacan becomes another poststructuralist, a thinker for whom the subject is a subject "of discourse."

Other scholars, following the lead of Jameson, show a more ardent eagerness to dismiss the clinical and psychoanalytic side of Lacan. Characteristically, this dismissal is formulated by means of a poststructuralist conceptualization of Lacan's subject. It emphasizes that Lacan's subject cannot be imagined through metaphors of containment, activity, or creativity. Eve Tavor Bannet argues:

There is in Lacan no autonomous, self-conscious subject in whom, as in a container, knowledge, experience and emotion inhere, whose relationship to the social environment can be measured in terms of creativity and self-recognition. Lacan's model for man is the computer. Man is a machine whose predetermined linguistically programmed circuits are governed by binary structures: closed-open, absent-present, or.[2]

If one reads Lacan hastily and uses quotations selectively, it is easy to find support for such claims. But anyone who reads Lacan carefully realizes that making generalizations about Lacan's teaching is a highly demanding task that requires facing—not ignoring—the contradictions in Lacan's conceptualizations.

Lacan frequently contradicts himself. Typically, these contradictions reveal Lacan in the process of thinking, in the process of finding the best metaphors or terms of comparison useful for elucidating the substance of his thought. For example, in relation to his earlier insistence that human beings are like machines (found in *Book II* of the Seminar and quoted by Bannet), Lacan later points out that human beings are not like machines. After considering the "originality" of human thought (a quality Bannet denies), Lacan points out:

That is where the power revealed by the originality of the machines we have at our disposal falls short. There is a third dimension of time which they undeniably are not party to, which I'm trying to get you to picture via this element which is neither belatedness, nor being in advance, but haste, the relation to time peculiar to the human being. That is where speech is to be found, and where language, which has all the time in the world, is not. That is why, furthermore, one gets nowhere with language.[3]

Here Lacan insists that there is an important difference between subjects and machines. Meaning, found in speech, differs from the information found in machine language because speech is responsive to time and to desire in a way that language is not. Speech, something produced by humans, is very different from language. "The question of meaning," Lacan points out in an earlier context, "comes with speech."[4] In order to emphasize the importance of this point Lacan makes a rather dramatic and self-contradictory assertion: "One gets nowhere with language."

Lacan's repudiation of "language" (which machines have) is a privileging of speech—something possessed uniquely by humans and charged with human qualities. Speech uniquely produces meaning because speech is a "language" uniquely "configured" by subject-functions. Meaning is produced as language is driven or operated by subject-functions such as desire, temporality, repression, the Imaginary. If we consider the relationships posited here between discourse and the subject we can see a metaphor of containment employed. Speech is something (in a sense) "contained" by subjects in so far as, though it circulates intersubjectively, it is something proper to, defined by, or "contained" by the nature of subjectivity. To understand speech, as opposed to language, one must understand what it means to be a subject. One must understand that a subject is not a machine programmed by a binary language.

In the process of arguing that speech differs from language, Lacan insists that "one gets nowhere with language." But of course Lacan is not really saying that one always "gets nowhere with language." Lacan is in many respects a poststructuralist; his understanding of language is central to his system. This is one of many passages showing that we must be sensitive to both the dialectical instability of Lacan's terms and to the various inflections Lacan gives to the term *language*. In an earlier discussion of the importance of language, Lacan responds to a remark by Lefebvre-Pontalis and points out that he distinguishes between "language and significations." "Language is a system of signs," says Lacan, "and as such, a complete system."[5] Emphasizing the importance of this observation, Lacan continues: "With that one can do anything."[6] Lefebvre-Pontalis responds to this emphasis on language (which he considers misleading) by saying, "On condition that there be speaking subjects."[7] In effect, Lefebvre-Pontalis points out that you can do "anything with language," but only if there are speaking subjects. Lacan agrees, but adds: "Of course, The question is to know what the function of speaking subject is in all this."[8] For both Lacan and his commentators, the key question is to know "the function of the speaking subject."

Later in the same seminar, where he explores the "function of the speaking subject" "in all this," Lacan uses the story of the three white disks to show how human meaning, unlike machine meaning, can be produced by human temporality.[9] This leads to emphasis on the distinction between speech and language and his declaration that one gets "nowhere" with language.

At the end of *Book II* Lacan returns to his comparison between man and the machine:

With a machine, whatever doesn't come on time simply falls by the wayside and makes no claims on anything. This is not true of man, the scansion is alive, and whatever doesn't come on time remains in suspense. That is what is involved in repression. No doubt something which isn't expressed doesn't exist. The repressed is always there, insisting, and demanding to be. The fundamental relation of man to this symbolic order is very precisely what found the symbolic order itself—the relation of non-being to being.

What insists on being satisfied can only be satisfied in recognition. The end of the symbolic process is that non-being comes to be, because it has spoken.[10]

Lacan's attention to repression, nonexistence, time, and recognition reveal psychoanalytic concerns that easily allow him to distinguish subjects from machines. Machines need not concern themselves with these phenomena; subjects are made subjects in being driven by these forces.

Characteristically, the Lacan of the Seminar is thinking and reformulating his pronouncements as he sees things in various and different relations. In *Book II,* after a lengthy and somewhat defensive discussion of whether St. John meant speech or language in his formulation "In the beginning was the word (logos)," Lacan dismisses the increasingly complicated argument: "I am not engaging you in an *ex cathedra* teaching. I don't think it would befit our object, language and speech, for me to bring something apodictic for you here, something you must just have to record and put in your pocket."[11] Repeatedly Lacan emphasizes that he is not engaged in the formulation of dogma, but in the process of thinking. In the "Overture to the Seminar" in *Book I* he says:

The master breaks the silence with anything—with a sarcastic remark, with a kick-start.

That is how a Buddhist master conducts his search for meaning, according to the technique of Zen. It behooves the students to find out for themselves the answer to their own questions. The master does not teach *ex cathedra* a ready made science.[12]

Of course, although the Lacan of the Seminar does not teach a ready-made science, interpreters of Lacan usually do. Explicators of Lacan feel it is their job to produce stable cognitive products (convenient conceptual summaries of ideas) and to avoid initiating unstable cognitive processes of the sort fostered by Lacan's texts. Written representations of Lacan's thought thus typically reduce the complexity of his thought as they generalize and simplify the teaching. This drive, finally, makes it all too easy to "fix" Lacan by appropriating him along the lines of existing theoretical assumptions. Rather than becoming involved in the disruptive conceptual complexities produced by Lacan's thinking, Lacan's commentators frequently distance themselves from him in order to preserve mastery of conceptual codings. This makes it easy to read Lacan as one more poststructuralist thinker.

Eve Bannet quotes Lacan selectively to argue that the "consequences" of the

takeover of perception, desire, imagination, thought experience and reality by the symbolic order are two-fold. First, it imposes conformity and abolishes individuality to the point where "the collective and the individual are the same thing." Secondly it leads to a situation in which "we are spoken more than we speak."[13]

Such a situation means, Bannet points out, that "as the conscious subject is little more than a mechanism which repeats the signifiers and significations already in language, so the unconscious is a mechanism which repeats what has been repressed."[14]

This representation of the Lacanian subject is not altogether wrong. But it is not right either. It reduces the subject to a loudspeaker system, "repeating the signifiers and significations already in language." It is quite easy to show that there is much more to Lacan's subject. But this description of the Lacanian subject seems plausible because it echoes concepts that poststructuralism has already established as critical dogma.

When Jameson imagines a Lacan who has fully displaced Freud, and when Bannet imagines Lacan's subject as a machine that merely "repeats the signifiers and significations already in language," both these gestures repeat a general tendency of structuralists and poststructuralists to deny Lacan's theoretical uniqueness by reading Lacan's subject as one more version of the poststructuralist subject.

There is a repeated "identity" pattern in poststructuralist thought that works to erase the human subject, to make "the subject of discourse" an entity composed, contained, derived from, and imprisoned by language (not speech). In *The Pursuit of Signs,* Jonathan Culler repeats claims made earlier by Levi-Strauss and argues that as structuralism investigates the self, it erases it:

These disciplines find, as their work advances, that the self is dissolved as its various functions are ascribed to impersonal systems which operate through it. As the self is broken down into component systems, deprived of its status as source and master of meaning, it comes to seem more and more like a construct: a result of systems of convention.[15]

The subject conceived by structuralism is an "effect" of discourse. It is an illusion produced by linguistic effects. The subject thus fades back, without a residue, into its constitutive element, language. The subject of discourse becomes a subject *of discourse.*

If we push Culler's position slightly further, we can arrive at the sort of pronouncement made by Diane Macdonell in *Theories of Discourse.* Macdonell surveys the various theories of ideology and discourse that have arisen since structuralism and (giving special attention to the work of Althusser) argues that "attempts to supply a theory of the subject (singular and general) for ideology or discourse will tend to idealism, speculating about what does not exist."[16] Such an absolute dismissal of the self has a certain plausibility. It might even be supported by certain strategic quotes from Lacan. In *Book II* Lacan insists that the subject is not an "entity," and later that the "subject is no one."[17] But these quotations, like many others, need to be read in terms of the context and contradictions within Lacan's thought, and not in terms of their agreement with existing poststructuralist ideas. Lacan is not saying that there is no subject; he is instead disputing the kinds of boundaries placed on the subject by traditional psychoanalytic theory. Lacan is disputing traditional interpretations of Freud, but he is not defining himself as a poststructuralist.

Macdonell's rejection of the self is a good example of Burke's logic of reduction: the tendency of any particular theory to purify its own language at the expense of good sense. Once something gets seen in terms of something else, Burke points out, it soon can be reduced to something that is "nothing but" that which it is seen in terms of. Because the characteristic gesture of structuralism is to see the subject in terms of language, the subject easily becomes nothing but language. These attempts to read Lacan's "subject of discourse" as a "nothing" that fades back into discourse, however, misread Lacan. Such an absolute dismissal of the subject is ill-considered—even for poststructuralist theory. It represents little more than an attempt to simplify discourse theory by banishing difficult concepts.

Lacan's theory of the subject offers a solution to the impasse attending the debates between Freudians and poststructuralists. For Lacan, relations between discourse and the subject are two-sided. The subject operates on discourse, and discourse operates the subject. This dialogical interaction between subject-functions shaping discourse, and social forces providing the matrix of discourse, is useful for understanding the particular nature of speech products. This model suggests, first, that there are specific subject-functions (repression, for example) that can always deflect and give idiosyncratic shape to social discourse. This is true because self-components within the self interact to produce particular and unique discourse effects. Second, Lacan forces us to recognize that we must study many different and distinct discourse functions (ideology, knowledge, narcissism, repetition) that operate on the subject as the subject interacts in a discourse community. It is a great oversimplification to represent these discourse functions in general terms—in terms either of general "subject-positions" plotted by social discourse, or in terms of some autonomous ego that defines itself through discourse.

To develop a more complex picture of the subject, we must more fully appreciate how Lacan's subject is distinct from the subject imagined by poststructuralist thought. Like the poststructuralists, Lacan "dissolves" the subject. But Lacan's insistence on the subject's radical self-division and his description of the constitution of the subject by discourse is easily misunderstood by thinkers who approach Lacan without extensive knowledge of psychoanalysis. We can examine the differences between the Lacanian subject and the poststructuralist self by reconsidering Culler's argument. The self, he says, is "dissolved" as "its various functions are ascribed to impersonal systems which operate through it." When Culler describes the self as "dissolved," he means in part that it is "deprived of its status as source and master of meaning" as it is "broken down into component systems." Like the self Culler describes, Lacan's subject finds "its various functions" operated by "impersonal systems" that operate it. Also like the self Culler describes, Lacan's subject is deprived of its status as "master" of meaning. Unlike Culler's self, however, Lacan's subject is not simply a linguistic construct, an illusion produced by language effects.

Human subjects, unlike human bodies, are hypothetical phenomena. Detecting their presence will always be an effect of systems of belief and theory brought to bear on the gestures and traces of an invisible entity. Lacan is very careful--and very subtle--in his account of the subject. In many ways Lacan's account of the subject is a very precise account of meaning effects produced by the "impersonal" subject-functions and subject-components alluded to by Culler. A review of this account of subject-systems, however, indicates that, whereas Lacan's subject disappears in one sense, it does not disappear in another sense. Lacan's subject disappears in the sense that a particular component (long idealized by psychoanalysis), the ego, can no longer aspire to control self-components and functions. Lacan's subject also disappears in the sense that human nature is not determined by a universal "inner nature" but by historical, social, and linguistic forces. Finally, Lacan's subject disappears in the sense that the psychoanalytic cure cannot be defined by a reintegration of the fragmented self-components. Yet Lacan's understanding of the subject, as composed of components and processes essentially divided and self-alienated, neither reduces, devalues, nor eliminates either the importance or phenomenal character of the subject.

Lacan's subject is perhaps best defined as the one who suffers. As a clinician, Lacan used his analysis of the subject not as a philosophical ground for ignoring unique human beings, but as a ground for under-standing the therapeutic action of psychoanalysis. In this sense, in terms of Lacan's commitment to psychoanalytic training, his commitment to the practice of analysis, and his commitment to the production of schol-arship, the subject is not simply "present," but central to the whole Lacanian enterprise.

Jacques Alain-Miller, comparing Lacan to Levi-Strauss, Barthes, Fou-cault, and Derrida, emphasizes this important but often neglected aspect of Lacan's work:

What did Levi-Strauss, Barthes, Foucault, and Derrida do for a living? They taught and they wrote. They gave classes. They were intellectuals. They were teachers. They were university people.

What did Lacan do during his lifetime? There is one answer. He saw pa-tients.[18]

Lacan's work shows a man constantly talking to people about the psy-choanalytic drama of the subject. Because Lacan found it important to understand the subject in terms of things apparently external to it, the subject can appear absent from his discussion, a sort of epiphenomenon animated by discourse. Such an assumption, however, is a misreading of Lacan. Lacan's subject is "de-centered," but this de-centered subject is the focus for his theoretical project. Lacan's analysis of discourse indi-cates his interest in two things: first, the subject's position in discourse, and second, those problems attending the analyst's attempt to use dis-course to re-position the subject.

In some respects Lacan's account of the subject follows the lines of a rhetorical analysis. Lacan is interested in figures of speech and how speech, creating systems of desire and identification, moves the subject. On the one hand, this analysis is highly theoretical: Lacan is fully engaged in all the conceptual resources formulated by poststructuralist thought. On the other hand, Lacan's analysis is highly practical. As an analyst Lacan confronted subjects who resisted, denied, and displaced linguistic effects. This forced him to formulate a description of a subject much more active and resistant than the subject imagined by poststruc-turalist thought.

We might best appreciate the relatively greater weight given to Lacan's subject by considering its potential for resistance. Poststructuralist the-ory posits the subject as a passive entity constituted by participation in social language. The idea of resistance questions this passivity and calls attention to a subject's unique ability to deny, dismiss, or deform social directives. Resistance implies agency, or an ability to counteract forces that in other contexts would successfully constitute subjects.

Paul Smith, a critic seeking to formulate a more adequate account of ideology, has critiqued the poststructuralist account of the subject in terms of its failure to explain resistance. "The stress, within current theorization, on the *subjection* of the subject," he says, "leaves little room to envisage the agent of a real and effective resistance."[19] Smith concedes that poststructuralist theory seems initially useful as a way to account for ideological operations in language. But in the final analysis, such an account oversimplifies the operations of ideology. "Marx's teleological 'real individual,' and left-wing post-structuralist's 'subject in process,' " Smith says, "are both less than adequate for the task of conceiving ideology and its subjects."[20] The problem, as Smith and others see it, is that if the subject is conceived (along the lines of Althusser) as a simple effect of ideology, a unified structure "called" into place by the interpellating force of language, then the subject has no resources for resisting ideology. If the subject is to resist the force of ideology (and it must if it wants to direct political change), then it must be something other than a *simple* effect of ideology. To develop a more complex account of both ideology and the subject, Smith turns to Lacan.

In *Discerning the Subject*, Smith describes the subject as an entity constructed by contradictory ideological interpellations. Subjects are formed by a disordering history, a "colligation of multifarious and multiform subject positions."[21] Describing the subject as both an entity always in process and an entity suffering conflict explains both the subject's constitution by ideology and the subject's potential for ideological resistance: The subject is formed by ideology, not in any unitary way, but through collections of differing ideological positions. "What is produced by ideological interpellation," Smith claims, "is contradiction."[22] The subject is thus constituted by ideology, but because no ideological position is ever absolute, the subject is always potentially able to resist (because of its inner "play" of various ideological configurations) an external univocal ideological force.

Smith's account of the subject's potential for resistance suggests a somewhat more cohesive subject than the one imagined by poststructuralism. Smith's subject is not a passive force completely animated by fluctuating currents of social discourse; it has a certain limited capacity for agency and resistance. Once agency and resistance are conceptualized as characteristics belonging to subjects, however, it is tempting to imagine the subject in traditional Freudian or "psychological" terms. The subject becomes certain "contained" characteristics. Smith, however, strongly resists this temptation. Agency, as he sees it, is only a temporary subject-effect resulting from a temporary subject position, and in addition, subject-structure is not stable: Discourse configurations are constantly leaking in and out. The subject has no permanent "inner" material and no boundary containing stable subject-characteristics.

Smith's account of the subject reflects an impressive theoretical synthesis of Althusser and Lacan. Smith agrees with Althusser that subjects are formed through ideological forces. But Smith also promotes Lacan's ideas in insisting that social discourse does not affect the subject in an immediate way. Social discourse is always mediated through unconscious structures.

Smith's account of the subject resembles Lacan's account in many ways. Lacan's subject, like Smith's, is characterized by conflict, has no "inner" unity, and has a porous "boundary." The Lacanian Other, in part a discourse structure, is always at the conflictual core of the subject. Lacan's subject thus is always most "outside" when it is most "inside." In addition to having an alien discourse structure at the center, Lacan's subject is also porous: discourse nodules and configurations are always leaking into the subject, producing various singular effects, and thus affecting subjectivity.

Smith's account of the subject resembles that of Lacan, but it also differs in important ways. Although deeply problematic, the metaphor of boundary describes Lacan's subject better than it describes Smith's. Lacan's subject, like Smith's, has a porous boundary, but Lacan's subject has more stability than the subject-in-process described by Smith. As a clinician, Lacan is very much concerned with something that used to be called individuality. Lacan discredits the term *individual* because it implies both traditional Freudian dogma and the unified self of ego-psychology. But Lacan is very much attentive to the singular and particular nature of the subject.

Lacan's account of the subject, because it describes a more "stable" subject than Smith's, better explains the particular tenacity of the subject's "resistance." Because the subject (as a discourse system) is very loosely "centered" around certain self-defining discourse patterns (Lacan, unlike Smith, emphasizes the subject's enormous capacity for repetition.), it resists other discourse patterns that generate conflict: It resists political influence, just as it resists psychoanalytic influence. Both forms of resistance show the subject's active attempt to counteract the manipulating effects of discourse. The subject, thus, is not just another discourse system subjected to the effects of discourse colligation. It is a discourse system with its own particular properties; it is a discourse system driven by particular subject-functions.

Lacan's subject is distinct and unique because, for Lacan, each subject has a singular configuration of subjectivity. In *Book II* of the Seminar Lacan speaks of analysis as a project through which "the subject discovers his truth, that is to say the signification taken on in his particular destiny by those givens which are peculiar to him and which one can call his lot."[23] The subject has a particular destiny, in part because the subject appropriates and employs language in a particular way. Lacan emphasizes that the job of the analyst is to listen carefully to the particular language of the subject. In the *Ecrits* he speaks of this language used by the subject in psychoanalysis as a "language that seizes desire at the very moment in which it is humanized."[24] This language, he says, "is absolutely particular to the subject."[25] This emphasis on the "absolutely particular" character of the subject's language and the "particular" character of the subject's destiny suggests that each subject has (in a loose sense anyway) properties that are somehow "proper to" or "contained" by it.

This absolute particularity of the subject's language is in part related to what rhetoricians call "style" or "voice." Subjects both appropriate and express discourse in their own unique way. More importantly for Lacan, this stylistic particularity of speech is related to various psychoanalytic phenomena—desire, repetition, resistance, trauma, and the symptom—that uniquely define and situate each subject. We should recognize that it is not simply that singular subjects have to some extent individualized discourse content in their conscious and unconscious, but that subjectivity is itself an individualized process of subject-functions that work on discourse. These unique subject-functions work on the content of social discourse and reproduce it in often strikingly deflected, mutilated, and oddly juxtaposed forms. These products then become material features of the social discourse to which other subjects respond.

Lacan insists that the early history of the subject (in part a history of discourse) stamps on the subject (especially in childhood) certain characteristic patterns that remain stable (though they play out their influence in various "registers") throughout later historical progression. Each subject, Lacan suggests, has unique features, constantly changing in their particularity, but nonetheless changing according to a pattern "proper to" or "contained" by the subject. The subject, Lacan says, has a "particular destiny" that is determined by "those givens which are peculiar to him." This fixed historical dimension of the subject helps explain the subject's potential for resistance because it explains the relatively fixed nature of the subject's "identity pattern" (its ideals and values).

While Lacan's subject exists in a state of self-division, it is important to see that this is not a simple state of self-division but a repetitive *pattern* of self-division. Analysts discover that a subject's identity pattern is not easy to change; it is not easy for discourse to "intervene" in the subject in such a way as to redirect behavior or redefine identity. Subjects seem to have vast resources for ideological and psychoanalytic resistance. In Smith's description of the subject, resistance seems to be a kind of semiotic play, an almost random expression of disunification. Lacan's psychoanalytic account of the subject suggests that resistance is more focused, determined, and motivated. Each subject has a particular style of resistance that expresses certain predictable patterns of repression and repetition.

Lacan's account of the subject's particular nature calls attention to a certain stability within self-structure that motivates resistance. To consider the full complexity of relations between resistance and the subject, we should consider two very different forms of resistance. One can, in the first instance, resist "bad" ideology. In the second instance, one can resist knowing that ideology is bad. Although closely related, these two instances are markedly different.

The first case (political resistance) seems to be motivated by knowledge and self-consciousness. One resists bad ideology because one knows (or believes) that the effects of such discourse cause suffering. Subjects, because of knowledge and self-consciousness, are able to intervene in the production of ideological effects and to displace or reveal those forces that usurp their well-being. Subjects know their own suffering and know how to act in order to reduce that suffering. The second case, subjects resisting knowledge that contradicts their self-understanding (resistance to analysis), seems almost exactly the opposite. Subjects do not act from knowledge; they resist knowledge. Subjects do not act from a self-consciousness of the cause of their own suffering; they act from a motivated lack of self-consciousness that hides the cause of their own suffering. This resistance, in effect, is motivated largely by repression. Repression is made possible by psychological forces that characterize the nature of human subjectivity.

We can easily imagine that the second case (the subject resisting knowledge that generates self-conflict) represents an action that human beings would not want to imitate or idealize. It represents a case where human beings, because of configurations in the structure of the subject, choose to continue suffering.

This situation, of course, is only too common. Because of certain relatively stable but precariously dominant values and identities, subjects are unable and unwilling to entertain other values and identities that question their identity. It is clear that Lacan sees analytic resistance in these terms. Repeatedly Lacan describes links between resistance and subject-structure. In *The Four Fundamental Concepts of Psycho-Analysis*, Lacan speaks of resistance, in rather classic Freudian terms, as related to the memory of trauma (a specific memory figuration "contained" by a specific subject). "Remembering," Lacan says in his description of resistance, "is gradually substituted for itself and approaches ever nearer to a sort of focus or centre, in which every event seems to be under an obligation to yield itself—precisely at that moment, we see manifest . . . —the resistance of the subject."[26] What we see here is a glimpse of the total structure of subject—history, trauma, repression—in terms of which resistance operates.

Resistance (in this case) is not simply a blocking force directed against something the subject does not know. It is a force employed by the subject (or an essential component of the subject) preventing the subject's knowing something that it knows or suspects, but wants (at some level) to repress. Because resistance is tied to self-image, repression, repetition, and trauma—essential dynamics of subjectivity—it has its own particular tenacity. In a real sense the life and death of the *subject* (as distinct from the biological individual) is at stake in its identity, at stake in its repression, and at stake in its resistance.

The resisting subject fails to see what is in front of it. Even when the missing knowledge is produced and placed in front of the subject, the consciousness of the subject seeks to deny, misinterpret, or dismiss such knowledge. One analyst in Lacan's Seminar describes resistance in the patient as something "he [she] was on the point of discovering, he [she] could have discovered [her-] himself, he [she] knows it without knowing that he [she] knows it, all he [she] has to do is take the trouble to look up and this damn idiot . . . doesn't do it."[27] Resistance of this sort, found in analysis, seems highly idiosyncratic and sharply linked to the particular character of each particular subject.

Political resistance, on the other hand, is different. It is motivated by knowledge and self-consciousness—not by repression and fear. In cases of political resistance, the subject, because of certain acknowledged and relatively stable self-interests, is able to use "knowledge" to resist ideologies that undermine its self-interest. As subjects learn knowledge, they can be motivated to change their actions, their beliefs, and even their identities.

Curiously, however, many Freudian and poststructuralist accounts of the subject insist that subjects cannot behave rationally. Subjects cannot use knowledge in a disinterested way because knowledge cannot be easily distinguished from subject-structure. To assume that there is a particular linguistic package, knowledge that is in some way different from another particular linguistic package, "the subject," is, they argue, fallacious.

Knowledge is seldom pure "data"; it is always itself implicated in— produced by—subject-functions. There is a certain limited agreement on this issue between Lacan and Althusser. Subjects and knowledge are not two absolutely different systems of discourse. The same forces that produce subjects also produce knowledge.

All systems of knowledge carry within them implications for subject-structure, so we might expect analytic resistance to operate in relation to all political knowledge, just as it operates in respect to psychoanalytic knowledge. Good Republicans, thus, would be forever destined to deny facts that render suspect their political philosophy. This suggests, in turn, that any resistance to ideology must always be prefigured in advance by a suitable subject-structure: Only those subjects constituted along patterns different from the ruling ideology could oppose the ruling ideology.

This extrapolation from theory, however, seems both pessimistic and inaccurate. It seems a mistake to argue that knowledge is always so intimately connected to subject-structure and repression. This would imply that knowledge could be received only in those cases when the recipient of the knowledge possessed a subject-structure congruent with the knowledge being transferred, and the truth of this claim does not seem supported by events we see taking place in the world.

It seems a mistake to claim that knowledge can never be easily transferred from one subject to another. Many institutions are founded precisely on the premise that such a universal and harmonious transferal can take place. Many kinds of knowledge—medicine, agriculture, metallurgy—seem easily transferred. There seem to be many cases where knowledge is received by differing sorts of people without resistance. There also seem to be cases where reformulation of political action is able to proceed relatively easily from the effects of similar knowledge.

These observations suggest that an understanding of resistance requires a more careful examination of the relation between knowledge and subject-structure. How is knowledge produced? What kind of "discourse element" is it? How is it "carried within" subjects? How is it related to subjectivity? How is it "passed" from one subject to another?

These questions return us to our introductory question: How exactly is discourse related to the subject of discourse? How is the particular discourse system we call the subject related to other discourse systems operating in society? What we need is not simply a better account of the relations between knowledge and the subject, but a better account of the relation between particular discourse systems in society and that other system—the subject.

Lacan offers this better account of the relations between discourse and the subject. Lacan explains both how subjects can resist ideology on the grounds of knowledge, and how subjects are also effects of social discourse. To grasp this in detail, we must appreciate the unique nature of Lacan's subject—its status as a particular discourse structure.

Lacan teaches that the subject is a unique, though self-divided, system differing in important respects from other discourse systems that situate, constitute, and intervene in it. In this respect Lacan is not a poststructuralist. Unlike the poststructuralist subject whose subjectivity is constantly operated by taking "positions" in response to social interaction, the Lacanian subject contains unique subject-driven mechanisms that both produce and feed on social discourse in quite unique and particular ways.

Lacan describes the subject as a system whose discourse inside is formed from taking in material from an outside field of discourse. This system (the subject) has a porous boundary that contains (in various layers of structure) the discourse that enters it. Poststructuralist accounts of the subject offer no distinctions between the various ways discourse can be contained. The subject is often imagined as a text or site where various strands of discourse have effects. Lacan's account of the subject, however, pays special attention to the *organization* of discourse within the subject. The particular organization of discourse within the subject produces the subject's uniqueness.

This uniqueness derives from two sources. In the first instance, both chance and the biological structure of the human organism determine what particular discourse configurations enter into the subject. Different subjects, as a result of the particular concrete state of personal history, contain different discourse matter. Lacan points out that "language is completely burdened with our history."[28] Each nation, each region, each city, each suburb is the site of particular overlays of dialect and inflection. A particular subject moves about in these geographical positions according to a particular itinerary and a particular configuration of attention and response. It thus encloses a particular concrete accumulation of speech.

In the second instance, subjects are unique not simply as a result of chance encounters with the social "other," but as a result of how their unique subjectivity directs itself toward, works on, and processes social interaction. As a boundary within which discourse components interact, the subject combines and modifies discourse components according to a variety of processes. These processes of discourse combination and modification are driven by various subject-functions—desire, repression, the Symbolic, the Imaginary, the Real—that are particular for each subject. These subject-functions produce the subject's *particularity* of discourse —a singular style of discourse that characterizes and organizes the subject.

In considering the particular discourse effects produced by a subject, we should keep in mind the important role played by the biological body. Lacan's subject is, in part, a rather unique discourse structure, because it is a discourse structure housed by a biological organism. Biology channels, and thus "operates," a variety of roles for discourse. It would be too lengthy to discuss all the roles shaped by biological processes, but I want to emphasize one rather significant role.

The discourse systems "contained" by Lacan's subject are "contained" by a biological body, thus contradictions between differing contained discourse subsystems have especially significant effects. A machine can contain contradiction as simply information about contradiction. In the human body, however, certain kinds of discourse contradiction can produce both conflict and suffering. For human subjects, suffering is not a "system" of discourse but a particularly discomforting mode of conflictual subjectivity often having biological consequences. Analysts can sometimes see the effects of discourse conflict (suffering) when certain body parts—the arm of the hysteric for example—are unable to function. The effects of discourse conflict can also be seen in speech itself, in hesitation, denial, inflated self-assertion. In politics we see the effects of discourse conflict in other ways: when one social group wages real or metaphorical war on another group. These conflicts exist not because discourse systems produce conflict, but because discourse systems housed by biological bodies produce conflict according to a logic peculiar to the nature of subjectivity.

Resistance is a particularly important concept in this context because the subject engages in both political and analytic resistance in order to "contain" biological conflict and suffering. Often, in fact, political resistance is hard to distinguish from analytic resistance. But when subjects are successfully engaged in political resistance, the "containment" of suffering maps out a course of thought and action that provides a real solution to human suffering. Harmful sources of power are contained by successful political action. Psychoanalysis, like political action, can of course also provide an effective containment of suffering (a real solution to human suffering). The resistance to psychoanalysis, on the other hand, is a form of negative containment. When subjects in analysis are unwilling to face the truth of their own subjectivity, containment maps out a course of thought and action that has negative effects. Containment becomes a strategy of repression and thus less a satisfactory *solution* to a problem of suffering and more a *source* of suffering resulting from the repression of conflictual knowledge.

This rather complex relationship between political resistance/containment and psychoanalytic resistance/containment has implications for understanding ideology. An ideology would be most powerful, not through its ability to produce unitary meaning, but through its ability to manage repression and thus contain conflict. Ideologies, in short, are able to make suffering seem desirable because they have strategies for generating analytic resistance to knowledge. Ideologies work precisely by making undesirable conditions seem worthwhile, pleasant, or unavoidable. The power of an ideology thus must lie in its ability to make certain modes of uncomfortable and conflictual subjectivity seem either desirable or unavoidable.

If ideologies do not exclude certain packages of knowledge and prescribe certain modes of suffering as desirable "containments" for conflict, they fail to control the ruptures within self-structure and thus fail to provide directives for social organization. Jameson, of course, insists on the importance of political containment in his account of the political unconscious, but fails to grasp containment in relation to those complex modes of resistance observed by analysts—unique "unconscious processes" and "blockages." Rather than seeking to understand the political implications of these modes of subjectivity, Jameson wants to dismiss them and to criticize Lacan's interest in them. In his haste to dismiss the particularity of the subject, Jameson fails to grasp the psychoanalytically complex nature of ideology. He fails to see how every political map for containment requires a psychoanalytic critique (an examination of what psychoanalytic knowledge has been repressed), just as every psychoanalytic map of containment requires a political critique (an examination of what political knowledge has been repressed).

I suggested earlier that part of Lacan's genius as a theorist lay in his ability to think beyond the limitations of both Freudian and poststructuralist conceptions of the subject. I argued that Lacan is able to explain both how subjects can resist ideology on the grounds of knowledge, and also how they are socially constituted by knowledge. To understand this apparent contradiction, we must review what it means for Lacan's subject to contain discourse.

Lacan argues that subject can take different "positions" in respect to its reception of discourse. Depending on its mode of reception, discourse can be contained by the subject in at least two very different ways. Discourse can be present in memory as a rather free-floating and inconsequential thing. This discourse "package" does not affect other discourse contents within the self-system; it is simply a unit of memory. In this context, discourse plays no role in the constitution of the self; discourse is simply heard speech that may suffer any number of fates. It may be remembered longer, or it may be forgotten. In being forgotten, however, it is not repressed; it is simply something no longer available for conscious consideration and has no apparent effect on the subject.

When discourse has the most important effects on the subject, it is not simply something remembered longer; it is something that works to organize or structure subject-components. The particularity of discourse, in this case, is not simply something *contained* by the self; it is something that in some sense *structures* the self. Discourse interacts with subject-components, giving them a particular form and consequence. In analysis, for example, an overly harsh superego can sometimes be made more mild by discourse that reveals its origin and operation. In this case both the experience and the general nature of the subject are changed as self-components responding to discourse begin to work in new ways. Overly critical people cannot only learn that it is in their own best interest to be less critical, they can discover inner resources for changing their behavior. The case here is not one where only one self-component, the superego, changes. Instead, change is facilitated as the ego, a synthesizing agent for self-components, "processes" discourse and "learns" to respond differently to the insistence of the unconscious.

Lacan describes the ego as a system that contains "a whole organization of certainties, beliefs, of coordinates, of references."[29] The ego thus contains, in various ways and in various "packages," knowledge. This object called knowledge, however, exists in many different states. Some knowledge packages, which are an important part of the *subject*, are prepackaged, preformed by external events, or by *social* interaction. It is easy to see the particularly powerful ideological force of these components. The particular content of these components is always already determined before the birth of the subject. The subject can do nothing other than largely internalize, and thus in some manner *be*, some particular manifestation of this discourse system.

Paul Smith cogently points out, however, that Lacan's subject is structured by and on self-division, and this means the subject can never purely be one thing. The subject is never *equivalent* to a particular organization of knowledge. The subject is a system *operated by* many internal agencies and *structured in terms of* various sublevels of organization. All of these components form a system, but the components of this system are never fully synthesized or harmonized. In most cases it is difficult to know if a "discourse component" of the self is best imagined as something like a paragraph held in memory, an emotional affect stimulated by remembered discourse, or as an agency constructed by a synthesis of abiding emotional affects.

Knowledge can be contained in different ways and in different "layers" within the subject. Different kinds of discourse conflicts within the subject can reflect the different ways discourse is contained by the *subject*. The conscious and the unconscious, for example, can contain different kinds of knowledge that can lead to conflict. Although some cases of contradiction can be contained by the subject without apparent conflict, other contradictions produce significant conflict, that is, suffering. This conflict is especially important because in certain ways this conflict rather precisely *is* the subject. Lacan describes the subject's *singularity* as an expression of the *symptom* produced by the subject's unconscious *conflict*.

This relationship between the subject's singularity and the conflict expressed by the subject is important. The presence of conflict within the subject makes it possible for the subject to "contain" discourse material that is not a simple reflection of the social discourse systems that "position" the subject. Conflict, in short, contributes to the production of original discourse. Many subject-functions can contribute to this originality. First, discourse brought in to the self-system is often filtered and selectively internalized and personally organized as a result of unconscious functions of repression and desire attending to external discourse. Second, as different discourse systems within the subject compete to operate the subject, conflict is generated. This conflict plays a role in a multitude of discourse deflections noted by analysts in the speech of patients: substitution, fetishism, parapraxis, symptomatic associations. As these functions produce uniquely juxtaposed discourse structures, they produce original meaning effects that can have social and personal consequences. Additionally, Lacan's subject can generate original discourse as a result of its patterned exclusion of the real. As this structured lack interacts with established social discourse patterns, it generates conflict and thus discourse.

We should acknowledge, as well, that subjects do not simply take in knowledge, they produce it. In rare moments subjects, in order to avoid suffering, construct knowledge about the cause of their conflict and suffering. This knowledge, always deeply implicated in the experience of conflict, can be both political and psychoanalytic. All these patterns of conflict and many others can produce not only unique discourse, but also lead to the formation within the subject of discourse components that do not mirror existing social and ideological structures. These new discourse structures, which can help define the subject, are new structures unique to the subject produced by the symptomatic nature of the subject interacting with the material of social discourse. Many subject-components begin as internalized nodules of social discourse and later become uniquely configured and relatively stable structures within a particular subject. Thus whereas it is true that the "boundaries" of subjects contain some structures that merely reflect discourse systems external to the subject, it is also true that subject "boundaries" contain elements—both discourse and subject-functions—unique to a particular subject. These elements are often not shared or even understood between subjects except through the psychoanalytic experience, but they have important effects. They have been produced by unique relationships of meaning within the subject, and they produce new meanings for both the subject and others.[30]

For example, when trauma (as Lacan describes it) contributes to the erasure of the real and the institution of the *object petit a*, this event is particularly configured within each singular subject. It is an effect of the particular personal history and linguistic history of the subject. This event influences the unique discourse of the subject and contributes to a singular rather than a common discourse pattern that defines the subject and its symptom. When the subject comes to the analyst with a symptom, analysis requires recognition of what Lacan calls the "singularity of a case."[31] Through analysis patients come to understand the effects of the singular nature of their speech and thus gain access to a new speech that represents and in some measure changes their nature.

Lacan's theory of the singular subject and his understanding of the role of conflict in the construction of the subject help explain the nature of literary rhetoric. The rhetorical force of any argument can be amplified by *originality* and *repetition*.

Literature can be original because it is often, as analysts claim, the *symptom* of a singular subject. It is a singular expression because it speaks to and speaks of singular narcissistic conflict, those forces closest to the substance and image of a particularly configured subjectivity. It may be the case, for example, that texts expressing the symptoms of subjectivity, rather than a simple fantasy of coherence, hold the strongest rhetorical power. Such texts are most successful in shifting libidinal investments, though they are perhaps least able to control the libidinal investments they release. It seems to me that some novels are like the subjects imagined by poststructuralists. They are simple collections of discourse. From the perspective of both the author and the reader, these simple discourse collections show little sign of conflict or conflictual libidinal organization. They simply reflect a principle of random discourse organization.

Conflictual texts churn the disordered content, the libidinal conflicts, and the divided organizations of self-systems to produce the experience of conflict. Such texts are the origins of style and have the style of originality. This originality is efficacious for rhetoric. It is usually easy for subjects to reject the persuasive appeal of arguments they have heard before. Our ego-systems have already developed discourse to counter such appeals. We need not involve ourselves in the complexity of such arguments. Original discourse is a different matter. In our attempts to reject it, we may get "involved" in its complexity, and this involvement is always a risk.

If the rhetoric of literature is original, like the subject, it is also repetitive, like the subject. The rhetoric of literature does not often employ the simple repetitions of a Pepsi lyric. But, like the subject, literary works keep coming back to knots of conflict. Like the traumatic memories and dreams of the soldiers that Freud considered in his ponderings on the death instinct, authors and readers keep coming back to the scene of texts. It is hard not to see in these returns and repetitions the drive to mastery. D. H. Lawrence observes: "One sheds one['s] illnesses in books, repeats and presents again one's emotions to be master of them."[32]

What forces authors to keep coming back to completed but "unfinished" manuscripts? What pushes authors, in their revisions, to "get things right?"[33] What kind of control does the author look for? What kind of control do critics look for when they also want to "get it right"? What is right? What is the experience of control and possession that signifies "right"?

Literature can be a highly rhetorical mode of discourse because it drives readers to make sense of and master unfinished business; it prompts us to resolve conflict and to see conflict in overly simple resolutions. The need to master conflict is not simply an intellectual entertainment; it is a fundamental need of the self. It is a narcissistic need. There are many ways to talk about how narcissistic need operates in human speech. In the course of this book I have tried to analyze and give examples of this need operating in language. At the end of a book, however, one needs to generalize; of all the generalizations I have seen, I like Lacan's formulation best: "What insists on being satisfied can only be satisfied in recognition. The end of the symbolic process is that non-being come to be, because it has spoken."[34] In writing, as in speaking, it is seldom the case that nothing more needs to be said. But we sometimes sense, with some relief, that "non-being" has "come to be, because it has spoken." Writers come to feel that they have "gotten it right." No one ever has the last word on a subject, but we all require some sense of completion as a prompt for abandoning any project of discussion or analysis.

Notes

1. Jameson, *The Political Unconscious*, 153.
2. Eve Tavor Bannet, *Structuralism and the Logic of Dissent* (Urbana: University of Illinois Press, 1989), 14.
3. Jacques Lacan, *The Seminar of Jacques Lacan: Books I and II*, ed. Jacques-Alain Miller (New York: Norton, 1988), book II, 291.
4. Ibid., 286.
5. Ibid., 287.
6. Ibid.
7. Ibid.
8. Ibid.
9. Ibid., 287–89.
10. Ibid., book II, 307–8.
11. Ibid., book I, 314.
12. Ibid., 1.
13. Bannet, *Structuralism and the Logic of Dissent*, 20.
14. Ibid., 21.
15. Culler, "In Pursuit of Signs," 104.
16. Diane Macdonell, *Theories of Discourse* (Oxford: Basil Blackwell, 1986), 42.
17. Lacan, *The Seminar*, book II, 53, 54.
18. Jacques-Alain Miller, "How Psychoanalysis Cures According to Lacan," *Newsletter of the Freudian Field* 1 (1987): 6.
19. Smith, *Discerning the Subject*, 39.
20. Ibid., 41.
21. Ibid., 32.
22. Ibid., 37.
23. Lacan, *The Seminar*, 326.
24. Lacan, *Ecrits*, 81.
25. Ibid.

26. Jacques Lacan, *The Four Fundamental Concepts of Psycho-Analysis*, ed. Jacques-Alain Miller (New York: Norton, 1978), 51.

27. Lacan, *The Seminar*, book I, 26.

28. Ibid., book II, 285.

29. Ibid., book I, 23.

30. Ibid., book I, 12.

31. Ibid.

32. D. H. Lawrence, *The Letters of D. H. Lawrence*, Vol. 2, *1913–1916*, ed. George J. Zytaruk and James T. Boulton (Cambridge: Cambridge University Press, 1979–84),90; quoted in Jeffrey Berman, *Diaries to an English Professor* (New York: New York University Press, in press).

33. I would like to thank Geoffrey Harpham for posing these questions for me.

34. Lacan, *The Seminar*, book II, 308.

SEVEN

Conclusion: What Do We Do with Rhetorical Criticism?

This book has employed psychoanalytic theory to explain the complex experiential effects, the conflictual rhetoric, of literary texts. But if *rhetoric* is really the central term, the umbrella word, then rhetorical criticism must both encompass and go beyond traditional psychoanalytic concerns. Good rhetoric, like effective psychoanalysis, is a response to suffering, and social formations are as likely to make us suffer as personal history. Good rhetoric must be concerned as much with politics and social history as with the psychological battles of the inner self.

Rhetorical criticism must explore those mediating verbal structures that are the textual interface between the inner world of the self and the outer world of politics. Rhetorical criticism should urge us to examine our resistance to history and to theory, just as it should urge us to examine each subject's singular resistance.[1] When successful, rhetorical criticism will help us to grasp how the inner world of the self is structured like the outer world of society; conversely, it will help us appreciate how the inner world is not structured like the outer world. Through this improved understanding we should be in a better position to grasp how conflicts in the outer world both reflect and draw energy from conflicts in the inner world. We must, in short, see a dialogue between the dialectical processes of social transformation and the psychological processes of self-transformation.

The concept of transference promises to be a conceptual tool for bridging the gap between rhetorical interests and psychoanalytic interests. In its simplest sense, it refers to the strategy employed by the analyst to effect changes in the speaking subject. Transference, as it was discovered by Freud, marks the discovery of a particularly effective rhetorical use of language. It is an effective device for rhetoric because it mobilizes speech to be used, not merely as a mask for a self, but as a verbal externalization of the self's own inner structure. When analysis engages transference, speech becomes libidinally charged. Pauses are signifying events; each word can become the focus of intensive care and attention. When transference is successful, words reflect and deflect the essential form of the self. When analysis is successful, changes in acting follow changes in speaking.

Recent research shows growing recognition of the importance of transference and rhetoric for literary study. Meredith Skura's *The Literary Use of the Psychoanalytic Process* contains a chapter on "Literature as Transference: Rhetorical Function."[2] Mark Bracher and I argue that reading can transform the self in a manner similar to workings of transference in analysis.[3] Peter Brooks's *Reading for the Plot* contains a chapter on "Narrative Transaction and Transference"; his essay "The Idea of a Psychoanalytic Literary Criticism," further develops the idea of transference as the most promising concept for a more fruitful form of a new criticism that would be both psychoanalytic and rhetorical.[4]

Brooks believes that a new form of rhetorical and psychoanalytic criticism based on an understanding of the transferential effects of reading can remedy the faults of contemporary rhetorical criticism. The more recent critical methodologies, Brooks says,

too often remain content with formal operations, simply bracketing the human realm from which psychoanalysis derives. Given its project and its strategies, such rhetorical/deconstructive criticism usually stays within the linguistic realm. It is not willing to make the crossover between rhetoric and reference.[5]

Like Brooks, I believe that a more flexible style of literary criticism needs to be both human and referential, both rhetorical and textual, both psychoanalytic and political. Contemporary ideological criticism offers some of this change. It is both human and referential. But it is too often impersonal. The current tendency of ideological criticism to minimize the psychoanalytic complexity of the subject is not only shortsighted; it is self-defeating.

Brooks emphasizes that the rhetoric of the text is very much a function of its personal transference effects. The transferential model, Brooks explains

illuminates the difficult and productive encounter of the speaker and the listener, the text and the reader, and how their exchange takes place in an "artificial" space—a symbolic and semiotic medium—that is nonetheless the place of real investments of desire from both sides of the dialogue. The transference actualizes the past in symbolic form so that it can be repeated, replayed, worked through to another outcome. The result is, in the ideal case, to bring us back to actuality, that is, to a revised version of our stories.[6]

Brooks's discussion of transference helps us understand how literature rhetorically reformulates emotion. Transference operates as "affects from the past become invested in the present."[7] The concept of transference explains why the projections we make in response to a text are not random responses but libidinally charged material reflecting the libidinally charged components of self-structure. Strong knots of emotional organization project themselves on to the text in our response to it. The reader's affects from the past thus appear in the semiotic medium of the text.

As these affects of the past appear in relation to the symbolic and semiotic medium of the text, they can be manipulated. Semiotic structures that are the sites of investments of desire can become, through the complex nature of textual and intertextual interaction, sites for the disinvestments of desire. As Brooks explains, "It is precisely . . . in the symbolic mode that the past and its ghosts may be destroyed, or laid to rest."[8] When we more clearly see the ghosts of the past as ideological ghosts intertwined with personal ghosts repeating themselves in the "transference exchanges" of the text, we will recover the broader rhetorical reach of literary response—a history of literature as site of transferential exchanges and interchanges.

In this book I have focused more on the elements of transference—projection, resistance, idealization—than on the concept of transference. I have done this because transference, as it operates in psychoanalytic practice, differs in important ways from the transference of the reading process. Certainly reading, like analysis, prompts transference projections. The *examination* of the traumas of the past, as they are discovered by the analysand's projecting of meanings onto the analyst, however, is not the material of reading, as they are the material of psychoanalysis. Texts draw us into transference relationships because we become attached to texts much as we become attached to people.[9] But if we respond to texts like we respond to analysts and project the themes of our past on them, the texts do not respond to us like analysts. Literature offers more opportunity for pleasurable projection and less clearly defined resistance to projection. There is no significant other in the text directing questions toward the reader's past or toward the reader's shield of resistance.

Stephen Mitchell points out:

One of the great, generally unacknowledged truths about analytic technique is that it is developed on a trial and error basis, personally designed in the interaction with each individual analysand. With some analysands, one can question illusions from the start; with others this is not possible. There is no way to know beforehand. One tests out different approaches: puzzlement, teasing, probing, intellectual challenge, raised eyebrow (literally and figuratively), until one finds which among the analyst's many voices and positions enables that particular analysand to feel both joined and nudged toward deeper understanding.[10]

Literature does not respond to our projections. It dumbly tells us a story while we project our experience on to it. What we do with literature and our transference response is very much dependent on us.

In classes, perhaps, teachers practice empathic responses to the resistances of classes, learning which voices and positions can be used in "joining and nudging students toward deeper understanding." Indeed, it may be that the rhetorical process of literary response is made best use of in classrooms where teachers function, not as analysts, but as facilitators for insight. Jeffrey Berman's forthcoming *Diaries to an English Professor* demonstrates how literary study combined with diary entry can provide a powerful impetus for insight and self-development.[11] A thorough rhetoric of literature should help us to realize that literary theory must be concerned with pedagogy as much as with textuality. It is past time for scholars to realize that, although we idealize texts, we spend much of our time talking about texts to people. The things we say about texts are often grounded in prior meanings we establish when talking to people.

Classrooms make the best use of the transference effects of literary response, and a psychoanalytic-based rhetorical criticism will help us to understand these effects. But to understand what happens in a classroom we must also understand what happens to individual readers lost, and on their own, in books. In this space, pleasure is paramount and the only resistance to the subject is self-resistance. The idea that literature offers the self plentiful opportunities for fantasy and pleasurable projections of identity confirmation has been carefully documented by Norman Holland.[12] If I distinguish my reading model from Holland's on the basis of my understanding of the text's resistance to reading, I should stress the importance of Holland's insights and my indebtedness to him. Holland insists on the importance of the individual subjectivity of the reader in the reading process, and he effectively documents how projection operates to shape private reading experience.

Holland's discussion of the pleasure principle explains many facets of the reading experience. Reading develops within an envelope of narcissistic security and allows the ego to play with representation because the space of reading offers a bubble of security that can keep us well distanced from the threats of reality. It is *precisely* because the pleasure principle is so secure in reading that reading can offer a site where consciousness can be tricked into seeing and feeling things it might otherwise dismiss or avoid.

Much has been made of the resistances to reading and the resistances to theory, but a case needs to be made, as well, for the pleasure of resistance. The pleasures of reading enable us to entertain perceptions, thoughts, and identifications we quickly turn from in real life. The conflicts of literature may seem merely imaginary, so the ego is able to give them a perceptual and enjoyable concreteness often too threatening to be imagined in real life. We are invited to position ourselves as imagined masters of this conflict. What we call "good" literature seems to designate literary works that contain strategies that multiply and complicate the pleasures of such a response.

The pleasures of reading put into motion feelings and values normally kept rigidly protected by the self-system, placing them in pleasurable tension and conflict through literary form. Literary texts help us to indulge, elaborate, and make fully conscious fantasies we might otherwise rigidly censor. They also help us to feel what we might otherwise repress, and to think what we might otherwise deny or avoid. But it is not simply that reading can help us see what we might otherwise miss. The new elements of perception and experience generated by reading become introduced within structures of fantasy, idealization, and reality and can contribute to changes within the entire self-system. Within the pleasurable and narcissistic space of reading, relationships between conflictual themes can be fluid and synthetically productive of transformative patterns of perception, reflection, and thought.

Consider the principles of resistance at work in reading in terms of the split nature of the subject. We are all split subjects, and we are split by means of the verbal structures that constitute us as subjects. If we are Freudians we can say we are split from our desires; if we are Lacanians we can say we are split from our essential being. Whatever psychoanalytic theory of the subject we entertain, the self does not appear to be at one with its heart's desire.

This situation where the self is not at one with itself is the condition of the power of literature. It is a cliché to say that literature *moves* us. But it is a cliché that we too often oversimplify. If literature moves us, it is because it enables us to pass through and circulate about the distances that normally separate our various divided and unsynthesized models of identity and desire. In effect, literature moves us from one desire and identification to another, often with a momentum that makes us dizzy. In this manner literature gives us a greater range of feeling and perception. It encourages us to experience through it that which we often are unable to experience without it. I would like to think that literature encourages us, in Blake's words, to embrace "contraries," or to feel the excitement and tension of conflict.[13] Literary conflict is never simply a battle between good guys and bad guys, a rhetoric with one cheering section and one fully embraced value position. Literary conflict is productive because there is no clear winner in the conflict. Literature offers both a perspective on and a desire for both those mutually incompatible forms of subjectivity in conflict. Thus the conflicts and resistances of literature (at least those we want to entertain and be entertained by) are always in some way promoting a desire for the synthesis of two apparently irreconcilable ideas.

Resistance can frustrate us, but it can also give us pleasure. If we sense that a text is pure fantasy, we are often inclined to dismiss it. It does not interest us; it does not seriously entertain us. The text presents us with nothing to master and offers us none of the pleasures of mastery. The psychoanalytics of mastery, however, is best imagined as an eternally interminable, unfinished program. Through my rhetorical reading of *Heart of Darkness,* I have tried to make two points. First, in being overtly concerned with questions of value, the work overtly seeks to idealize. It seeks to accurately describe a world of moral confusion, but also to move beyond this confusion to formulate ethical principles. Second, though confusing, this specific text is recognized within literary culture as a "strong" text. This means precisely that this text prompts readers to respond to it. The text produces a great deal of criticism, which expresses widely diverging styles of idealization. The text thus seems emphatically able to encourage idealization, but oddly unable to control the form of the idealization it engenders.

In my attempt to make sense of this situation, I suggest that this text, like many similar ones, mobilizes a fluidity of narcissistic ambitions. If idealization is funded by narcissistic energy, then texts must release and rebind the narcissistic energy to promote idealization. Literary rhetoric depends on its ability to release libidinal narcissistic energy. But because this release is so central to the literary experience, literary texts become self-defeating if they seek to rigidly control libido and insist on a didactic rhetoric of mastery. Literary texts offer readers many positions of mastery; but they resist any wholesale narcissistic investment in such totalizing positions of mastery.

In reading *Heart of Darkness* I have sought to describe the narcissistic structure of the author and the narcissistic structure of a reader. An understanding of narcissism helps bridge the gap between the apparent pleasures of reading and the changes in self-awareness these pleasures enable. Initially this seems to be another paradox. Narcissism appears to be a force most dedicated to defending a static self-structure. However, as Kohut and Kernberg show us, narcissism is an energy that—in driving the self to exist more fully in order to master all situations—is also involved with self-change. And the self's imaginative potential for change is protean. Narcissism can keep self-boundaries fluid, encouraging us to identify with people we want to be like, with people we do not fully understand, with situations that are exotic and inexplicable. Narcissism explains the mechanisms and pleasures of self-conflict and our curiously obsessive investments in often distant social conflict.

As we appreciate the narcissistic forces at work in textual response, we can examine relationships between narcissism and literary theory. It seems that the authority of theory is always a form of narcissism. No theory ever offers enough evidence to justify its policing of thought and imagination. We choose theories not because they are true, but because we become caught within their imagined conflicts; we become absorbed by their ability to resolve conflicts according to prescribed methods. We find a compelling resonance between the objects we want to believe and the things theories describe. We are drawn toward a vision of mastery that theories offer.

I would hope good theories offer us the subtle rewards of more complex forms of narcissism. Good theories discipline us as we use them. Good theories purge us of our more superfluous desires and draw us closer toward finer discriminations and more adequate models of understanding and insight. Our narcissistic conflicts with theories contribute to their rhetoric of truth effects. These effects, however, can be achieved only when there is some form of resistance to narcissistic needs. Narcissistic needs that are immediately fulfilled by some *purely* imaginative fantasy offer little impetus for growth and development. Good theories, like good readings, always require an artful sense of resistance.

Literary professionals find ample scope for introducing resistance into literary response. As interpretation becomes a "discipline," readers adopt a systematic theoretical perspective and are encouraged to subordinate purely personal responses to one or more codes of public intelligibility. A rigorous pursuit of experienced truth effects would thus, within its own terms, justify any theoretical orientation. A reader's imagining of an author, for example, may be a projection of human qualities onto a signifier "author," but it is also an introduction of a force of resistance and a principle of authority into the reading process. With the introduction of an author, readers want to know if they have gotten the "message" of the text "right."

Both deconstruction and reader-response theory have largely discredited the notion of the author, as well as the notion of character. But such a dismissal, although true in an important sense, is also beside the point. Characters and authors are not people, but we often perceive them according to our own internal structures that represent people for us. If the benefits of reading are gained by resistances, gained by our projections of a structured other into to the semiotics of a text, notions of an author and character can produce useful reading discoveries.

One might easily argue that some notion of authority is essential for any discipline of reading. It would be worthwhile to consider all the various "authorities" introduced into interpretation theory—New Criticism, phenomenology, structuralism, poststructuralism, New Historicism, Freudian theory, Marxist theory—and reflect on how they are employed often quite eclectically according to the personal interests of readers. These employments reward reading and convert textuality into diverse but particular forms of experience. They are thus all potentially useful gambits for introducing play into the habitual codes of interpretation.

We will never know what form of authority to adopt as the master code of resistance. But this is not really a problem. The use of theory, like the use of a text, requires its own resistance, its own opposition. Just as we tend to perform rather limited theoretical readings of texts, we perform limited literary readings of theories, projecting on them our past, our characteristic fears, and our aspirations. We will never be able to pick a master code of resistance. Nor is it necessary. We only need to continue to use theories that reward us and resist theories that do not through productive discourse.

These observations lead me to certain principles that may be self-evident. First, the most important consequence of reading is a pragmatics of self-reflexivity. This would seem fairly simple; we read in order to learn something that will be important to us. We do not read to learn a correct interpretation of a text. Shoshana Felman usefully explains that the Lacanian and "new Freudian model of reflexivity differs from the traditional humanistic mode of reflexivity, from the classical psychological and philosophical epistemology of self-reflection."[14] Felman describes this model as

a reflexivity whose self-reference, whose process of turning back upon itself, is not based on a symmetry but on asymmetry; asymmetry between the self departed from and the self returned to; asymmetry between the turn and the return; a reflexivity, therefore, which, passing through the Other, returns to itself without quite being able to rejoin itself; a reflexivity which is thus untotalizable, that is irreducibly dialogic, and in which what is returned to the self from the Other is, paradoxically, the ignorance or the forgetfulness of its own message; a reflexivity, therefore, which is a new mode of cognition or information gathering whereby ignorance itself becomes structurally informative.[15]

Felman points out that this model of reflexivity requires an additional model of knowledge. "Such knowledge," she says, "cannot be acquired (or possessed) once and for all; each case, each text, has its own specific, singular symbolic functioning and requires a different interpretation." I am inclined to add that this knowledge is even more unstable than Felman claims. It is not simply that each text "has its own specific, singular symbolic functioning and requires a different interpretation"; it is also the case that each context of teaching a text requires the production of a new knowledge about it. This leads me to my second claim: When we learn to teach text we must also learn forms for teaching it most appropriate for the context in question. Just as each analyst must respond to a patient's resistance with a trial-and-error experimentation with response, each teacher must engage in similar strategies.

Rhetorical criticism, by paying more attention to who we teach, will better explain what we teach, when we think we are teaching a text. We cannot afford to simply assume that when we teach the ideological structures of a text we are drawing attention to structures that have had real affects on readers. We cannot afford to simply assume that, even when these structures do affect readers, our discussion of such structures will structure for others a recognition of the social and political forces that affect their lives.

We can seldom know in advance how to best teach a text, but we gain experience about how to adapt to different teaching conditions. We must approach texts in ways to stimulate enthusiasm and insight differently, depending on whether the context of our study is an undergraduate class, a graduate class, or the privacy of our own study. Even as we follow certain principles in our teaching context, we also often modify those principles as we find students, or simply ourselves, responding to the particularity of discourse that the textual engagement produces. As a teacher I am constantly astonished at how often a fully coherent (and for a moment), totally convincing interpretation of a text can be produced on the basis of a strong mood that is expressed in the first five minutes of class discussion.

Mood creates for a moment a "real" interpretive ground that all questions about the text work to answer. I would imagine, however, that mood too often produces an authoritative ground for interpretive tasks. Literature may work best when it responds to the force fields of mood. But we should keep in mind that beyond mood and the vagaries of individual subjectivity, the rhetoric of interpretation must always engage another larger interpretive concern. If mood is important, we must understand the larger causes of mood. We will understand these many causes when we pay attention to issues that sometimes seem well outside the text. We have learned from Lacan and Freud, however, that those things that seem most outside the text are often the very things at the center of the text. A rhetoric of the literary will be most useful when we more fully grasp how the rhetoric of interpretation is always implicated in an often unacknowledged rhetoric we all share, which is always at the center of a text—the rhetoric of the "good" person and the "good" society. Of course part of the nature of rhetoric requires that the meaning of these words and the relationships among them be fiercely contested.

Notes

1. Robert Con Davis has collected an interesting set of essays about resistance to teaching in *College English* 49, no. 6/7 (1987).
2. Skura, *The Literary Use of the Psychoanalytic Process*, 171–99.
3. Marshall W. Alcorn, Jr., and Mark Bracher, "Literature, Psychoanalysis, and the Re-Formation of the Self: A New Direction for Reader Response Theory," *PMLA* 100 (1985): 342–54.
4. Brooks, *Reading for the Plot;* and Brooks, "The Idea of a Psychoanalytic Literary Criticism," 341.
5. Brooks, *Reading for the Plot,* 337.
6. Ibid., 344.
7. Ibid., 341.
8. Ibid., 345.
9. I would like to thank Jeffrey Berman for pointing out some of these relations to me.
10. Mitchell, *Relational Concepts in Psychoanalysis,* 212.
11. Berman, *Diaries to an English Professor.*
12. Holland, *Five Readers Reading.*
13. William Blake, *Selected Poems,* ed. P. H. Butler (London: J. M. Dent, 1991), 52.
14. Shoshana Felman, *Jacques Lacan: The Adventure of Insight* (Cambridge: Harvard University Press, 1987), 61.
15. Ibid., 60.

Bibliography

Achebe, Chinua. "An Image of Africa: Racism in Conrad's Heart of Darkness." *Massachusetts Review* 18 (1977): 782–94.

Alcorn, Marshall W., Jr., and Mark Bracher. "Literature, Psychoanalysis, and the Re-Formation of the Self: A New Direction for Reader Response Theory." *PMLA* 100 (1985): 342–54.

———. "Loss and Figuration: Paradigms of Constructive and Deconstructive Mourning." *Centennial Review* 35 (1991): 501–18.

Althusser, Louis. *Lenin and Philosophy.* New York: Monthly Review Press, 1971.

Aristotle. *Rhetoric.* In *The Basic Works of Aristotle*, edited by Richard McKeon. New York: Random House, 1941.

Bain, Carl E., Jerome Beatty, and J. Paul Hunter, eds. *The Norton Introduction to Literature*, 4th ed. New York: Norton, 1986.

Baldwin, James. "Sonny's Blues." In *Going to Meet the Man.* New York: Doubleday, 1948. Reprinted in *Norton Introduction to Literature*, 5th ed., ed. Carl E. Bain, Jerome Beatty, and J. Paul Hunter. New York: Norton, 1991.

Bannet, Eve Tavor. *Structuralism and the Logic of Dissent.* Urbana: University of Illinois Press, 1989.

Barrett, Harold. *Rhetoric and Civility.* New York: State University of New York Press, 1991.

Barthes, Roland. *Image, Music, Text.* New York: Hill, 1977.

Barzilai, Shuli. "Borders of Language: Kristeva's Critique of Lacan." *PMLA* 106 (1991): 294–305.

Baumlin, James S., and Tita French Baumlin. "Psyche/Logos: Mapping the Terrains of Mind and Rhetoric." *College English* 3 (1989): 245–61.

Beach, Joseph Warren. "Impressionism: Conrad." In *The Twentieth Century Novelists: Studies in Techniques*, 337–65. New York: Appleton-Century.

Belsey, Catherine. *Critical Practice.* London: Routledge, 1980.

Bergmann, Martin S. "The Legend of Narcissus." *American Imago* 41 (1984): 389–411.

Berman, Jeffrey. *Joseph Conrad: Writing as Rescue.* New York: Astra Books, 1977.

Berman, Jeffrey. *Diaries to an English Professor.* New York: New York University Press, in press.

———. *Narcissism and the Novel.* New York: New York University Press, 1990.

———. "Writing as Rescue: Conrad's Escape from the Heart of Darkness." *Literature and Psychology* 25 (1975): 65–78.

Bleich, David. "Intersubjective Reading." *NLH* 17 (1986): 412

———. *Subjective Criticism.* Baltimore: Johns Hopkins University Press, 1978.

Bonney, William. *Thorns and Arabesques: Contexts for Conrad's Fiction.* Baltimore: Johns Hopkins University Press, 1980.

Borman, Ernest B. *Discussion and Group Methods: Theory and Practice.* New York: Harper & Row, 1975.

Bowie, Malcolm. *Lacan.* Cambridge: Harvard University Press, 1991.

Bracher, Mark. "Lacan's Theory in the Four Discourses." *Prose Studies* 11 (1988): 32–49.

Brantlinger, Patrick. *Rule of Darkness.* Ithaca, N.Y.: Cornell University Press, 1991.

Brenkman, John. "Narcissus in the Text." *Georgia Review* 30 (1976): 293–327.

Brooks, Peter. *Reading for the Plot.* New York: Random House, 1985.

———. "The Idea of a Psychoanalytic Literary Criticism." *Critical Inquiry* 13 (1987): 334–48.

Burke, Kenneth. *A Rhetoric of Motives.* Berkeley and Los Angeles: University of California Press, 1969.

Bursten, Ben. "The Narcissistic Course." In *The Narcissistic Condition,* edited by Marie Cole. New York: Human Sciences Press, 1977.

Caramagno, Thomas C. "Manic-Depressive Psychosis and Critical Approaches to Virginia Woof's Life and Art." *PMLA* 103 (1988): 10–23.

Carrithers, Michael, Steven Collins, and Steven Lukes, eds. *The Category of the Person.* Cambridge: Cambridge University Press, 1985.

Chasseguet-Smirgel, Janine. *The Ego Ideal: A Psychoanalytic Essay on the Malady of the Ideal.* New York: Norton, 1985.

Cohen, Ira. H. *Ideology and Unconsciousness: Reich, Freud and Marx.* New York: New York University Press, 1982.

Coombes, H. *Literature and Criticism.* Middlesex, England: Penguin, 1965.

Conrad, Joseph. *Heart of Darkness.* In *Youth and Two Other Stories.* Garden City, N.Y.: Doubleday, Page & Co., 1921.

———. "Henry James." In *Notes on Life and Letters.* Garden City, N.Y.: Doubleday, Page & Co., 1926.

———. *Lord Jim.* Garden City, N.Y.: Doubleday, Page & Co., 1921.

———. *A Personal Record.* London: J. M. Dent, 1919.

———. "Preface." In *The Nigger of the "Narcissus."* Garden City, N.Y.: Doubleday, Page & Co., 1921.

Corder, Jim W. "Hunting for Ethos Where They Say It Can't Be Found." *Rhetoric Review* 7 (1989): 299–315.

Crews, Frederick. "The Power of Darkness." *Partisan Review* 34 (1967): 507–25.

Culler, Johnathan. "In Pursuit of Signs." *Daedalus* 106 (1977): 95–112.

———. *Structuralist Poetics.* Ithaca, N.Y.: Cornell University Press, 1975.

Davis, Robert Con, ed. Special issue on "Psychoanalysis and Pedagogy." *College English* 49, no. 6/7 (1987).

de Man, Paul. *Allegories of Reading.* New Haven, Conn.: Yale University Press, 1979.

Derrida, Jacques. *Of Grammatology.* Translated by Gayatri Spivak. Baltimore: Johns Hopkins University Press, 1976.

Eagleton, Terry. *Against the Grain.* London: Verso, 1986.

———. *Literary Theory: An Introduction.* Minneapolis: University of Minnesota Press, 1983.

Edelson, Marshall. *Language and Interpretation in Psychoanalysis.* Chicago: University of Chicago Press, 1975.

Ehrenzweig, Anton. *The Hidden Order of Art.* Berkeley and Los Angeles: University of California Press, 1984.

Eliot, T. S. *Selected Essays.* New York: Harcourt Brace, 1950.

Elster, Jon, Ed. *The Multiple Self.* Cambridge: Cambridge University Press, 1986.

Felman, Shoshana. *Jacques Lacan: The Adventure of Insight.* Cambridge: Harvard University Press, 1987.

Fish, Stanley. *Is There a Text in This Class?* Cambridge: Harvard University Press, 1980.

———. "Why No One's Afraid of Wolfgang Iser." *Diacritics* 11 (1981): 2–13.

Fishbein, Martin, and Icek Ajzen. *Belief, Attitude, Intention, and Behavior.* Reading, Mass.: Addison-Wesley, 1975.

Foucault, Michel. *Language, Counter Memory, Practice.* Ithaca, N.Y.: Cornell University Press, 1977.

Fowles, J. "Notes on Writing a Novel." *Harpers,* July 1968, 88–97.

Freud, Sigmund. *The Standard Edition of Complete Psychological Works of Sigmund Freud.* 24 vols. Edited and translated by James Strachey. London: Hogarth Press, 1953–74.

———. Civilization and Its Discontents. 1930. *The Standard Edition,* vol. 21.

———. "Formulations Regarding the Two Principles in Mental Functioning." 1911. *The Standard Edition,* vol. 12.

———. "Instincts and Their Vicissitudes." 1915. *The Standard Edition,* vol. 14.

———. *Leonardo da Vinci and a Memory of His Childhood.* 1910. *The Standard Edition,* vol. 11.

———. "Mourning and Melancholia." 1917. *The Standard Edition,* vol. 14.

———. "On Narcissism: An Introduction." 1914. *The Standard Edition,* vol. 14.

———. "Remembering, Repeating and Working-Through." 1914. *The Standard Edition,* vol. 12.

———. *Three Essays on the Theory of Sexuality.* 1905. *The Standard Edition,* vol. 7.

Freud, Sigmund. "The Uncanny." 1919. *The Standard Edition*, vol. 17.
————. "The Unconscious." 1915. *The Standard Edition*, vol. 14.
Fyvel, T. R. *George Orwell: A Personal Memoir*. London: Hutchinson, 1983.
Gallop, Jane. *Reading Lacan*. Ithaca, N.Y.: Cornell University Press, 1985.
Garnett, Edward, ed. *Letters from Joseph Conrad, 1895–1924*. Indianapolis: Charter Books, 1962.
Geertz, Clifford. *The Interpretation of Cultures*. New York: Basic Books, 1973.
————. *Local Knowledge*. New York: Basic Books, 1983.
Glassman, Peter. *Joseph Conrad and the Literature of Personality*. New York: Columbia University Press, 1976.
Green, Andre. "Moral Narcissism." *International Journal of Psychoanalytic Psychotherapy* 8 (1980–81): 244–62.
Green, Martin. *Dreams of Adventure, Deeds of Empire*. New York: Basic Books, 1979.
Greenacre, P. "The Childhood of the Artist." In *Psychoanalytic Study of the Child*, vol. 12, 47–72. New York: International Universities Press, 1957.
————. "The Fetish and the Transitional Object." In *Psychoanalytic Study of the Child*, vol. 24, 144–64. New York: International Universities Press, 1969.
Grunberger, Bela. *Narcissism: Psychoanalytic Essays*. New York: International Universities Press, 1979.
Habermas, Jurgen. *Theorie des kommunikativen Handelns*, vol. 2. Frankfurt: Suhrkamp, 1981.
Halloran, Michael S. "Aristotle's Concept of *Ethos*, or If Not His Somebody Else's." *Rhetoric Review* 1 (1982): 58–64.
Harpham, Geoffrey Galt. "The Fertile Word: Augustine's Ascetics of Interpretation." *Criticism* 28 (1986): 237–53.
————. "Language, History, and Ethics." *Raritan* 7 (1987): 128–46.
————. *On the Grotesque*. Princeton, N.J.: Princeton University Press, 1982.
Hartmann, H., Ernest Kris, and R. Lowenstein. "Comments on the Formation of Psychic Structure." In *The Psychoanalytic Study of the Child*, vol. 2, 11–38. New York: International Universities Press, 1946.
Hassan, Ihab. "Pluralism in Postmodern Perspective." *Critical Inquiry* 12 (1986): 503–20.
Hawthorn, Jeremy. *Conrad: Language and Fictional Self-Consciousness*. Lincoln: University of Nebraska Press, 1979.
Hilgard, Josephine. *Personality and Hypnosis: A Study of Imaginative Involvement*. Chicago: University of Chicago Press, 1979.
Holland, Norman. *The Dynamics of Literary Response*. New York: Oxford University Press, 1968.
————. *Five Readers Reading*. New Haven, Conn.: Yale University Press, 1975.
————. *The I*. New Haven, Conn.: Yale University Press, 1985.
————. "Recovering the Purloined Letter." In *The Reader in the Text*, edited by Susan R. Suleiman and Inge Crosman. Princeton, N.J.: Princeton University Press, 1980.
————. "A Transactive Account of Transactive Criticism." *Poetics* 7 (1978): 177–89.

Horowitz, Mardi Jon. *Image Formation and Psychotherapy*. New York: Jason Aronson, 1983.

Iser, Wolfgang. *The Act of Reading*. Baltimore: Johns Hopkins University Press, 1978.

Jameson, Fredric. "The Imaginary and Symbolic in Lacan: Marxism, Psychoanalytic Criticism, and the Problem of the Subject." In *Literature and Psychoanalysis, The Question of Reading: Otherwise*, edited by Shoshana Felman. Baltimore: Johns Hopkins University Press, 1982.

———. *The Political Unconscious: Narrative as a Socially Symbolic Act*. Ithaca, N.Y.: Cornell University Press, 1981.

Jauss, Hans Robert. *Aesthetic Experience and Literary Hermeneutics*. Translated by Michael Shaw. Minneapolis: University of Minnesota Press, 1982.

Jean-Aubrey, G., ed. *Joseph Conrad: Life and Letters*. Garden City, N.Y.: Doubleday, Page & Co., 1927.

Jonson, Barbara. *The Critical Difference*. Baltimore: Johns Hopkins University Press, 1980.

———. "Rigorous Unreliability." *Critical Inquiry* 11 (1984): 278–85.

Johnson, Ben. "Poetaster." In *The Complete Plays of Ben Jonson*, edited by G. A. Wilkes. Oxford: Clarendon Press, 1981.

Karl, Frederick. *Joseph Conrad: The Three Lives*. New York: Farrar, Straus & Giroux, 1979.

Kernberg, Otto. *Borderline Conditions and Pathological Narcissism*. New York: Jason Aronson, 1975.

———. *Internal World, External Reality*. New York: Jason Aronson, 1980.

———. *Object Relations Theory and Clinical Psychoanalysis*. New York: Jason Aronson, 1976.

Kinneavy, James. *A Theory of Discourse*. Englewood Cliffs, N.J.: Prentice-Hall, 1971.

Klein, Melanie. "Mourning and Its Relation to Manic-Depressive States." In *Love, Guilt, and Reparation and Other Works, 1921–1945*. New York: Dell, 1975.

Kohut, Heinz. *The Analysis of the Self: A Systematic Approach to the Psychoanalytic Treatment of Narcissistic Personality Disorders*. New York: International Universities Press, 1971.

———. "Creativeness, Charisma, Group Psychology." In *Self Psychology and the Humanities: Reflections on a New Psychoanalytic Approach*, edited by Charles B. Strozier. New York: Norton, 1985.

———. *How Does Analysis Cure?* Edited by Arnold Goldberg. Chicago: University of Chicago Press, 1984.

———. *The Restoration of the Self*. New York: International Universities Press, 1980.

———. "The Self in History." In *Self Psychology and the Humanities: Reflections on a New Psychoanalytic Approach*, edited by Charles B. Strozier. New York: Norton, 1985.

Kris, Ernst. *Psychoanalytic Explorations in Art*. New York: International Universities Press, 1962.

Kristeva, Julia. *Black Sun: Depression and Melancholia.* Translated by Leon S. Roudiez. New York: Columbia University Press, 1989.

———. *Tales of Love.* Translated by Leon S. Roudiez. New York: Columbia University Press, 1987.

Kraft, Quentin G. "On Character in the Novel: William Beatty Warner versus Samuel Richardson and the Humanists." *College English* 50 (1988): 32–47.

Kucera, Henry. "Computers in Language Analysis and Lexicography." In *The American Heritage Dictionary.* Edited by William Morris. Boston: Houghton Mifflin, 1981.

La Capra, Dominick. "Culture and Ideology: From Geertz to Marx." *Poetics Today* 9, no. 2 (1988): 377–94.

LaBarre, W. *The Ghost Dance: Origins of Religion.* New York: Delta, 1972.

Lacan, Jacques. *Ecrits.* Translated by Alan Sheridan. New York: Norton, 1977.

———. *The Four Fundamental Concepts of Psycho-Analysis.* Edited by Jacques-Alain Miller. New York: Norton, 1978.

———. "Les psychoses, 1955–56." In *Le séminaire de Jacques Lacan,* edited by Jacques-Alain Miller. Paris: Edition du Seuil, 1975–81.

———. *The Seminar of Jacques Lacan: Books I and II.* Edited by Jacques-Alain Miller. New York: Norton, 1988.

Laplanche, Jean. *Life and Death in Psychoanalysis.* Translated by Jeffrey Mehlman. Baltimore: Johns Hopkins University Press, 1976.

Laplanche, Jean, and B. Pontalis, eds. *The Language of Psychoanalysis.* Translated by Donald Nicholson-Smith. New York: Norton, 1973.

Lawrence, D. H. *The Letters of D. H. Lawrence.* Vol 1., *1901–1913,* edited by James T. Bouton. Vol. 2, *1913–1916,* edited by George J. Zytaruk and James T. Boulton. Vol. 3, *1916–1921,* edited by James T. Boulton and Andrew Robertson. Cambridge: Cambridge University Press, 1979–84.

Layton, Lynne, and Barbara Ann Schapiro, eds. *Narcissism and the Text: Studies in Literature and the Psychology of Self.* New York: New York University Press, 1986.

Lesser, Simon O. *Fiction and the Unconscious.* Chicago: University of Chicago Press, 1957.

Levey, Mark. "The Concept of Structure in Psychoanalysis." *Annual of Psychoanalysis* 22–23 (1984–85): 137–55.

Lichtenstein, Heinz. *The Dilemma of Identity.* 1977. Reprint. New York: Jason Aronson, 1983.

Macdonell, Diane. *Theories of Discourse.* Oxford: Basil Blackwell, 1986.

Mack, Maynard. "The Jacobean Shakespeare: Some Observations on the Construction of the Tragedies." In *Essays in Shakespearean Criticism,* edited by James L. Calderwood and Harold E. Toliver. Englewood Cliffs, N.J.: Prentice-Hall, 1970.

Mailloux, Steven. *Interpretive Conventions: The Reader in the Study of American Fiction.* Ithaca, N.Y.: Cornell University Press, 1982.

Meissner, W. W. *Internalization in Psychoanalysis.* New York: International Universities Press, 1981.

Menaker, Esther. "The Ego-Ideal: An Aspect of Narcissism." In *The Narcissistic Condition*, edited by Marie Coleman Nelson. New York: Human Sciences Press, 1977.

Meyer, Bernard. *Joseph Conrad: A Psychoanalytic Biography*. Princeton, N.J.: Princeton University Press, 1970.

Miller, Arthur. *Death of a Salesman*. New York: Penguin, 1985.

Miller, Jacques-Alain. "How Psychoanalysis Cures According to Lacan." *Newsletter of the Freudian Field* 1 (1987): 4–30.

Mitchell, Stephen. *Relational Concepts in Psychoanalysis: An Integration*. Cambridge: Harvard University Press, 1988.

Mitchell, W. J. T. "What Is an Image?" *NLH* 15 (1984): 503–38.

Neel, Jasper. *Plato and Derrida*. Carbondale: University Southern Illinois Press, 1987.

Neisser, Ulric. "The Processes of Vision." In *The Nature of Human Consciousness*, edited by Robert Ornstein. San Francisco: W. H. Freeman, 1973.

Nell, Victor. *Lost in a Book*. New Haven, Conn.: Yale University Press, 1990.

Nelson, Marie Coleman, ed. *The Narcissistic Condition*. New York: Human Sciences Press, 1977.

Nettles, Elsie. "Heart of Darkness and the Creative Process." *Conradiana* 5 (1973): 66–73.

Norris, Christopher. *Deconstruction: Theory and Practice*. London: Routledge, 1988.

Ogden, Thomas H. *The Matrix of the Mind*. Northvale, N.J.: Jason Aronson, 1986.

Ong, Walter, S. J. *Orality and Literacy*. New York: Methuen, 1982.

Orwell, George. *The Road to Wigan Pier*. New York: Medallion Books, 1961.

———. "Shooting an Elephant." In *The Orwell Reader: Fiction, Essays, and Reportage by George Orwell*. New York: Harcourt Brace, 1949.

Pollock, George H. "Mourning and Adaptation." *International Journal of Psycho-Analysis* 42 (1961): 341–60.

Quintilian. *Institutio oratoria*. Translated by H. E. Butler. Cambridge: Harvard University Press, 1960.

Ragland-Sullivan, Ellie. *Jacques Lacan and the Philosophy of Psychoanalysis*. Urbana: University of Illinois Press, 1986.

———. "The Magnetism between Reader and Text: Prolegomena to a Lacanian Poetics." *Poetics* 13 (1984): 381–406.

———. "Rhetoric and Unconscious Desire: The Battle for the Postmodern Episteme." *Studies in Psychoanalytic Theory* 1 (1992): 2–24.

Rai, Alok. *Orwell and the Politics of Despair*. Cambridge: Cambridge University Press, 1990.

Reed, Walter. *An Exemplary History of the Novel*. Chicago: Chicago University Press, 1981.

Rendall, Steven. "Fish vs. Fish." *Diacritics* 12 (1982): 49–57.

Rodden, John. *The Politics of Literary Reputation: The Making and Claiming of "St. George" Orwell*. Oxford: Oxford University Press, 1989.

Roland, Alan. "Imagery and the Self in Artistic Creativity and Psychoanalytic Literary Criticism." *Psychoanalytic Review* 68 (1981): 409–24.

Rorty, Amelie Oksenberg. "A Literary Postscript: Characters, Persons, Selves, Individuals." In *The Identities of Persons*, edited by Amelie Oksenberg Rorty. Berkeley and Los Angeles: University of California Press, 1976.

Rose, Gilbert. *Trauma and Mastery in Life and Art*. New Haven, Conn.: Yale University Press, 1987.

Rothstein, Arnold. *The Narcissistic Pursuit of Perfection*. New York: International Universities Press, 1984.

Said, Edward. *Joseph Conrad and the Fiction of Autobiography*. Cambridge: Harvard University Press, 1966.

Schaefer, Roy. "Narration in the Psychoanalytic Dialogue." *Critical Inquiry* 7 (1980): 29–53.

Schwab, Gabriele. "Genesis of the Subject, Imaginary Functions, and Poetic Language." *NLH* 15 (1984): 453–74.

Schwarz, Daniel R. *Conrad: Almayer's Folly to Under Western Eyes*. Ithaca, N.Y.: Cornell University Press, 1980.

Shelden, Michael. *Orwell: The Authorized Biography*. London: Minerva, 1991.

Skura, Meredith Ann. *The Literary Use of the Psychoanalytic Process*. New Haven, Conn.: Yale University Press, 1981.

Smith, Hallet, ed. *Twentieth Century Interpretations of The Tempest*. Englewood Cliffs, N.J.: Prentice-Hall, 1969.

Smith, Paul. *Discerning the Subject*. Minneapolis: University of Minnesota Press, 1988.

Staten, Henry. "Conrad's Mortal Word." *Critical Inquiry* 12 (1986): 720–40.

Steiner, George. "Narcissus and Echo." *American Journal of Semiotics* 1 (1980): 3–16.

Suleiman, Susan R. "Introduction: Varieties of Audience-Oriented Criticism." In *The Reader in the Text*, edited by Susan R. Suleiman and Inge Crosman. Baltimore: Johns Hopkins University Press, 1980.

Suleiman, Susan R., and Inge Crosman, eds., *The Reader in the Text*. Baltimore: Johns Hopkins University Press, 1980.

Tate, Claudia. *Domestic Allegories of Political Desire: The Black Heroine's Text at the Turn of the Century*. New York: Oxford University Press, 1992.

Tellegen, A., and G. Atkinson. "Openness to Absorbing Self-Altering Experiences ("Absorption"), a Trait Related to Hypnotic Susceptibility." *Journal of Abnormal Psychology* 83: 268–77.

Thomas, D. M. *The White Hotel*. New York: Pocket Books, 1981.

Thornburn, David. *Conrad's Romanticism*. New Haven, Conn.: Yale University Press, 1974.

Tompkins, Jane, ed. *Reader-Response Criticism*. Baltimore: Johns Hopkins University Press, 1980.

Trilling, Lionel. "George Orwell and the Politics of Truth." In *The Opposing Self*. New York: Viking, 1955.

Valéry, Paul. *Aesthetics*. Vol. 13 of *The Collected Works of Paul Valéry*, edited by Jackson Mathews, translated by Ralph Manheim. New York: Pantheon, 1964.

Volosinov, V. N. *Marxism and the Philosophy of Language.* Cambridge: Harvard University Press, 1986.

Watt, Ian. *Conrad in the Nineteenth Century.* Berkeley and Los Angeles: University of California Press, 1979.

Weber, Max. *On Charisma and Institution Building.* Edited by S. N. Eisenstadt. Chicago: University of Chicago Press, 1968.

Welleck, René, and Austin Warren. *Theory of Literature* New York: Harcourt, Brace & World, 1956.

White, Hayden. *Tropics of Discourse.* Baltimore: Johns Hopkins University Press, 1978.

———. "The Value of Narrativity in the Representation of Reality." *Critical Inquiry* 7 (1980): 5–27.

White, James Boyd. *When Words Lose Their Meaning: Constitutions and Reconstitutions of Language, Character, and Community.* Chicago: University of Chicago Press, 1984.

Williams, Raymond. *Culture and Society: 1780–1950.* New York: Columbia University Press, 1983.

Winer, Jerome A., Thomas Jobe, and Carlton Ferrono, "Toward a Psychoanalytic Theory of the Charismatic Relationship." *The Annual of Psychoanalysis* 22–23 (1984–85): 155–77.

Winnicott, D. W. "Transitional Objects and Transitional Phenomena." *International Journal of Psycho-Analysis* 34 (1953): 89–97.

Wolf, Ernest S. "Psychoanalytic Psychology of the Self and Literature." *NLH* 12 (Autumn 1980): 41–61.

Woodcock, George. *The Crystal Spirit: A Study of George Orwell.* Boston: Little Brown, 1966.

Wyatt, Jean. *Reconstructing Desire: The Role of the Unconscious in Women's Reading and Writing.* Chapel Hill: University of North Carolina Press, 1990.

Zizek, Slavoj. "The Object as a Limit of Discourse: Approaches to the Lacanian Real." *Prose Studies* 11 (1988): 94–120.

———. "Why Lacan Is Not a 'Post-structuralist.'" *Newsletter of the Freudian Field* 1 (1987): 31–39.

Index